학습 진도표와 함께 목표를 달성해 보세요.

_____의 **Grammar Gateway Basic** Light Version 학습 진도표

목표와 다짐을 적어보세요.

나는 _____ 을 하기 위해

_____ 년 _____ 월 _____ 일까지 이 책을 끝낸다.

학습플랜을 정하세요.

- ☐ 30일 완성 (하루에 UNIT 4개씩)
- ☐ 40일 완성 (하루에 UNIT 3개씩)
- ☐ 60일 완성 (하루에 UNIT 2개씩)
- ☐ ___ 일 완성 (하루에 UNIT ___ 개씩)

학습을 마친 UNIT의 번호를 지워 보세요.

1	2	3	4	5	6	7	8	9	10	11	12	13	14	15	16	17	18	19	20
21	22	23	24	25	26	27	28	29	30	31	32	33	34	35	36	37	38	39	40
41	42	43	44	45	46	47	48	49	50	51	52	53	54	55	56	57	58	59	60
61	62	63	64	65	66	67	68	69	70	71	72	73	74	75	76	77	78	79	80
81	82	83	84	85	86	87	88	89	90	91	92	93	94	95	96	97	98	99	100
101	102	103	104	105	106	107	108	109	110	111	112	113	114	115	116	117	118	119	120

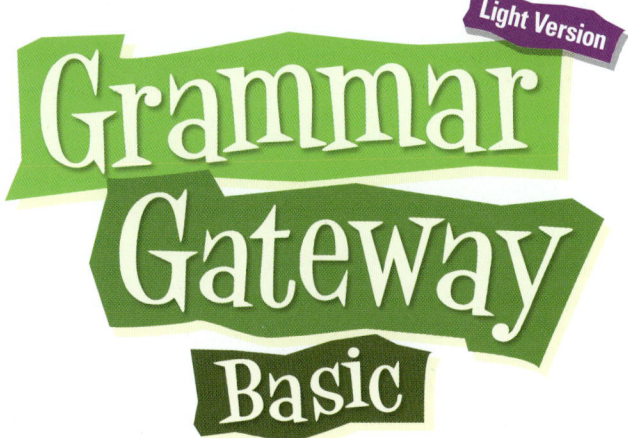

해커스 어학연구소

GRAMMAR GATEWAY BASIC

www.Hackers.co.kr

PREFACE

Grammar Gateway Basic은 문법을 처음 시작하는 초보 학습자들이 영어의 기초를 탄탄하게 다질 수 있는 기초 영어 문법서입니다.

본 교재는 영어를 모국어로 사용하는 사람들이 어떻게 말하고 쓰는지 분석·관찰하여 가장 중요한 문법 포인트를 총 120개의 UNIT으로 담아냈습니다. 한 UNIT을 꼭 필요한 문법 설명과 문제풀이까지 1페이지로 구성하여 부담 없이 문법을 익힐 수 있습니다. 나아가 실생활에서 바로 사용할 수 있는 예문과 다양한 유형의 연습문제를 통해 문법뿐만 아니라 말하기와 쓰기 능력도 기를 수 있습니다. 또한, 영문법에 두려움을 가진 학습자를 위해 어려운 문법 용어 대신 쉬운 문법 설명과 다양한 삽화를 통해 재미있게 공부할 수 있도록 하였습니다.

강의를 들으면서 공부하고 싶은 학습자들은 해커스 동영상강의 포털 해커스인강(www.HackersIngang.com)에서 동영상강의와 함께 학습이 가능합니다. 더불어, 실시간 토론과 정보 공유의 장인 해커스영어 사이트(www.Hackers.co.kr)와 점프해커스(www.JumpHackers.com)에서 교재 학습 중 궁금한 점을 다른 학습자들과 나누고, 다양한 무료 영어 학습 자료를 이용할 수 있습니다.

Grammar Gateway Basic을 통해 막연하고 어렵게만 여겨지는 영문법에 한걸음 더 가까이 다가설 수 있으실 거라 확신합니다. 여러분의 꿈을 이루는 길에 Grammar Gateway Basic이 함께하기를 기원합니다.

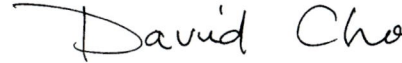

CONTENTS

책의 특징 8
책의 구성 10

현재와 현재진행

UNIT 1	He **is** a student.	be동사 (am/is/are)	12
UNIT 2	He **is not** hungry.	be동사 부정문	13
UNIT 3	**Is** she from China?	be동사 의문문	14
UNIT 4	She **is talking** on the phone.	현재진행 시제	15
UNIT 5	He **is not driving**.	현재진행 시제 부정문	16
UNIT 6	**Is** it **raining**?	현재진행 시제 의문문	17
UNIT 7	He **likes** music.	일반동사 현재 시제 (1)	18
UNIT 8	He **drives** to work every morning.	일반동사 현재 시제 (2)	19
UNIT 9	He **doesn't like** fish.	현재 시제 부정문	20
UNIT 10	**Do** you **speak** English?	현재 시제 의문문	21
UNIT 11	I **am doing** vs. I **do**	현재진행 시제와 현재 시제 비교	22
UNIT 12	He **wants** a new watch.	현재진행 시제로 쓰지 않고 현재 시제로 쓰는 동사	23

과거와 과거진행

UNIT 13	She **was** in the hospital.	be동사 과거 시제 (was/were)	24
UNIT 14	I **was not** good at math in high school.	be동사 과거 시제 부정문과 의문문	25
UNIT 15	He **walked** to school yesterday.	일반동사 과거 시제	26
UNIT 16	I **didn't go** to work yesterday.	과거 시제 부정문과 의문문	27
UNIT 17	He **was playing** the guitar.	과거진행 시제	28
UNIT 18	I **wasn't sleeping**.	과거진행 시제 부정문과 의문문	29
UNIT 19	He **used to** be a football player.	used to	30

현재완료

UNIT 20	She **has washed** the dishes.	현재완료 시제 (1)	31
UNIT 21	He **has known** her **for** five years.	현재완료 시제 (2) 현재까지 계속되는 일	32
UNIT 22	She **hasn't seen** this movie.	현재완료 시제 (3) 지금까지 경험해본 일	33
UNIT 23	I **did** vs. I **have done**	과거 시제와 현재완료 시제 비교	34
UNIT 24	We**'ve just started**.	just, already, yet	35

미래

UNIT 25	She **will** run tomorrow.	미래 시제 (1) will	36
UNIT 26	He**'s going to** make dinner tonight.	미래 시제 (2) be going to	37
UNIT 27	I **will** vs. I**'m going to**	미래 시제 (3) will과 be going to 비교	38
UNIT 28	She **is leaving** tomorrow.	미래 시제 (4) 미래를 나타내는 현재진행과 현재 시제	39

조동사

UNIT 29	He **can** speak Italian.	can과 could	40
UNIT 30	**Can I** use your phone?	Can I ~ ?, Can you ~ ?	41
UNIT 31	He **might** go out.	might	42
UNIT 32	He **must** be thirsty.	must (강한 확신)	43

UNIT 33	They **must**/**have to** stay in their seats.	must와 have to (의무)	44
UNIT 34	People **must not** run near the pool.	must not과 don't have to	45
UNIT 35	He **should** go home.	should	46
UNIT 36	**Would you like** some help?	would like (to)	47

수동태

| UNIT 37 | The newspaper **is delivered** every day. | 수동태 | 48 |
| UNIT 38 | She **caught** a fish. A fish **was caught**. | 능동태와 수동태 비교 | 49 |

부정문과 의문문

UNIT 39	She **is not** afraid.	부정문	50
UNIT 40	**Is** the water too hot?	의문사가 없는 의문문	51
UNIT 41	**Who** is he? **What** is it?	who와 what	52
UNIT 42	**Which** do you want?	which	53
UNIT 43	**Where** is the bathroom?	where, when, why	54
UNIT 44	**How** can I help you?	how	55
UNIT 45	Do you know **where the station is**?	간접의문문	56

-ing와 to+동사원형

UNIT 46	**Exercising** is good for health.	-ing (1) 주어	57
UNIT 47	She **enjoys listening** to music.	-ing (2) 목적어	58
UNIT 48	He **wants to open** a restaurant.	to+동사원형	59
UNIT 49	They **like visiting**/**to visit** art museums.	-ing와 to+동사원형 모두 뒤에 올 수 있는 동사	60
UNIT 50	She **wants him to finish** the report.	동사 + 사람 + to+동사원형	61
UNIT 51	He **made her scream**.	make/have/let + 사람 + 동사원형	62
UNIT 52	They're running **to catch** the bus.	목적을 나타내는 to+동사원형과 명사 + to+동사원형	63

명사와 대명사

UNIT 53	**a girl**, **snow**	셀 수 있는 명사와 셀 수 없는 명사	64
UNIT 54	**a dog**, **two dogs**	단수와 복수	65
UNIT 55	**a fish**, **some fish**	단수, 복수에 주의해야 할 명사	66
UNIT 56	**a glass of** water, **two cans of** soda	a glass/can/… of ~	67
UNIT 57	**a** lamp, **the** lamp	a/an과 the	68
UNIT 58	I want to travel around **the** world.	the를 쓰는 경우와 쓰지 않는 경우 (1)	69
UNIT 59	They **went to the movies**.	the를 쓰는 경우와 쓰지 않는 경우 (2) 장소	70
UNIT 60	**She** is my friend.	사람과 사물을 가리키는 대명사	71
UNIT 61	**It** is Monday.	비인칭 주어 it	72
UNIT 62	This is **my** camera.	소유를 나타내는 표현	73
UNIT 63	It's **Amy's** book.	명사의 소유격	74
UNIT 64	How much is **this**/**that**?	this/these와 that/those	75
UNIT 65	How about this **one**?	one과 ones	76

CONTENTS

수량 표현

UNIT 66	There are **some** children on the bus.	some과 any	77
UNIT 67	There are **no** rooms.	no와 none	78
UNIT 68	**Someone** left this briefcase in the lobby.	someone/anything/nowhere ⋯	79
UNIT 69	**many** cars, **much** sugar	many와 much	80
UNIT 70	She received **a lot of** letters.	a lot of	81
UNIT 71	**a few** cookies, **a little** milk	a few와 a little	82
UNIT 72	**few** cookies, **little** milk	few와 little	83
UNIT 73	**All** dogs have tails.	all	84
UNIT 74	**Every** house has a roof.	every	85
UNIT 75	**all of** the pie, **some of** the pie	all/most/some/none of ~	86
UNIT 76	He enjoys playing **both**.	both/either/neither	87

형용사와 부사

UNIT 77	He's wearing a **black** jacket.	형용사	88
UNIT 78	They are walking **carefully**.	부사	89
UNIT 79	Jake is a **nice** guy. Jake always dresses **nicely**.	형용사와 부사 비교	90
UNIT 80	It's **late**. I got home **late**.	주의해야 할 형용사와 부사	91
UNIT 81	He **always** eats cereal for breakfast.	always, often, never ⋯	92
UNIT 82	The bag is **too** small.	too	93
UNIT 83	They aren't big **enough**.	형용사/부사 + enough	94
UNIT 84	There aren't **enough** seats on the bus.	enough + 명사	95
UNIT 85	An airplane is **faster**.	비교급	96
UNIT 86	I'm looking for a **larger** one.	주의해야 할 비교급 형태	97
UNIT 87	Chris is **the tallest** person.	최상급	98
UNIT 88	Where is **the closest** café from here?	주의해야 할 최상급 형태	99
UNIT 89	Chris is **as heavy as** Paul.	as ~ as	100
UNIT 90	She isn**'t as old as** him.	not as ~ as	101

전치사와 구동사

UNIT 91	**at** the bus stop, **in** the living room, **on** the floor	장소 전치사 at, in, on (1)	102
UNIT 92	I don't have to wear a suit **at** work.	장소 전치사 at, in, on (2)	103
UNIT 93	The bus stops **in front of** my house.	위치 전치사 (1) in front of, behind, by, next to	104
UNIT 94	She is standing **between** Emily and Lynn.	위치 전치사 (2) between, among, over, under	105
UNIT 95	Where is the letter **from**?	방향 전치사 (1)	106
UNIT 96	The Nile River flows **through** Egypt.	방향 전치사 (2)	107
UNIT 97	It arrives **at** 5:30.	시간 전치사 (1) at, on, in	108
UNIT 98	Bats sleep **during** the day.	시간 전치사 (2) during, for, in, within	109
UNIT 99	Dr. Kim sees his patients **from** 9 a.m. **to** 6 p.m.	시간 전치사 (3) from ~ to, by, until	110
UNIT 100	The house **with** the yellow roof is ours.	기타 전치사 with, without, by	111
UNIT 101	They are talking **about visiting** Susan.	전치사 + -ing	112
UNIT 102	Are you **sure about** that?	형용사 + 전치사	113
UNIT 103	**Look at** that baby.	동사 + 전치사	114
UNIT 104	She is **trying on** a hat.	구동사	115

GRAMMAR GATEWAY BASIC LIGHT VERSION

접속사와 절

UNIT 105	The door opened, **and** he came in.	and, but, or	116
UNIT 106	The movie was boring, **so** they didn't enjoy it.	so와 because	117
UNIT 107	She was watching TV **when** he came in.	when과 while	118
UNIT 108	The restaurant closed **before** they arrived.	before와 after	119
UNIT 109	The city has changed a lot **since** I moved here.	since와 until	120
UNIT 110	**If** it **rains**, she'll stay at home.	if (1) if + 현재 시제	121
UNIT 111	**If** he **had** time, he would have breakfast.	if (2) if + 과거 시제	122
UNIT 112	**if I do** vs. **if I did**	if (3) if + 현재 시제와 if + 과거 시제 비교	123
UNIT 113	He knows the girl **who** won the race.	관계대명사 who, which, that (1) 주격	124
UNIT 114	They enjoyed the dinner **which** James made.	관계대명사 who, which, that (2) 목적격	125

다양한 문장들

UNIT 115	**There is** a boat in the sea.	there + be동사	126
UNIT 116	He **gave his wife a ring**.	동사(give/make 등) + 사람 + 사물	127
UNIT 117	**Come** here. **Let's go** inside.	명령하기, 권유하기	128
UNIT 118	He **said that** I could use his car.	다른 사람의 말을 전달하기 (간접화법)	129
UNIT 119	I like it **too**. I don't like them **either**.	too와 either	130
UNIT 120	**So** am I. **Neither** am I.	so와 neither	131

CHECK-UP TEST

TEST 1 현재와 현재진행	134
TEST 2 과거와 과거진행	136
TEST 3 현재완료	138
TEST 4 미래	140
TEST 5 조동사	142
TEST 6 수동태	144
TEST 7 부정문과 의문문	146
TEST 8 -ing와 to + 동사원형	148
TEST 9 명사와 대명사	150
TEST 10 수량 표현	152
TEST 11 형용사와 부사	154
TEST 12 전치사와 구동사	156
TEST 13 접속사와 절	158
TEST 14 다양한 문장들	160

부록

1 품사와 문장 성분	164
2 불규칙 동사	168
3 주의해야 할 형태 변화	170
4 축약형	173
5 주의해야 할 명사와 the 용법	174
6 알아두면 유용한 형용사 + 전치사 표현	176
7 알아두면 유용한 동사 표현	178

정답	185
INDEX	205

책의 특징

쉽게 이해할 수 있는 문법책, Grammar Gateway!

- 어려운 문법 용어 대신 설명을 쉬운 말로 풀어 써서 이해하기 쉽습니다.
- 표와 그래프를 통해 문법 설명을 한눈에 볼 수 있어 학습자가 보다 쉽게 이해할 수 있습니다.

재미있게 공부할 수 있는 문법책, Grammar Gateway!

- 생생한 삽화가 그려져 있어 딱딱하기만 했던 영문법을 재미있게 공부할 수 있도록 도와줄 뿐만 아니라 효과적으로 공부할 수 있게 해줍니다.
- 다양한 유형의 연습문제가 수록되어 있어 영문법 공부에 흥미를 더해줍니다.

GRAMMAR GATEWAY BASIC

끝낼 수 있는 문법책, Grammar Gateway!

- 한 UNIT이 한 페이지로 가볍게 구성되어 간단하게 학습을 마칠 수 있습니다.
- 학습 진도표를 활용해 스스로 학습 진도를 점검하며 꾸준히 공부한다면 책을 완전히 끝낼 수 있습니다.

말하기/쓰기에 활용할 수 있는 문법책, Grammar Gateway!

- 실생활에서 사용할 수 있는 예문들이 실려 있어 실제 말하기/쓰기에 바로 적용할 수 있습니다.
- 문장과 대화를 직접 완성해보는 연습을 통해 말하기/쓰기 실력을 향상시킬 수 있습니다.

책의 구성

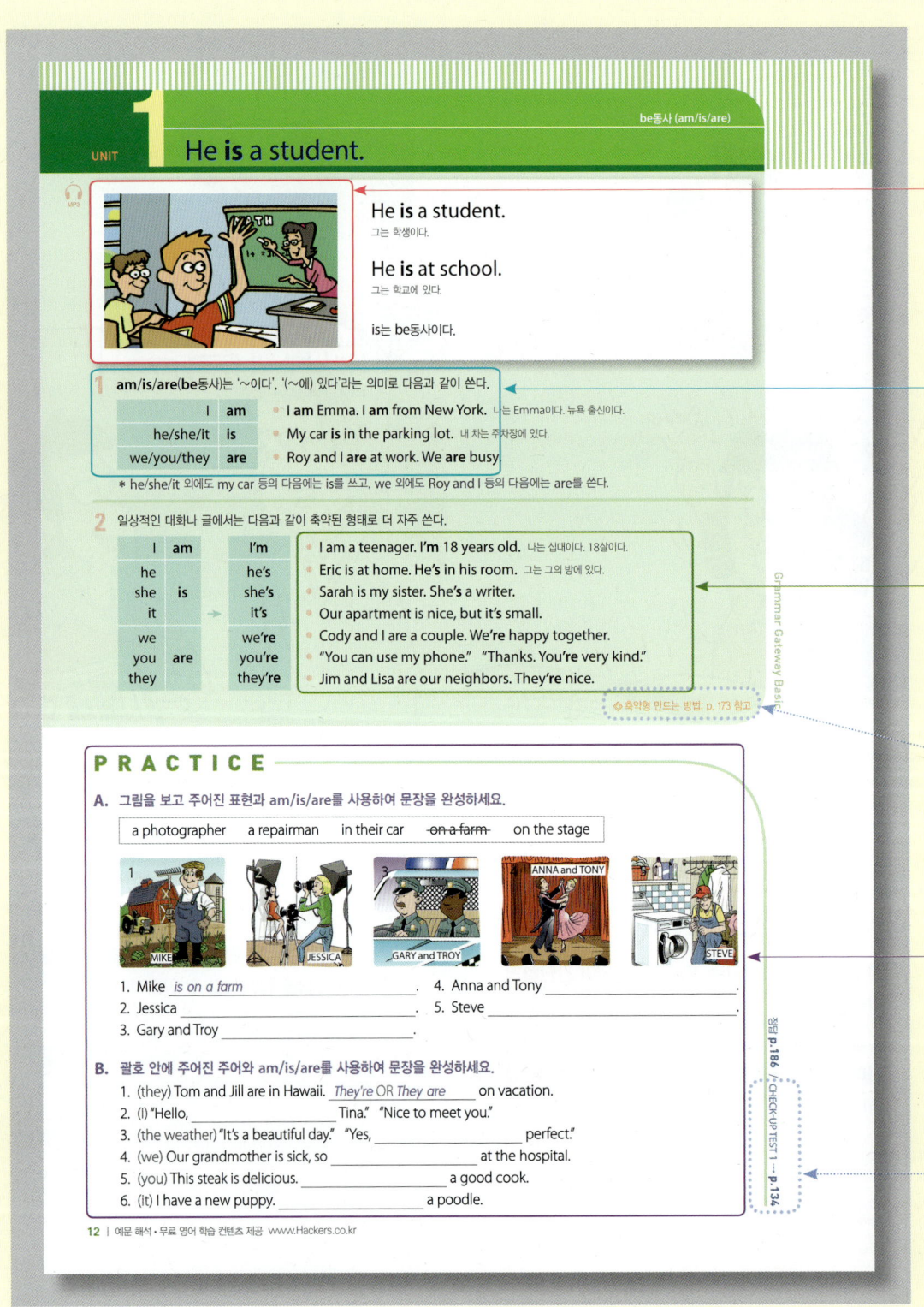

GRAMMAR GATEWAY BASIC

● **삽화**
실제 상황을 보는 듯 생생하고 재미있는 삽화를 통해 공부할 내용을 효과적으로 파악할 수 있어요.

● **문법 설명 + 표/그래프**
문법 용어를 사용하지 않고 쉽게 풀어 쓴 설명을 읽고, 표/그래프를 통해 읽은 내용을 다시 확인할 수 있어요.

● **예문**
예문을 통해 문법이 어떻게 활용되었는지 확인할 수 있어요.
- 예문을 직접 해석해보고, 온라인 무료 예문 해석(Hackers.co.kr)을 활용하여 내가 해석한 의미가 맞는지 점검해보세요.
- MP3(talk.Hackers.com)로 예문을 듣고 소리 내어 따라하며 말하기 연습도 해보세요.

● 부록 페이지에서 더 알아두면 좋은 내용을 보충할 수 있어요!

● **문제**
공부한 내용을 Practice에서 바로 연습할 수 있어요.
- 실제 상황에서 이뤄지는 대화와 문장을 완성하는 연습문제를 풀어보며 말하기/쓰기 연습도 해보세요.

● 여러 UNIT의 내용을 종합적으로 점검해볼 수 있는 CHECK-UP TEST도 풀어 볼 수 있어요!

UNIT 1　He **is** a student.

be동사 (am/is/are)

He **is** a student.
그는 학생이다.

He **is** at school.
그는 학교에 있다.

is는 be동사이다.

1 am/is/are(be동사)는 '~이다', '(~에) 있다'라는 의미로 다음과 같이 쓴다.

I	am
he/she/it	is
we/you/they	are

- I **am** Emma. I **am** from New York. 나는 Emma이다. 뉴욕 출신이다.
- My car **is** in the parking lot. 내 차는 주차장에 있다.
- Roy and I **are** at work. We **are** busy.

* he/she/it 외에도 my car 등의 다음에는 is를 쓰고, we 외에도 Roy and I 등의 다음에는 are를 쓴다.

2 일상적인 대화나 글에서는 다음과 같이 축약된 형태로 더 자주 쓴다.

I	am		I'm
he			he's
she	is	→	she's
it			it's
we			we're
you	are		you're
they			they're

- I am a teenager. **I'm** 18 years old. 나는 십대이다. 18살이다.
- Eric is at home. **He's** in his room. 그는 그의 방에 있다.
- Sarah is my sister. **She's** a writer.
- Our apartment is nice, but **it's** small.
- Cody and I are a couple. **We're** happy together.
- "You can use my phone." "Thanks. **You're** very kind."
- Jim and Lisa are our neighbors. **They're** nice.

◇ 축약형 만드는 방법: p. 173 참고

PRACTICE

A. 그림을 보고 주어진 표현과 am/is/are를 사용하여 문장을 완성하세요.

| a photographer | a repairman | in their car | ~~on a farm~~ | on the stage |

MIKE　　JESSICA　　GARY and TROY　　ANNA and TONY　　STEVE

1. Mike _is on a farm_ .
2. Jessica _____ .
3. Gary and Troy _____ .
4. Anna and Tony _____ .
5. Steve _____ .

B. 괄호 안에 주어진 주어와 am/is/are를 사용하여 문장을 완성하세요.

1. (they) Tom and Jill are in Hawaii. _They're OR They are_ on vacation.
2. (I) "Hello, _____ Tina." "Nice to meet you."
3. (the weather) "It's a beautiful day." "Yes, _____ perfect."
4. (we) Our grandmother is sick, so _____ at the hospital.
5. (you) This steak is delicious. _____ a good cook.
6. (it) I have a new puppy. _____ a poodle.

UNIT 2 He **is not** hungry.

be동사 부정문

I'm full.

긍정 He **is** full. 그는 배부르다.

부정 He **is not** hungry. 그는 배고프지 않다.

1 am/is/are + not: ~이 아니다, (~에) 없다

I	am	
he/she/it	is	not
we/you/they	are	

- I **am not** from Japan. I'm Korean. 나는 일본 출신이 아니다.
- Carla **is not** in her office. She is out for lunch. Carla는 사무실에 없다.
- These apples **are not** expensive. Let's get some.

2 I am not, he is not 등은 다음과 같이 축약된 형태로 더 자주 쓴다.

I	am not		I'm not
he			he's not / he isn't
she	is not	→	she's not / she isn't
it			it's not / it isn't
we			we're not / we aren't
you	are not		you're not / you aren't
they			they're not / they aren't

- **I'm not** tall, but I'm good at basketball. 키가 크지 않다.
- Where is John? He **isn't** here. 여기에 없다.
- Amanda is in her bed, but she**'s not** asleep.
- Today **isn't** Saturday. It's Sunday.
- We**'re not** brothers. We're cousins.
- Don't worry. You**'re not** late.
- Those boxes are big, but they **aren't** heavy.

PRACTICE

A. 괄호 안에 주어진 주어와 am/is/are not을 사용하여 문장을 완성하세요.

1. (I) _I'm not OR I am not_ an adult. I'm only 17 years old.
2. (this water) _____ cold. It needs ice.
3. (you) It's time for school, but _____ ready.
4. (Mark) _____ at the restaurant. He's at the café.
5. (we) We can meet you tonight. _____ busy.
6. (the exam) _____ difficult. The questions are easy.
7. (she) Sharon is my friend, but _____ my best friend.
8. (my books) _____ in my room. I can't find them.

B. am/is/are 또는 am/is/are not을 축약된 형태로 사용하여 문장을 완성하세요.

1. Tara is in France, but she _'s not OR isn't_ in Paris.
2. I can play the guitar, but I _____ good at it.
3. We're not at the airport. We _____ still in the taxi.
4. My parents _____ Spanish. They're from Mexico.
5. Moscow isn't a country. It _____ a city.
6. "Do you want some juice?" "No thanks. I _____ thirsty."
7. That movie is OK, but it _____ great.
8. Cindy and Luke aren't here. They _____ at the beach.

UNIT 3 Is she from China?

be동사 의문문

긍정 **She is** from China. 그녀는 중국 출신이다.

의문 **Is she** from China? 그녀는 중국 출신인가요?

1 be동사 의문문에서 am/is/are는 주어 앞에 쓴다.

am	I ... ?
is	he ... ? / she ... ? / it ... ?
are	we ... ? / you ... ? / they ... ?

- Excuse me. **Am I** near Main Street? 제가 Main Street 근처에 있나요?
- "**Is he** your father?" 저 분이 네 아버지시니? "No, he's my uncle."
- "**Is Diane** in her room?" "No, she's out."
- "**Is it** warm outside?" "Yes, the weather is great."
- "**Are we** in the same class?" "Yes, I'm Danny."
- "**Are you** still sick?" "No, I'm better now."
- "**Are those cookies** good?" "Yes, they're delicious."

2 다음과 같이 의문에 짧게 답할 수 있다.

Yes,	I	am.
	he/she/it	is.
	we/you/they	are.

No,	I	'm not.
	he/she/it	's not. / isn't.
	we/you/they	're not. / aren't.

- "**Are you** Pamela?" 당신이 Pamela인가요? "**Yes, I am.**" (= Yes, I am Pamela.)
- "**Is the radio** too loud?" 라디오가 너무 시끄러운가요? "**No, it isn't.**" (= No, it isn't too loud.)
- "**Is Mom** in the kitchen?" "**Yes, she is.**"
- "**Are the guests** here?" "**No, they're not.**"

PRACTICE

A. 괄호 안에 주어진 주어와 am/is/are를 사용하여 의문문을 완성하세요.

1. (Jackie) " _Is Jackie_____ in Europe?" "Yes, she is."
2. (it) "_____ cloudy today?" "No, there's not a cloud in the sky."
3. (I) I'm looking for Mr. Smith's office. _____ in the right building?
4. (you) "_____ an artist?" "Yes, I'm a painter."
5. (today) "_____ your birthday?" "Yes, it is."
6. (Joel and Mary) "_____ at the movies?" "I think so, but I'm not sure."
7. (she) "My sister is an actress." "_____ famous?"
8. (we) "_____ ready for the meeting?" "Yes. Let's begin."

B. 주어진 의문문을 보고 예시와 같이 짧게 답하세요.

1. Are you and Claire Italian?   _Yes, we are_____. We're from Rome.
2. Are you busy?   _____. I'm free right now.
3. Is Brandon a scientist?   _____. He's a doctor.
4. Are these gloves on sale?   _____. They're half price.
5. Is your house on 21st Avenue? _____. It's on 22nd Street.

UNIT 4 She **is talking** on the phone.

현재진행 시제

She **is talking** on the phone.
그녀는 전화로 이야기하는 중이다.

is talking은 현재진행 시제이다.

1 현재진행 시제는 '지금 ~하는 중이다'라는 의미로 **am/is/are** + **-ing**로 쓴다.

I	am (= 'm)	cooking looking visiting cleaning
he she it	is (= 's)	
we you they	are (= 're)	

- I'm **cooking** pasta now. 파스타를 요리하는 중이다.
- "I'm **looking** for my glasses." 안경을 찾는 중이야. "They're on your desk."
- Ralph isn't here. He's **visiting** his grandparents in England.
- Rebecca **is cleaning** her room right now.
- Look outside! It's **snowing**.
- (전화상에서) "Where are you?" "We're **eating** dinner at a restaurant."
- Please slow down. You're **driving** too fast.
- Frank and Brenda are in the library. They're **studying** for an exam.

2 **-ing**를 붙일 때 주의해야 할 동사들이 있다.

come → co**ming**	sit → si**tting**	lie → **lying**
have → ha**ving**	shop → sho**pping**	tie → **tying**
take → ta**king**	run → ru**nning**	die → **dying**

◇ -ing 붙이는 방법: 부록 p. 170 참고

- Hurry up! The train **is coming**. 기차가 오고 있어.
- A couple **is sitting** on the grass, and their dogs **are lying** beside them.

PRACTICE

A. 그림을 보고 주어진 표현을 사용하여 예시와 같이 문장을 완성하세요.

~~cross the street~~   enter the bank   fly in the sky   play the violin   stand at the bus stop

1. Carl and Rita _are crossing the street_ .
2. Jack _____.
3. Melinda _____.
4. Two birds _____.
5. Kim _____.

B. 괄호 안에 주어진 단어들을 사용하여 현재진행 시제 문장을 완성하세요.

1. (I, pack) _I'm packing_ OR _I am packing_ for my trip. I'm very excited.
2. (he, have) "Where's Tim?" "_____ lunch at the cafeteria."
3. (Mitchell, practice) _____ for a concert. It's tomorrow night.
4. (the children, help) _____ their dad in the garden.
5. (they, run) "Where are Alex and Ed?" "_____ in the park."
6. (I, tie) Please wait for me. _____ my shoes.

UNIT 5 He is **not driving**.

현재진행 시제 부정문

긍정 He **is eating** lunch. 그는 점심을 먹는 중이다.

부정 He **is not driving**. 그는 운전하고 있지 않다.

1 현재진행 시제 부정문은 am/is/are + not + -ing로 쓴다.

I	am not (= 'm not)	
he she it	is not (= 's not / isn't)	doing using traveling cooking
we you they	are not (= 're not / aren't)	

- I'm not busy. **I'm not doing** anything now. 아무것도 하고 있지 않다.
- **I'm not using** this chair. You can use it. 이 의자를 사용하고 있지 않다.
- Tom is in London with Ann. He **isn't traveling** alone.
- My mom **isn't cooking**. She's washing the dishes.
- It's cloudy, but it **isn't raining**.
- We**'re not working** today. We're on vacation.
- You **aren't drinking** your coffee. Is it too hot?
- Where are the children? They **aren't playing** in the garden.

PRACTICE

A. 주어진 동사를 사용하여 현재진행 시제 문장을 완성하세요. 부정문으로 쓰세요.

| enjoy   move   speak   swim   ~~watch~~   wear |

1. "Can I change the channel?" "Sure. I _'m not watching OR am not watching_ this show."
2. The bus _____ because of the traffic.
3. This book is boring. I _____ it at all.
4. You _____ your seat belt. That's dangerous.
5. Mr. Taylor _____ Russian. It's German.
6. We _____ because the water is too cold.

B. 그림을 보고 괄호 안에 주어진 표현을 사용하여 현재진행 시제 문장을 완성하세요. 필요한 경우 부정문으로 쓰세요.

1. (listen to music) He _'s listening to music OR is listening to music_ .
   (sleep) The dog _isn't sleeping OR is not sleeping_ .
2. (play soccer) They _____ .
   (rain) It _____ .
3. (drive) She _____ .
   (talk on the phone) She _____ .

UNIT 6 Is it raining?

현재진행 시제 의문문

긍정 It **is raining**. 비가 내리는 중이다.
의문 **Is** it **raining**? 지금 비가 내리는 중인가요?

1 현재진행 시제 의문문은 **am/is/are + 주어 + -ing**로 쓴다.

am	I	
is	he / she / it	speaking ... ? coming ... ? taking ... ? working ... ?
are	we / you / they	

- **Am** I **speaking** too quickly? 제가 너무 빨리 말하고 있나요?
- Where's Bob? **Is** he **coming** home now? 그가 지금 집에 오는 중인가요?
- "**Is** Sarah **taking** a walk?" "Yes, she's at the park."
- "**Is** the printer **working**?" "No, it's not."
- "**Are** we **winning** the game?" "Yes, we are."
- "**Are** you **drinking** tea?" "No, it's coffee."
- "**Are** the kids **flying** a kite?" "I think so."

2 **Yes, she is.** 또는 **No, I'm not.** 등과 같이 의문문에 짧게 답할 수 있다.
- "**Is** Stacy **studying** right now?" Stacy는 지금 공부하는 중인가요? "**Yes, she is.**" (= Yes, she's studying right now.)
- "**Are** you **sleeping**?" "**No, I'm not.**" (= No, I'm not sleeping.)

PRACTICE

A. 괄호 안에 주어진 단어들을 사용하여 현재진행 시제 의문문을 완성하세요.
1. (you, listen) _Are you listening_ to the radio?
2. (Glen, look) _____ for me?
3. (you, call) _____ Wendy?
4. (I, talk) _____ too loudly?
5. (you and Vicky, make) _____ chicken soup?
6. (the wind, blow) _____ a lot today?
7. (Emily, wear) _____ new glasses?
8. (your brothers, ride) _____ their bicycles?

B. 주어진 의문문을 보고 예시와 같이 짧게 답하세요.

1. Are you doing your homework?   _Yes, I am_ . I'm busy.
2. Is Helen exercising at the gym?   _____ . She's at the bookstore.
3. Are you drawing a picture?   _____ . I'm writing a report.
4. Are the children having breakfast? _____ . They're eating cereal.
5. Is David taking a shower?   _____ . He's cleaning the bathroom.
6. Is it snowing outside?   _____ . Let's make a snowman.

UNIT 7

일반동사 현재 시제 (1)

He **likes** music.

He is listening to music.

He **likes** music.
그는 음악을 좋아한다.

likes는 현재 시제이다.

1 현재 시제는 다음과 같이 쓴다.

I/we/you/they	visit live
he/she/it	sells snows

- I **visit** my aunt in Miami every year. 매년 Miami에 사는 이모를 방문한다.
- We **live** in an apartment downtown. 우리는 시내에 있는 아파트에 산다.
- "What is Kevin's job?" "He **sells** cars."
- It often **snows** here in January.

주어가 **he/she/it** 등일 때 동사 끝에 **-s**를 붙이는 것에 주의한다.
- Emily **wants** a computer for her birthday. Emily는 생일 선물로 컴퓨터를 원한다.
- My son usually **eats** toast for breakfast.

2 **-s**가 아니라 **-es**를 붙이는 동사들이 있다.

teach → teach**es**	go → go**es**	study → stud**ies**	miss → miss**es**
finish → finish**es**	do → do**es**	fly → fl**ies**	pass → pass**es**

◆ -(e)s 붙이는 방법: 부록 p. 170 참고

- This train **goes** to Washington DC. 이 열차는 워싱턴까지 간다.
- Larry is a college student. He **studies** art history.

단, **have**는 주어가 **he/she/it** 등일 때 **has**로 쓴다.
- I have a dog, and Tina **has** a cat. 나는 개가 있고, Tina는 고양이가 있다.

PRACTICE

A. 둘 중 맞는 것을 고르세요.

1. I (**wear** / wears) a suit to work.
2. My cousin (call / calls) me every week.
3. Jackie often (listen / listens) to jazz music.
4. Many shops (close / closes) early on holidays.
5. Mr. Harris (get / gets) a haircut every month.
6. We (ride / rides) our bikes on the weekends.
7. This jacket (cost / costs) $30. It's on sale today.
8. Erica and I (work / works) in the same building.

B. 괄호 안에 주어진 동사를 사용하여 문장을 완성하세요.

1. (drink) Henry _drinks_ milk every morning.
2. (do) Mark _____ his laundry every Saturday.
3. (have) New York _____ many tall buildings.
4. (speak) My parents are from Türkiye, so I _____ Turkish at home.
5. (play) "You _____ the violin well." "Thank you."
6. (finish) I can meet you at 5:30. My class _____ at 5.
7. (cry) The baby _____ a lot every night.
8. (buy) Kim and Marco usually _____ bread from a bakery on Larch Street.

UNIT 8   He **drives** to work every morning.

일반동사 현재 시제 (2)

He **drives** to work every morning.
그는 매일 아침 운전해서 회사에 간다.

1 반복적으로 일어나는 일에 대해 말할 때 현재 시제를 쓴다.
- I usually **meet** my friends on Fridays. 나는 금요일에 보통 친구들을 만난다.
- We **go** to the movies every weekend. 우리는 주말마다 영화를 보러 간다.
- Jessica **travels** a lot in the winter.
- Sam sometimes **exercises** at night.

2 일반적인 사실에 대해 말할 때도 현재 시제를 쓴다.
- Mexicans **speak** Spanish. 멕시코인들은 스페인어를 쓴다.
- Edward is a lawyer. He **works** for a big company. 그는 큰 회사에서 일한다.
- That store **sells** fresh fruit. Let's go there.
- Peter and Nicole are my neighbors. They **live** next door.

3 변하지 않는 사실 또는 과학적인 사실을 말할 때도 현재 시제를 쓴다.
- The sun **rises** in the east. 해는 동쪽에서 뜬다.
- Leaves **fall** from the trees in autumn. 가을에 나뭇잎이 나무에서 떨어진다.
- Rain **comes** from clouds.

P R A C T I C E

A. 다음 스케줄을 보고 Karen의 일상에 대해 말해보세요.

WEEKDAY SCHEDULE
07:00 wake up
08:00 leave home
09:00 start work
NOON go to lunch
06:00 finish work

1. Karen _wakes up_ at 7 o'clock.
2. She _____ at 8 o'clock.
3. She _____ at 9 o'clock.
4. She _____ at noon.
5. She _____ at 6 o'clock.

B. 주어진 동사를 사용하여 문장을 완성하세요.

| bake | ~~give~~ | like | need | play | sleep |

1. Many people _give_ presents on Christmas.
2. Plants _____ water and sunlight to live.
3. Carl _____ the summer. He hates cold weather.
4. Bats _____ during the day and hunt at night.
5. Brenda _____ golf every day after work.
6. My sister often _____ pies at home. They taste great.

UNIT 9 He **doesn't like** fish.

현재 시제 부정문

> I don't like fish.

긍정 She **likes** fish. 그녀는 생선을 좋아한다.

부정 He **doesn't like** fish. 그는 생선을 좋아하지 않는다.

1 현재 시제 부정문은 **do/does not** + 동사원형으로 쓴다.

I we you they	do not (= don't)	work know need travel
he she it	does not (= doesn't)	

- I **don't work** on weekends. 주말에 일하지 않는다.
- We **don't know** this city well. We're new here. 우리는 이 도시를 잘 모른다.
- You **don't need** a jacket. It's warm today.
- My parents **don't travel** a lot. They usually stay home.
- Ray has a guitar, but he **doesn't play** it much.
- Dina **doesn't swim**. She's afraid of the water.
- The store **doesn't open** early in the morning.

* 일상적인 대화나 글에서는 do not/does not 보다는 don't/doesn't를 더 자주 쓴다.

2 주어가 **he/she/it**일 때 **does not** (= **doesn't**)을 쓰는 것에 주의한다.

- "Is that Anita?" "No, Anita **doesn't wear** glasses." (Anita don't wear로 쓸 수 없음)

이때, **does not** (= **doesn't**) 다음에 동사원형을 쓰는 것에 주의한다.

- Martin **doesn't cook** at home. He usually eats out. (Martin doesn't cooks로 쓸 수 없음)

PRACTICE

A. 괄호 안에 주어진 표현을 사용하여 부정문을 완성하세요.

1. (have a watch) "What time is it?" "Sorry. I _don't have a watch_ OR _do not have a watch_."
2. (understand Chinese) Scott has many Chinese friends, but he _____.
3. (look well) "You _____." "I think I have a cold."
4. (have a lot of homework) "I usually _____." "Wow, you're so lucky!"
5. (watch) Judy _____ TV. She prefers to read.
6. (make much noise) My apartment is quiet. My neighbors _____.
7. (clean) Brad _____ his room often. It's usually dirty.
8. (run after midnight) We need to take a taxi. The subway _____.

B. 그림을 보고 괄호 안에 주어진 동사를 사용하여 문장을 완성하세요. 필요한 경우 부정문으로 쓰세요.

 This is our car.
 You're Ted, right? / Yes, I am.

 I hate the rain.

1. (know) He _doesn't know_ the answer.
2. (have) They _____ a car.
3. (remember) She _____ his name.
4. (want) They _____ any more food.
5. (like) She _____ rainy days.

UNIT 10 Do you speak English?

현재 시제 의문문

긍정 You **speak** English. 당신은 영어를 한다.

의문 **Do** you **speak** English? 영어를 하시나요?

1 현재 시제 의문문은 **do/does** + 주어 + 동사원형으로 쓴다.

do	I we you they	look … ? have … ? like … ? visit … ?
does	he she it	

- **Do** I **look** OK in this dress? 제가 이 옷을 입으니 괜찮아 보이나요?
- "**Do** we **have** any eggs?" 달걀이 있니? "Look in the fridge."
- **Do** you **like** Italian food? I know a good restaurant.
- "**Do** your friends **visit** you often?" "Yes. Every week."
- "**Does** Andrew **work** in a restaurant?" "Yes, he's a chef."
- "**Does** Janine **live** in Vancouver?" "No, she lives in Toronto."
- "**Does** that café **sell** tea?" "Yes. It has several kinds."

2 다음과 같이 의문문에 짧게 답할 수 있다.

Yes,	I/we/you/they	do.
	he/she/it	does.

No,	I/we/you/they	don't.
	he/she/it	doesn't.

- "**Do** you **know** Susie?" Susie를 아나요? "Yes, I do." (= Yes, I know Susie.)
- "**Does** Harry **play** the cello?" "No, he doesn't." (= No, he doesn't play the cello.)

PRACTICE

A. 괄호 안에 주어진 표현을 사용하여 예시와 같이 질문해 보세요.

1. (you, remember me) *Do you remember me* ? Of course! Hi, Cathy.
2. (Ann, have a boyfriend) _____ ? Yes, his name is Mike.
3. (you, read the newspaper) _____ ? No, I don't.
4. (Jack, play any sports) _____ ? Yes. Volleyball.
5. (your parents, call you) _____ often? Yes, they do.
6. (you, own a bicycle) _____ ? No, but I want one.
7. (the bus, usually arrive) _____ on time? No, it doesn't.
8. (your kids, like dogs) _____ ? Yes. They love them.

B. 주어진 의문문을 보고 예시와 같이 짧게 답하세요.

1. A: Do you often wear jeans?
   B: *Yes, I do* .

2. A: Do I need a haircut?
   B: _____ . Your hair is fine.

3. A: Does Steve usually eat out for lunch?
   B: _____ . He always brings his lunch.

4. A: Do you use the Internet a lot?
   B: _____ . I check my e-mail daily.

5. A: Does your daughter go to college?
   B: _____ . She's in high school.

6. A: Do your neighbors have any children?
   B: _____ . They have three sons.

UNIT 11 I am doing vs. I do

현재진행 시제와 현재 시제 비교

현재진행 시제 **He is playing** a computer game now.
그는 지금 컴퓨터 게임을 하는 중이다.

현재 시제 **He plays** soccer often,
but he's not playing soccer now.
그는 축구를 자주 하지만, 지금은 축구를 하고 있지 않다.

1

현재진행 시제 (I am doing ~)

I'm jogging now.

과거   지금   미래

현재진행 시제는 지금 말하고 있는 시점에 일어나고 있는 일을 나타낸다.

- I'm jogging now. (지금 조깅하고 있음)
- Jeff isn't wearing a suit today.
  (오늘 정장을 입고 있지 않음)
- Lisa is cooking Chinese food. It smells good.
- Is it snowing a lot outside?
- Look! Lena and Nancy are dancing.
- My sisters aren't watching TV. They're talking.

현재 시제 (I do ~)

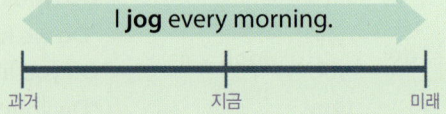

I jog every morning.

과거   지금   미래

현재 시제는 반복적으로 일어나는 일이나 일반적인 사실을 나타낸다.

- I jog every morning. (매일 아침 조깅을 함)
- Jeff doesn't usually wear suits.
  (보통 정장을 입지 않음)
- Lisa cooks Chinese food often.
- Does it snow much here in December?
- Lena and Nancy dance very well.
- My sisters don't watch TV much.

PRACTICE

A. 그림을 보고 괄호 안에 주어진 동사들을 한 번씩 사용하여 문장을 완성하세요.

Name: ANTON
Job: car mechanic

Name: LIZ
Job: sales clerk

Name: GINO
Job: fashion designer

Name: GEORGE
Job: painter

1. (fix, eat) Anton _fixes_ cars. He _'s eating OR is eating_ a sandwich.
2. (ride, work) Liz _____ a horse. She _____ at a shop.
3. (play, design) Gino _____ soccer. He _____ clothes.
4. (paint, sleep) George _____ pictures. He _____ right now.

B. 괄호 안에 주어진 단어들을 사용하여 현재진행 시제 또는 현재 시제 문장을 완성하세요.

1. (he, wash) "Is Dad in the garage?" "Yes, _he's washing_ _____ the car right now."
2. (Angela, go) _____ to the dentist every month.
3. (I, look) " _____ for my cell phone." "Oh, it's on the kitchen table."
4. (the post office, not deliver) _____ mail on Sundays.
5. (we, buy) _____ our groceries at that supermarket every week.
6. (Jason and Frank, not study) _____ now. They're at the gym.
7. (he, not answer) Mr. Smith's phone is ringing, but _____ it.

UNIT 12 He **wants** a new watch.

현재진행 시제로 쓰지 않고 현재 시제로 쓰는 동사

He **wants** a new watch.
그는 새 시계를 원한다.

1 다음과 같은 동사들은 현재진행 시제로 쓰지 않고 주로 현재 시제로 쓴다.

want	love	prefer	know	agree	remember
need	like	hate	believe	understand	forget

- Claire **loves** tea. She drinks it every morning. Claire는 차를 좋아한다.
- Margaret and I are very different. She never **agrees** with me. 그녀는 결코 나에게 동의하지 않는다.
- "**Do** you **need** some help?" "Yes. I **don't understand** this question."
- "I sometimes **forget** people's names." "Me too."

2 have와 has

'(어떤 물건 등을) 가지고 있다'라는 의미로 말할 때는 현재진행 시제로 쓰지 않고 현재 시제로 쓴다.

- Steve **has** a big house. It's beautiful. (Steve is having a big house로 쓸 수 없음)

그러나 '~을 먹다'라는 의미로 말할 때는 현재진행 시제와 현재 시제 둘 다 쓸 수 있다.

- I usually **have** dinner with my family, but now I'm **having** dinner alone.
  보통 가족과 저녁을 먹지만, 지금은 혼자 먹고 있는 중이다.

PRACTICE

A. 주어진 동사를 사용하여 현재진행 시제 또는 현재 시제 문장을 완성하세요.

| attend | ~~hate~~ | play | remember | spend | swim |

1. Michelle _hates_ snakes. She's afraid of them.
2. The ducks are in the water now. They _____.
3. My sister studies hard. She _____ a lot of time at the library.
4. _____ you _____ Harriet's telephone number?
5. Carla is at a church now. She _____ a wedding.
6. "Do you have any hobbies?" "I sometimes _____ the drums on weekends."

B. 다음 문장을 읽고 틀린 부분이 있으면 바르게 고치세요. 틀린 부분이 없으면 ○로 표시하세요.

1. Howard is knowing my brother. They go to the same school.   _is knowing → knows_
2. Are Matt and Tammy having lunch together?   _____
3. Tom and Sally are at the mall. They shop.   _____
4. "I'm not lying. I promise." "I believe you."   _____
5. Brian isn't having a car. He takes the bus to work.   _____
6. I don't sleep right now. I'm reading a book.   _____

UNIT 13 She **was** in the hospital.

be동사 과거 시제 (was/were)

어제

지금

She **is** at home now.

Yesterday, she **was** in the hospital.
어제 그녀는 병원에 있었다.

1 am/is의 과거는 **was**로 쓰고, are의 과거는 **were**로 쓴다.
- I **was** a student five years ago. Now I**'m** a teacher. 5년 전에 학생이었다. 지금은 선생님이다.
- It **was** cloudy yesterday, but it**'s** sunny today. 어제는 흐렸지만 오늘은 화창하다.
- Melisa and Dan **were** on their honeymoon last week. Now they**'re** back.

2 was/were는 다음과 같이 쓴다.

| I / he/she/it | was |
| we/you/they | were |

- I **was** in Florida last month. 지난 달에 플로리다에 있었다.
- My grandfather **was** a taxi driver many years ago. 할아버지는 수년 전에 택시 운전기사였다.
- Fred and I **were** roommates in college.

was/were는 축약된 형태로 쓰지 않는 것에 주의한다.
- When **I was** young, **I was** interested in airplanes. (I's로 쓸 수 없음)
- Our children were at the zoo yesterday. **They were** so excited. (They're로 쓸 수 없음)

PRACTICE

A. 괄호 안에 주어진 주어와 was 또는 were를 사용하여 문장을 완성하세요.

1. (I) _I was_ _____ in Italy three weeks ago.
2. (the stars) _____ beautiful last night.
3. (Andy) _____ very nice to me at the party yesterday.
4. (my friends and I) _____ at a concert last weekend.
5. (these gloves) "_____ in my car." "Oh, those are mine."
6. (he) "Do you know Mr. Evans?" "Yes, _____ my boss two years ago."
7. (it) _____ very hot on Sunday, so we were at the pool all day.
8. (we) _____ at the new restaurant last night. The food was great.

B. am/is/are 또는 was/were를 써넣으세요.

1. I can't find my keys. They _were_ here a minute ago.
2. I _____ short in middle school. Now I _____ tall.
3. "You _____ in a hurry this morning." "Yes, I was late for an appointment."
4. "When is your birthday?" "It _____ last Friday."
5. "Jenny _____ sick yesterday." "_____ she OK now?"
6. Kelly and Sam _____ my neighbors six years ago.
7. "These cups _____ $10 each." "Really? They _____ on sale last week."
8. Patrick _____ in London last weekend. He _____ in Paris now. He _____ very busy these days.

UNIT 14
I **was not** good at math in high school.

be동사 과거 시제 부정문과 의문문

1 was/were 부정문은 다음과 같이 쓴다.

| I / he/she/it | was not (= wasn't) |
| we/you/they | were not (= weren't) |

- I **was not** good at math in high school. 고등학교 때 수학을 잘하지 못했다.
- My vacation was fun, but it **wasn't** very long. 휴가가 즐거웠지만 길지 않았다.
- Melanie and I **weren't** friends a year ago. Now we're best friends.
- "You **weren't** at the office last week." "I was on a business trip."

* 일상적인 대화나 글에서는 was not/were not 보다는 wasn't/weren't를 더 자주 쓴다.

2 was/were 의문문은 다음과 같이 쓴다.

was	I ... ?
	he/she/it ... ?
were	we/you/they ... ?

- I told you the hotel was nice. **Was I** right? 내가 맞았니?
- **Was Tom** at his desk this morning? Tom이 오늘 아침에 자리에 있었나요?
- "**Were you** busy yesterday?" "Not really."

다음과 같이 의문문에 짧게 답할 수 있다.

| Yes, | I/he/she/it | was. |
| | we/you/they | were. |

| No, | I/he/she/it | wasn't. |
| | we/you/they | weren't. |

- "**Were you** at the mall last night?" 어젯밤에 쇼핑몰에 있었니? "**Yes, I was.**" (= Yes, I was at the mall.)
- "**Was the movie** good?" "**No, it wasn't.**" (= No, it wasn't good.)

PRACTICE

A. 다음은 어제 Philip에게 있었던 일입니다. was 또는 wasn't를 사용하여 문장을 완성하세요.

1  2  3  4  5

1. (tired) Philip _was tired_____ .
2. (asleep) He _____ on the bus.
3. (on time) He _____ .
4. (angry) His boss _____ with him.
5. (happy) He _____ .

B. 괄호 안에 주어진 주어와 was 또는 were를 사용하여 문장을 완성하세요.

1. (it) "How was the date yesterday?" " _It was_____ great."
2. (you) "_____ with Jessica on Saturday?" "No, I was alone."
3. (Howard) "_____ at the meeting yesterday?" "No, he wasn't."
4. (they) The boxes weren't heavy. _____ empty.
5. (the party) "_____ fun?" "Yes, it was."
6. (my parents) "_____ in New York last month." "I was there, too."
7. (the sky) _____ clear last night. There wasn't a cloud in the sky.
8. (you) "_____ at the gym this morning?" "No, I was at the store. Why?"

UNIT 15 He **walked** to school yesterday.

일반동사 과거 시제

어제

He **walks** to school every day.

He **walked** to school yesterday.
어제 그는 학교에 걸어갔다.

walked는 과거 시제이다.

1 '~했다'라는 의미로 과거에 일어난 일에 대해 말할 때 과거 시제를 쓴다. 과거 시제는 주로 동사원형 끝에 **-ed**를 붙인다.

동사원형	clean	finish	watch	laugh	wait
과거 시제	**cleaned**	**finished**	**watched**	**laughed**	**waited**

- I **cleaned** the house last Friday. 지난 금요일에 집을 청소했다.
- The soccer game **finished** at 5 o'clock yesterday.

2 다음과 같이 **-ed**를 붙일 때 주의해야 할 동사들이 있다.

| live → liv**ed** | die → di**ed** | study → stud**ied** | plan → plan**ned** |

◆ -(e)d 붙이는 방법: 부록 p. 171 참고

- Vincent van Gogh **died** in 1890. 빈센트 반 고흐는 1890년에 사망했다.
- We **planned** our vacation a month ago.

과거 시제로 쓸 때 **-ed**를 붙이지 않고 형태가 달라지는 동사들이 있다.

| have → **had** | get → **got** | buy → **bought** | go → **went** |

◆ 불규칙 동사: 부록 p. 168 참고

- Emily **had** bacon and eggs for breakfast this morning. Emily는 오늘 아침에 베이컨과 달걀을 먹었다.
- "I **bought** a new sofa last week." "It's really nice."

PRACTICE

A. 주어진 동사를 사용하여 과거 시제 문장을 완성하세요.

| cry | ~~freeze~~ | go | invite | play | work |

1. The lake _froze_ last winter, so I went skating a lot.
2. I _____ football in high school.
3. My neighbors _____ me for dinner last Friday.
4. The baby was sick last night. She _____ all night.
5. Joe _____ to the store this afternoon for some milk.
6. Jessica _____ at a bookstore when she was in college.

B. 괄호 안에 주어진 단어들을 사용하여 현재 시제 또는 과거 시제 문장을 완성하세요.

1. (the company, hire) _The company hired_ new employees three weeks ago.
2. (it, close) "Is the mall still open?" "Yes. _____ at 10 p.m. every day."
3. (Laura and Nick, get) _____ married last year.
4. (the Earth, travel) _____ around the Sun.
5. (everyone, laugh) _____ at Ken's joke. It was very funny.
6. (I, forget) "I'm sorry. _____ your book." "That's OK. Just bring it next time."
7. (he, fly) Jeff travels a lot. _____ to Singapore on business every month.
8. (I, need) It's so cold out here! _____ a scarf.

UNIT 16 I didn't go to work yesterday.

과거 시제 부정문과 의문문

1 과거 시제 부정문은 **did not** + 동사원형으로 쓴다.

| I / he/she/it / we/you/they | did not (= didn't) | go / arrive / sleep |

- I **didn't go** to work yesterday. 어제 회사에 가지 않았다.
- The bus **didn't arrive** on time this morning. 오늘 아침에 버스가 제시간에 도착하지 않았다.
- We **didn't sleep** much last night because of the storm.

* 일상적인 대화나 글에서는 did not 보다는 didn't를 더 자주 쓴다.

did not (= didn't) 다음에 동사원형을 쓰는 것에 주의한다.
- I **didn't stay** at home last weekend. I went out with my friends. (I didn't stayed로 쓸 수 없음)
- Danny **didn't fix** the printer. I did. (Danny didn't fixed로 쓸 수 없음)

2 의문문은 **did + 주어 + 동사원형**으로 쓴다.

| Did | I / he/she/it / we/you/they | leave ... ? / tell ... ? / like ... ? |

- "**Did I leave** my jacket here?" 제가 여기에 재킷을 두고 갔나요? "Yes, here you go."
- **Did** Susie **tell** you about her wedding? Susie가 결혼식에 대해 얘기했니?
- I didn't enjoy the show. **Did** you **like** it?

다음과 같이 의문문에 짧게 답할 수 있다.

| Yes, | I/he/she/it we/you/they | did. | No, | I/he/she/it we/you/they | didn't. |

- "**Did** you **take** these pictures?" 네가 이 사진들을 찍었니? "**Yes, I did.**" (= Yes, I took these pictures.)
- "**Did** Mark **get** a haircut?" "**No, he didn't.**" (= No, he didn't get a haircut.)

PRACTICE

A. 다음 목록을 보고 Miranda가 어제 한 일과 하지 않은 일들에 대해 말해보세요.

1. do the laundry — X
2. read the newspaper — X
3. go to the gym — O
4. wash the car — X
5. attend the cooking class — O
6. have dinner with Jackie — O

1. *She didn't do the laundry* OR *She did not do the laundry*.
2. _____.
3. _____.
4. _____.
5. _____.
6. _____.

B. 괄호 안에 주어진 단어들을 사용하여 과거 시제 의문문을 완성하세요.

1. (you, lose) *Did you lose* some weight? Yes, I lost five pounds.
2. (Sarah, pass) _____ her math exam? Yes, she's so happy.
3. (you, read) _____ this book? Yes. It was very good.
4. (someone, knock) _____ on the door? No. I don't think so.
5. (you, get) _____ my e-mail? I sent it yesterday. Yes, I did.
6. (we, miss) _____ the train? No. We're on time.
7. (Dave, grow) _____ up in France? No. He's from Italy.
8. (the Smiths, buy) _____ a house? Yes, it's very nice.

UNIT 17 He **was playing** the guitar.

과거진행 시제

At 7 o'clock he was at school.

He **was playing** the guitar.
그는 기타를 치는 중이었다.

was playing은 과거진행 시제이다.

1 과거진행 시제는 was/were + -ing로 쓴다.

I he/she/it	was	taking studying having cleaning
we/you/they	were	

- I **was taking** a shower when Lisa called. Lisa가 전화했을 때 샤워하는 중이었다.
- Ted **was studying** in London in 2001. 2001년에 런던에서 공부하고 있었다.
- At 1 o'clock today, we **were having** lunch.
- Benny and Mike **were cleaning** the kitchen this morning.

2 '~하는 중이었다'는 의미로 과거의 특정한 시점에 진행 중이었던 일에 대해 말할 때 과거진행 시제를 쓴다.

I was sleeping.

2:30 잠자기 시작 — 3:00 — 3:30 잠에서 깸

- I **was sleeping** at 3 o'clock yesterday. 나는 어제 3시에 자고 있었다.
- Jen **was looking** for you an hour ago. Where were you?
  Jen이 한 시간 전에 너를 찾고 있었어.
- I saw Joe and Rita. They **were talking** at the bookstore.
- My parents **were working** in the same company when they first met.

PRACTICE

A. 주어진 동사를 사용하여 과거진행 시제 문장을 완성하세요.

| attend   cross   eat   ~~listen~~   play   wait |

1. I _was listening_ to loud music, so I didn't hear the doorbell.
2. Oscar _____ breakfast when the mail arrived.
3. Many people _____ in line at the bank this morning.
4. Tara and I _____ a swimming class at 10:30 this morning.
5. I saw John and Fred at the park. They _____ basketball.
6. I _____ the street when someone called my name.

B. 괄호 안에 주어진 단어들을 사용하여 과거진행 시제 문장을 완성하세요.

1. (she, hide) "Did you find your cat?" "Yes, _she was hiding_ under the sofa."
2. (Jim and Monica, drink) _____ wine together at a bar last night.
3. (Alice, lie) _____ in bed when her mom knocked on the door.
4. (I, visit) "Were you in town on Christmas?" "No. _____ my family in Texas."
5. (Becky and I, do) At 9 o'clock yesterday, _____ homework at the library.
6. (the phone, ring) _____ when I entered the house.
7. (we, stand) _____ at the bus stop when someone asked for directions.
8. (it, snow) _____ outside when I woke up this morning.

UNIT 18 I wasn't sleeping.

과거진행 시제 부정문과 의문문

1 과거진행 시제 부정문은 다음과 같이 쓴다.

I / he/she/it	was not (= wasn't)	sleeping jogging
we/you/they	were not (= weren't)	waiting eating

- "Did I wake you?" "No, I **wasn't sleeping**." 자고 있지 않았어.
- Ken **wasn't jogging** at 8. He was at home.
  Ken은 8시에 조깅하고 있지 않았다.
- "Sorry I'm late." "Don't worry. We **weren't waiting** long."
- Nick and Joe **weren't eating**. They were still looking at the menu.

2 과거진행 시제 의문문은 다음과 같이 쓴다.

was	I / he/she/it	talking ... ? driving ... ?
were	we/you/they	working ... ? attending ... ?

- **Was I talking** too loudly? 내가 너무 크게 말하고 있었니?
- "**Was** Lou **driving**?" Lou가 운전하고 있었니? "No. I was driving."
- "**Were** you **working** in LA in 2010?" "No, I was in Seattle."
- **Were** you and Pete **attending** a wedding when I called on Sunday?

다음과 같이 의문문에 짧게 답할 수 있다.

Yes,	I/he/she/it	was.
	we/you/they	were.

No,	I/he/she/it	wasn't.
	we/you/they	weren't.

- "**Was** Diane **washing** her car when you saw her?" Diane이 세차하고 있었니?
  "**Yes, she was**." (= Yes, she was washing her car.)
- "**Were** your roommates **watching** a football game when you got up?"
  "**No, they weren't**." (= No, they weren't watching a football game.)

PRACTICE

A. 다음은 어제 Jay가 파티에 도착했을 때의 모습입니다. 괄호 안에 주어진 동사를 사용하여 문장을 완성하세요. 필요한 경우 부정문으로 쓰세요.

1 ANN

2 MIKE EMMA

3 JENNY

4 JACK BILL

5 RYAN

When Jay arrived at the party…

1. (sing) Ann _was singing_ a song.
2. (sit) Mike and Emma _____ at a table.
3. (carry) Jenny _____ a gift.
4. (have) Jack and Bill _____ cake.
5. (wear) Ryan _____ a suit.

B. 주어진 단어들을 사용하여 과거진행 시제 문장을 완성하세요. 필요한 경우 부정문으로 쓰세요.

| ~~look~~ | make | practice | ride | walk | work |

1. (I) "I saw you at the mall. Were you shopping?" "Yes. _I was looking_ for a new tie."
2. (Victor) "I heard the piano. _____ for his concert?" "Yes, he was."
3. (Eric and I) _____ in the office at noon. We were out for lunch.
4. (we) The food wasn't ready on time. _____ it when the guests arrived.
5. (you) You are all wet! _____ home from school when the rain started?
6. (Nick) _____ his bicycle. He was on his skateboard.

UNIT 19 He **used to** be a football player.

He is a golfer now.

He **used to be** a football player.
그는 미식축구 선수였다. (지금은 아니다.)

1 used to + 동사원형: (과거에는) ~ 했었다 (지금은 아니다)

| I we/you/they he/she/it | used to | be work cry |

- I'm a music teacher, but I **used to be** a singer. (과거에는 가수였지만 지금은 아님)
- "Do you know Sandra?" "Yes, we **used to work** together." (과거에는 함께 일했지만 지금은 아님)
- My little sister **used to cry** a lot, but now she doesn't cry often.

2 used to는 지금은 더 이상 계속되지 않는 과거의 습관이나 상태에 대해 말할 때 쓴다.

- My father **used to smoke** every day. Now he doesn't smoke anymore. (과거에는 담배를 매일 피웠지만 지금은 아님)
- I **used to live** alone, but now I have a roommate. (과거에는 혼자 살았지만 지금은 아님)

현재에 대해 말할 때는 **used to**를 쓰지 않는 것에 주의한다.

- Cindy used to study French. Now she **studies** Italian. (she uses to study로 쓸 수 없음)
- I used to believe in Santa Claus, but I **don't believe** in him anymore. (I don't use to believe로 쓸 수 없음)

PRACTICE

A. 그림을 보고 used to를 사용하여 예시와 같이 문장을 완성하세요.

1. He _used to play_ basketball.
2. He _____ afraid of dogs.
3. He _____ his car.
4. They _____ in San Francisco.

B. 주어진 동사를 사용하여 문장을 완성하세요. used to를 함께 쓰거나 현재 시제로 쓰세요.

| exercise   go   listen   ~~play~~   remember   ride |

1. "Do you play video games?" "No, I _used to play_ them, but I don't anymore."
2. Jennifer _____ every day. She wants to lose some weight.
3. "Do you know that woman's name?" "Yes. I _____ her name. It's Marsha."
4. Eddie _____ to rock music. Now he prefers jazz.
5. The Smiths _____ fishing a lot, but they're too busy these days.
6. We _____ the bus to school. Now we take the subway.

UNIT 20

현재완료 시제 (1)

She **has washed** the dishes.

She **has washed** the dishes.
(설거지를 해서 지금은 그릇들이 깨끗해졌음)

has washed는 현재완료 시제이다.

1 현재완료 시제는 **have/has + 과거분사**로 쓴다.

긍정

I/we/you/they	have (= 've)	washed
he/she/it	has (= 's)	lived
		watched

부정

I/we/you/they	have not (= haven't)	washed
he/she/it	has not (= hasn't)	lived
		watched

과거분사는 주로 동사원형 끝에 **-(e)d**를 붙인다.

live-lived-**lived**   ask-asked-**asked**   talk-talked-**talked**   ◆ -(e)d 붙이는 방법: 부록 p. 171 참고

그러나 다음과 같이 형태가 불규칙적으로 변하는 동사도 있다.

buy-bought-**bought**   have-had-**had**   make-made-**made**   ◆ 불규칙 동사: 부록 p. 168 참고

2 현재완료 시제는 과거부터 현재까지를 포괄하는 시제로, 과거에 있었던 일을 현재와 관련지어 말할 때 쓴다.

- I **have lived** in LA since 2008. (2008년부터 지금까지 LA에 계속 살고 있음)
- We **haven't been** to Egypt before. (과거부터 지금까지 이집트에 가본 경험이 없음)
- Bob **has watched** that TV show for five years. He never misses it.

I **have lived** in LA.
과거 ─────────── 현재 (지금)

PRACTICE

A. 주어진 동사의 과거형과 과거분사를 쓰세요.

1. give - *gave* - *given*
2. go   - _____ - _____
3. stop - _____ - _____
4. talk - _____ - _____
5. eat   - _____ - _____
6. play - _____ - _____
7. write - _____ - _____
8. make - _____ - _____
9. drive - _____ - _____
10. know - _____ - _____
11. watch - _____ - _____
12. meet - _____ - _____

B. 괄호 안에 주어진 동사를 사용하여 현재완료 시제 문장을 완성하세요. 필요한 경우 부정문으로 쓰세요.

1. (hear) "Do you know this song?" "Yes, I *'ve heard* OR *have heard* it before."
2. (eat) I woke up late this morning, so I _____ breakfast yet.
3. (grow) Your daughter _____ so much! She was so little when I saw her last time.
4. (speak) Is Carla angry with me? She _____ to me for three days.
5. (ride) "Did you see Dave's new car?" "Yes, we _____ in it already."
6. (see) "I _____ Mary since Monday." "She's in Toronto."
7. (find) The Andersons lost their dog last night, and they _____ him yet.
8. (attend) Peter enjoys music. He _____ many concerts.

UNIT 21 He **has known** her **for** five years.

현재완료 시제 (2) 현재까지 계속되는 일

2008년 (5년 전)

지금

Justin met Sandy five years ago.
They're still friends.

He **has known** her **for** five years. 또는
5년 동안 알고 지내왔다.

He **has known** her **since** 2008.
2008년부터 알고 지내왔다.

1 현재완료 시제는 '(과거부터 지금까지) 계속 ~해왔다'라는 의미로 말할 때 쓸 수 있다. 이때, **for** 또는 **since**와 자주 함께 쓴다.

have/has + 과거분사 + **for** + 기간 (three months 등)
: ~ 동안 계속 …해왔다

have/has + 과거분사 + **since** + 시작된 시점 (May 등)
: ~부터 계속 …해왔다

―― 3개월 동안 ――
I **have studied** French **for** three months.
May   June   July   지금

5월부터 ――
I **have studied** French **since** May.
May   지금

- I **have studied** French **for** three months.
  3개월 동안 계속 프랑스어를 공부해왔다.
- Lily **has lived** in England **for** two years.
  Lily는 2년 동안 계속 영국에서 살아왔다.
- We **haven't seen** Kathy **for** a week.

- I **have studied** French **since** May.
  5월부터 계속 프랑스어를 공부해왔다.
- Lily **has lived** in England **since** 2011.
  Lily는 2011년부터 계속 영국에서 살아왔다.
- We **haven't seen** Kathy **since** Thursday.

2 How long have you ~ ? : ~한 지 얼마나 되었나요?
- "How long have you been here?" 여기에 온 지 얼마나 되었나요? "For three weeks."
- "How long have you had your driver's license?" "Since last year."

PRACTICE

A. 괄호 안에 주어진 표현을 사용하여 현재완료 시제 문장을 완성하세요. **for** 또는 **since**를 함께 쓰세요.
1. (not talk to Ben) I _haven't talked to Ben for_ two weeks. I've been so busy lately.
2. (be married) Stan and Louise _____ eight years. They have two kids.
3. (not rain) Farmers are worried because it _____ June.
4. (drive his car) Ken _____ nine hours. He's very tired right now.
5. (lose 10 pounds) "Emily _____ last month." "Wow. That's amazing!"
6. (not eat anything) What's wrong with Luke? He _____ yesterday.

B. How long ~ ?을 사용하여 예시와 같이 의문문을 완성하세요.
1. A: I work at a coffee shop.
   B: _How long have you worked_ there?
2. A: Steve collects comic books.
   B: _____ them?
3. A: Alex and Sam go to the same school.
   B: _____ to the same school?
4. A: My daughter takes ballet lessons.
   B: _____ them?
5. A: Jimmy is asleep.
   B: _____ asleep?
6. A: I have a roommate.
   B: _____ a roommate?

UNIT 22 She **hasn't seen** this movie.

현재완료 시제 (3) 지금까지 경험해본 일

She **hasn't seen** this movie.
그녀는 이 영화를 본 적이 없다.

1. 현재완료 시제는 '(과거부터 지금까지) ~해본 적이 있다'라는 의미로 말할 때 쓸 수 있다.
   - We **have visited** Europe many times. 유럽에 여러 번 가본 적이 있다.
   - I **haven't tried** Indian food. Is it good? 인도 음식을 먹어본 적이 없다.
   - Tony **has met** the president before.
   - Mandy **hasn't taken** art lessons, but she's a good artist.

   We **have visited** Europe.
   과거 ─────────── 지금

2. **Have you ever** + 과거분사: 지금까지 ~해본 적이 있나요?
   - **Have you ever stayed** up all night? 지금까지 밤을 새본 적이 있나요?
   - "**Have you ever made** cookies?" "Yes. How about you?"

   have/has never + 과거분사: ~해본 적이 전혀 없다
   - I **have never owned** a pet. 나는 반려동물을 가져본 적이 전혀 없다.
   - Bruce always studies very hard. He**'s never failed** an exam.

   have/has been (to ~): (~에) 가본 적이 있다
   - Mr. Miller **has been to** many countries. Miller씨는 많은 나라에 가본 적이 있다.
   - I went to the new restaurant yesterday. **Have** you **been** there?

PRACTICE

A. 주어진 표현과 **I've** 또는 **I've never**를 사용하여 자신에 대해 말하세요.

1. be to Sweden
2. play chess before
3. live in the country
4. ride a roller coaster
5. see a kangaroo

1. I've (never) been to Sweden   .
2. _____.
3. _____.
4. _____.
5. _____.

B. 주어진 표현과 **Have you ever ~ ?**를 사용하여 문장을 완성하세요.

| be to Paris | ~~eat sushi~~ | go skiing |
| run a marathon | swim in the ocean | watch an opera |

1. A: *Have you ever eaten sushi*   ?
   B: Yes, it's delicious.
2. A: _____?
   B: Yes, last year. The music was amazing.
3. A: _____?
   B: No, I don't like winter sports.
4. A: _____?
   B: Yes, I go to the beach every summer.
5. A: _____?
   B: Yes, it's a beautiful city.
6. A: _____before?
   B: Yes, but I didn't finish the race.

UNIT 23 I did vs. I have done

과거 시제와 현재완료 시제 비교

They **moved** to New York City in 1990.
(1990년에 뉴욕시로 이사를 했음)

They **have lived** in New York City since 1990.
(1990년부터 지금까지 뉴욕시에서 살고 있음)

1 지금과 관련 짓지 않고 과거에 끝난 일이나 상황 자체에 대해서만 말할 때는 과거 시제를 쓴다.

- Christine **went** to the beach an hour ago.
  (한 시간 전에 해변에 갔음)
- Mike **changed** his phone number last week.
  (지난주에 전화번호를 바꿨음)

과거에 일어난 일이나 상황이 지금과 관련되어 있음을 말할 때는 현재완료 시제를 쓴다.

- Christine **has gone** to the beach.
  (해변에 가서 지금 여기에 없음)
- Mike **has changed** his phone number.
  (전화번호를 바꿔서 지금은 번호가 다름)

2 지금까지 어떤 일이 계속되고 있다는 의미로 말할 때는 현재완료 시제를 쓴다. 이때, 과거 시제를 쓰지 않는 것에 주의한다.

- My parents **have been** married for 30 years. (지금까지 결혼한 상태이므로 과거 시제 were married로 쓸 수 없음)
- I miss Jenna. I **haven't seen** her since last year. (지금까지 그녀를 보지 못하고 있으므로 과거 시제 didn't see로 쓸 수 없음)

이미 지나간 과거의 시점(last night, two days ago 등)에 대해 말할 때는 과거 시제만 쓰는 것에 주의한다.

- I **watched** a football game **last night**. (last night은 이미 지나간 과거 시점이므로 과거 시제 watched를 썼음)
- Aaron is on vacation. He **left** for Hawaii **two days ago**. (two days ago는 이미 지나간 과거 시점이므로 과거 시제 left를 썼음)

PRACTICE

A. 주어진 동사를 사용하여 현재완료 시제 또는 과거 시제 문장을 완성하세요.

| ~~call~~   grow   invent   see   study   work |

1. "Have you talked to Pam lately?" "Yes, she _called_ me last Friday."
2. Richard is a doctor at this hospital. He _____ here for two years.
3. Alexander Graham Bell _____ the telephone in 1876.
4. "Do you speak Japanese?" "A little. I _____ it since January."
5. I _____ a huge snake at the zoo last weekend.
6. "Your son _____ since last year." "Yes. He's taller now."

B. 다음 문장을 읽고 틀린 부분이 있으면 바르게 고치세요. 틀린 부분이 없으면 O로 표시하세요.

1. Julia hasn't gone to work yesterday.   *hasn't gone → didn't go*
2. My brother graduated from college last May.   _____
3. Randy has visited India in 1998.   _____
4. I knew Ann for 10 years. We are best friends. _____
5. We have stayed in this hotel for a week. Everything has been perfect. _____
6. I didn't use my computer since last week.   _____
7. I had an omelet for breakfast this morning. It was delicious. _____
8. How long did you play the trumpet? You play so well. _____

UNIT 24 We've just started.

just, already, yet

1 have/has + just + 과거분사: 방금 막 ~했다
- "Am I late for the meeting?" "No. We've just started." 방금 막 시작했어요.
- The plane from Boston has just arrived at the airport. Boston에서 온 비행기가 공항에 방금 막 도착했다.
- "Excuse me, you've just dropped your wallet." "Oh, thank you."

have/has + already + 과거분사: (예상보다 앞서) 이미 ~했다
- "Let's invite Andy to our party." "I've already invited him." 이미 그를 초대했어.
- "Jamie was looking for you." "I've already talked to her." 이미 그녀와 얘기했어.
- "We need to buy a cake for Dad's birthday." "Mom has already made one."

haven't/hasn't + 과거분사 + yet (부정문): 아직 ~하지 않았다
- Don't touch the chair. The paint hasn't dried yet. 페인트가 아직 마르지 않았어.
- "Did you do the laundry?" "No, I haven't done it yet."

Have/Has ~ + 과거분사 + yet? (의문문): 아직 ~하지 않았나요?
- "Has Anna returned from her trip yet?" Anna가 여행에서 아직 돌아오지 않았니? "No. She'll be back next week."
- "Max gave me a CD." "Have you listened to it yet?"

2 just, already, yet은 현재완료 시제와 함께 쓸 수도 있고, 과거 시제와 함께 쓸 수도 있다. 이때, 의미 차이가 없다.
- I've just finished lunch. 또는 I just finished lunch. 방금 막 점심 식사를 마쳤어.
- Monica has already spent all of her money. 또는 Monica already spent all of her money. 이미 돈을 다 썼어.
- "Did we miss the bus?" "No, it hasn't come yet." 또는 "No, it didn't come yet."

PRACTICE

A. 그림을 보고 주어진 동사와 just를 사용하여 현재완료 시제 문장을 완성하세요.

| dive | ~~leave~~ | meet | open |

1. She _'s just left_ OR _has just left_ the house.
2. He _____ into the pool.
3. The mall _____.
4. They _____ each other.

B. 괄호 안에 주어진 표현을 사용하여 예시와 같이 문장을 완성하세요. 필요한 경우 부정문으로 쓰세요.
1. (she, receive it, yet) I sent a postcard to Lisa, but _she hasn't received it yet_ OR _she didn't receive it yet_.
2. (I, find a job, yet) "_____. I'm so worried."
   "I'm sure you'll find one soon."
3. (I, already, have some) "Would you like some coffee?"
   "Thanks, but _____."
4. (Lily, call you back, yet) "_____?" "No. Maybe she's busy."
5. (Dave, already, finish his painting) "_____."
   "Wow. He's very fast."
6. (you, visit him, yet) "My uncle is in the hospital." "_____?"

UNIT 25 She will run tomorrow.

미래 시제 (1) will

She **runs** every day. She **ran** yesterday.
She **will run** tomorrow.
그녀는 내일 달릴 것이다.

will run은 미래 시제이다.

1 will + 동사원형: ~할 것이다

긍정			부정			의문		
I/we/you/they he/she/it	will (= 'll)	be make	I/we/you/they he/she/it	will not (= won't)	be make	will	I/we/you/they he/she/it	be …? make …?

- **I'll be** in the office this afternoon. 오늘 오후에 사무실에 있을 것이다.
- "The baby is sleeping." "OK. I **won't make** any noise." 시끄럽게 하지 않을게요.
- "**Will** Rob **finish** the report by tomorrow?" "I hope so."

2 will은 미래의 사실이나 미래에 일어날 것이라고 생각하는 일에 대해 말할 때 쓴다.

- Sharon **will be** 18 years old next year. Sharon은 내년에 18살이 될 것이다.
- "**Will** it **snow** tomorrow?" 내일 눈이 올까? "Maybe."
- "I'm worried about the test on Monday." "Don't worry. You**'ll do** fine."

will은 말하고 있는 시점인 지금 어떤 일을 하기로 결정하는 경우에도 쓴다.

- "Larry, the music is too loud!" "OK, I**'ll turn** down the volume." (음악을 줄이기로 지금 결정함)
- I think we're lost. I**'ll ask** for directions. (길을 물어보기로 지금 결정함)
- "The party for Patty is a surprise." "All right. I **won't tell** her about it."

PRACTICE

A. 괄호 안에 주어진 단어들과 will을 사용하여 문장을 완성하세요. 필요한 경우 부정문으로 쓰세요.

1. (I, have) "Are you ready to order?" "Yes, _I'll have OR I will have_ the chicken salad, please."
2. (it, take) "Is the museum far from here?" "No, we can walk. _____ long."
3. (you, drive) "_____ to work tomorrow?" "Probably."
4. (I, wear) "This tie doesn't match your suit." "Really? _____ it, then."
5. (you, meet) "_____ Mr. Mays at the airport?" "No, at his hotel."
6. (you, find) "Where is Mr. Scott's office?"
   "Go to the 11th floor. _____ it next to the elevator."

B. 주어진 동사를 사용하여 문장을 완성하세요. 과거 시제 또는 현재 시제로 쓰거나 will을 함께 쓰세요.

| ~~buy~~ explain go listen love snow |

1. "I like your dress." "Thanks. I just _bought_ it last week."
2. "I don't understand this question." "Don't worry. I _____ it to you."
3. Bill _____ to music every day. He likes music very much.
4. "I'm planning a trip to Singapore." "It's beautiful there. You _____ it."
5. Dan _____ to bed late last night, so he's tired today.
6. It _____ a lot in Alaska. It's very cold there.

UNIT 26 He's going to make dinner tonight.

미래 시제 (2) be going to

I'm going to make dinner tonight.

He's going to make dinner tonight.
그는 오늘 저녁 식사를 준비할 것이다.

is going to make는 미래 시제이다.

1 be going to + 동사원형: ~할 것이다

긍정·부정

I	am			be
he/she/it	is	(not)	going to	drive
we/you/they	are			clean

의문

am	I		be ... ?
is	he/she/it	going to	drive ... ?
are	we/you/they		clean ... ?

- It's going to be very hot today. 오늘은 매우 더울 것이다.
- Traffic is bad. We're not going to drive. 운전하지 않을 것이다.
- "Are you going to clean your room?" "Yes, but I'm going to wash the dishes first."

2 이미 하기로 결정한 미래의 일에 대해 말할 때 be going to + 동사원형을 쓴다.

- Susan is going to move to Chicago. She bought a house there. (시카고로 이사하기로 이미 결정했음)
- We're not going to eat out tonight. Mom already made dinner at home. (외식을 하지 않기로 이미 결정했음)

be going to는 지금 상황을 근거로 미래에 어떤 일이 일어날 것이 확실하다고 말할 때도 쓴다.

- The sun is going down. It's going to be dark soon. (해가 지고 있는 것을 보아 곧 어두워질 것 같음)
- The bus is leaving! We're going to miss it. (버스가 떠나고 있는 것을 보아 버스를 놓칠 것 같음)

PRACTICE

A. 괄호 안에 주어진 단어들과 be going to를 사용하여 문장을 완성하세요. 필요한 경우 부정문으로 쓰세요.

1. (I, attend) _I'm going to attend_ a seminar tomorrow. It's about African art.
2. (they, get) Andy proposed to Hannah. _____ married soon.
3. (I, go) _____ to the musical tonight. I'm not feeling well today.
4. (you, buy) "_____ that car?" "I'm still thinking about it."
5. (Brian, join) _____ us for lunch. He has an important meeting at noon.
6. (Tina, meet) "_____ us at the train station?" "Yes. At around 10 o'clock."

B. 그림을 보고 주어진 표현과 be going to를 사용하여 문장을 완성하세요.

| have a sale | play golf | take an exam | ~~watch a movie~~ |

1  2  3  4

1. She _'s going to watch a movie_ .
2. He _____ .
3. They _____ .
4. She _____ .

UNIT 27 I will vs. I'm going to

미래 시제 (3) will과 be going to 비교

Those shoes are so nice.
I'll buy them. (지금 사기로 결정함)

I saw some nice shoes.
I'm going to buy them. (이미 사기로 결정했음)

1 말하고 있는 시점인 지금 어떤 일을 하기로 결정하는 경우 **will**을 주로 쓴다.

말하고 있는 시점 이전에 이미 어떤 일을 하기로 결정해 놓았을 경우 **be going to**를 주로 쓴다.

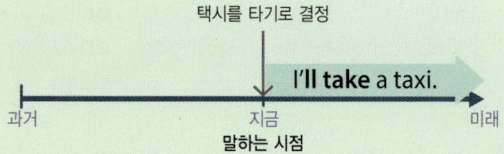

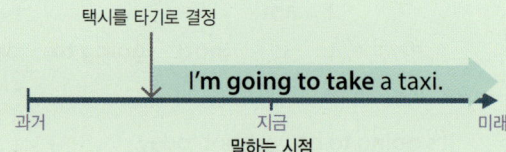

- "You're late for work."
  "Oh no! I'**ll take** a taxi, then."
  (말하고 있는 시점인 지금 택시를 타기로 결정함)
- "I can't lift this box."
  "I'**ll help** you."
  (말하고 있는 시점인 지금 도와주기로 결정함)
- "It's going to snow a lot today."
  "Really? I'**ll wear** my boots."

- "You're late for work."
  "I know. I'**m going to take** a taxi."
  (말하고 있는 시점 이전에 이미 택시를 타기로 결정했음)
- "Do you need my help?"
  "That's all right. Tom **is going to help** me."
  (말하고 있는 시점 이전에 이미 도와주기로 결정했음)
- "It's going to snow a lot today."
  "I saw the news. I'**m going to wear** my boots."

PRACTICE

A. 둘 중 더 적절한 것을 고르세요.

1. "Can I see the menu, please?" "Of course. (**I'll bring** / I'm going to bring) you one."
2. "I forgot my wallet." "Oh. (I'll pay / I'm going to pay), then."
3. "Do you and Eva have any plans for Saturday?" "Yes. (We'll go / We're going to go) to the beach."
4. "I feel so sleepy." "(I'll make / I'm going to make) some coffee for you, then."
5. (We'll visit / We're going to visit) our cousins in Tokyo next week. We've already bought the tickets.
6. "Why is Anne buying so many eggs?" "(She'll bake / She's going to bake) a cake for my birthday."

B. Shelly는 Brad와 함께 파티에 갈 계획을 한 뒤, Emma에게 그 계획에 대하여 처음으로 말하고 있습니다. 괄호 안에 주어진 표현과 **will** 또는 **be going to** 중 더 적절한 것을 사용하여 대화를 완성하세요.

SHELLY: 1. Brad and I _are going to attend Jessie's party tonight_ .
(attend Jessie's party tonight) We're leaving right now.
EMMA: I'm going too! Let's go together.
SHELLY: Good idea.
2. Traffic is bad today, so we _____. (walk there)
EMMA: 3. OK. I _____. (get my coat)
SHELLY: We must stop at the store.
4. We _____. (buy some snacks)
EMMA: All right. 5. I _____, then. (buy some wine)

UNIT 28 She **is leaving** tomorrow.

미래 시제 (4) 미래를 나타내는 현재진행과 현재 시제

She is leaving tomorrow.
그녀는 내일 떠날 예정이다.

is leaving은 현재진행의 형태이지만 미래의 의미이다.

1 구체적으로 계획을 세워 둔 미래의 일(약속, 예약 등)에 대해 말할 때 **am/is/are + -ing**를 쓴다.
- **I'm seeing** Bob on Friday. **We're going** to the opera. 금요일에 Bob을 만날 예정이다. 오페라를 볼 예정이다.
- Michelle and I **are having** dinner tonight. Will you join us? 오늘 밤에 Michelle과 저녁 식사를 할 예정이에요.
- Sally **isn't moving** to Florida. She changed her mind.

이때, **am/is/are + -ing** 대신 **am/is/are going to + 동사원형**을 쓸 수도 있다.
- **I'm opening** my new business next month. 또는 **I'm going to open** my new business next month.
  다음 달에 새로운 사업을 시작할 예정이다.
- **Are** you **running** in the marathon this weekend? 또는
  Are you **going to run** in the marathon this weekend?

2 대중교통, 수업 등 이미 짜여 있는 시간표, 일정표 상의 일에 대해 말할 때는 미래의 일이라 할지라도 현재 시제를 쓸 수 있다.
- The train **arrives** in Paris at 9:30 p.m. (기차 시간에 대해 말하고 있으므로 현재 시제 arrives를 썼음)
- "Why are you going to bed now? It's only 9 o'clock." "My class **starts** early in the morning."
  (수업 시간에 대해 말하고 있으므로 현재 시제 starts를 썼음)

PRACTICE

A. 다음 수첩을 보고 **be + -ing**를 사용하여 Stephanie의 다음 주 일정에 대해 말해보세요.

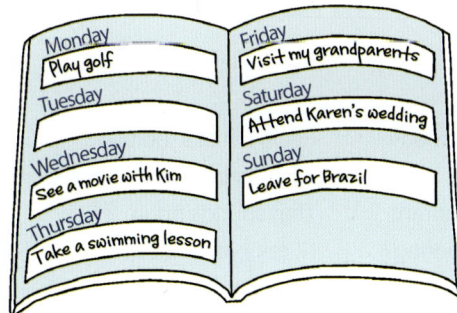

1. She _'s playing golf_ on Monday.
2. She _____ with Kim on Wednesday.
3. She _____ on Thursday.
4. She _____ on Friday.
5. She _____ on Saturday.
6. She _____ on Sunday.

B. 다음 시간표를 보고 괄호 안에 주어진 동사를 사용하여 예시와 같이 문장을 완성하세요.

1 Movie Schedule		2 Flight Departures		3 Train Arrivals		4 Class Schedule	
5:30	Funny People	12:30	London	1:00	New York	9:00	Computer
6:30	Space War	2:15	Berlin	2:00	Boston	10:30	English

1. (start) Funny People _starts at 5:30_ .
2. (leave) I'm going to Berlin. My flight _____ .
3. (arrive) Jerome is coming from Boston. His train _____ .
4. (begin) My computer class _____ .

UNIT 29 He can speak Italian.

can과 could

He **can speak** Italian.
그는 이탈리아어를 할 수 있다.

He **can't speak** Japanese.
그는 일본어를 할 수 없다.

1
can + 동사원형: ~할 수 있다
cannot + 동사원형: ~할 수 없다

어떤 일을 할 수 있는 능력 또는 어떤 일이 일어날 가능성이 있거나 없다고 할 때 **can**을 쓴다.

긍정·부정

I/we/you/they he/she/it	can cannot (= can't)	sing dance

의문

can	I/we/you/they he/she/it	sing ... ? dance ... ?

- Julie **can sing** well, but she **can't dance** well. Julie는 노래를 잘할 수 있지만, 춤은 잘 출 수 없다.
- "**Can** you **meet** me tonight?" "No, I'm too busy."

2
과거에 대해 말할 때는 **could**를 쓴다.

긍정

I/we/you/they he/she/it	could	swim finish

부정

I/we/you/they he/she/it	could not (= couldn't)	swim finish

- Ten years ago, Liz **could swim** 50 meters in 30 seconds. Liz는 10년 전엔 30초에 50미터를 수영할 수 있었다.
- Most students **couldn't finish** the exam. It was too difficult.

PRACTICE

A. 주어진 동사와 can을 사용하여 대화를 완성하세요. 필요한 경우 부정문으로 쓰세요.

| attend | eat | fix | ~~go~~ | lift | talk |

1. Sara _can't go OR cannot go_ to the beach with us today. — Really? That's too bad.
2. _____ your parrot _____ ? — Yes, it knows some basic words.
3. We _____ at the hotel. It has a restaurant. — That sounds good.
4. _____ Mr. Park _____ the meeting? — I'll call him and ask.
5. I _____ this box. It's too heavy. — I'll help you.
6. You should take the computer to Tom. He _____ it. — OK. Thanks.

B. 괄호 안에 주어진 동사와 can/can't 또는 could/couldn't를 사용하여 문장을 완성하세요.

1. (take) "Where is city hall?" "On Main Street. You _can take_ the subway there."
2. (see) I left my glasses at home, so I _____ the movie very well last night.
3. (walk) My sister is only 10 months old, but she _____ !
4. (buy) When I was a child, I _____ a soda for 25 cents. Now sodas cost much more.
5. (remember) "When is Lisa's birthday? I _____." "It's May 8."
6. (cook) My wife _____ very well before we got married, but now she's a great cook.

UNIT 30

Can I use your phone?

Can I ~ ?, Can you ~ ?

Can I use your phone?
네 전화기를 써도 될까?

Can you come to the party?
파티에 와주시겠어요?

1 **Can I ~ ?**: ~해도 될까요?

- It's very late. **Can I** stay here tonight? 오늘 밤 여기에서 머물러도 될까요?
- "**Can I** bring my friend to the picnic?" "Of course."

Can I ~ ?와 같은 의미이지만 더 공손하게 말할 때 **Could I ~ ?**를 쓸 수 있다.

- "**Could I** ask you something?" 무언가 물어봐도 될까요? "Sure. What is it?"
- "**Could I** check my e-mail on your computer?" "All right."

2 **Can you ~ ?**: ~해주시겠어요?

- "**Can you** lend me 10 dollars?" 10달러를 빌려주시겠어요? "Sorry. I didn't bring my wallet."
- "**Can you** recommend a good restaurant in this town?" "The Thai Grill is good."

Can you ~ ?와 같은 의미이지만 더 공손하게 말할 때 **Could you ~ ?**를 쓸 수 있다.

- I'm sorry. **Could you** say that again? 다시 말씀해주시겠어요?
- "**Could you** give this letter to Jason?" "No problem."

PRACTICE

A. 그림을 보고 주어진 표현과 **Can I ~ ?**를 사용하여 문장을 완성하세요.

| close the window | ~~come in~~ | have some water | take this seat |

1. *Can I come in* ?
2. _____ ?
3. _____ ?
4. _____ ?

B. 괄호 안에 주어진 표현과 **Could you ~ ?**를 사용하여 대화를 완성하세요.

1. (take me home) *Could you take me home* ? Of course.
2. (come to my office) _____ ? What time?
3. (sign this form) _____, please? OK.
4. (move your car) _____ ? Sure.
5. (read me another story) _____ ? No. It's time for bed.

UNIT 31 He **might** go out.

He **might go** out.
그는 나갈지도 모른다.

He **might not go** out.
그는 나가지 않을지도 모른다.

1 **might + 동사원형**: ~할지도 모른다
might not + 동사원형: ~하지 않을지도 모른다

어떤 일이 일어나거나, 일어나지 않을 가능성이 있다고 할 때 **might**를 쓴다.

긍정·부정

I/we/you/they he/she/it	might might not	see finish

- Let's go to Hollywood. We **might see** a famous person. 유명한 사람을 볼지도 몰라.
- I have a lot of work to do. I **might not finish** it all today. 나는 오늘 다 끝내지 않을지도 모른다.
- "Where's Eric?" "I'm not sure. He **might be** in his bedroom."
- Emily **might not enjoy** this movie. She doesn't like comedies.

PRACTICE

A. 주어진 대화를 보고 might를 사용하여 상황에 맞게 문장을 완성하세요.

1. BILL: Are you meeting Jenny tomorrow? TOM: I'm not sure.
2. JANE: Are you traveling by train? ROBERT: I'm thinking about it.
3. TINA: Are you going to Martin's wedding? CAROL: Maybe.
4. PETER: Are you moving next month? RACHEL: I don't know yet.

1. Tom _might meet Jenny tomorrow_ .   3. Carol _____ .
2. Robert _____ .   4. Rachel _____ .

B. 괄호 안에 주어진 동사와 **might** 또는 **might not**을 사용하여 문장을 완성하세요.

1. (win) Our soccer team is playing well. We _might win_ the game.
2. (help) Fred isn't very busy today. He _____ us with our homework.
3. (come) "Emma is sick. She _____ with us." "That's too bad."
4. (try) "Have you been to that restaurant?" "No, but I _____ it next week."
5. (fit) That dress looks too small. It _____ me.
6. (like) Carla and Jake _____ seafood. Let's cook some steaks.
7. (invite) "Do you have plans this Friday?" "Well, I _____ some friends to my house."
8. (buy) I _____ this suitcase. I think it's too heavy.

UNIT 32 He must be thirsty.

must (강한 확신)

He must be thirsty.
그는 분명히 목마를 것이다.

1 must + 동사원형: 분명히 ~할 것이다
must not + 동사원형: 분명히 ~하지 않을 것이다
어떤 일에 대해 강하게 확신할 때 must를 쓴다.

긍정·부정

I/we/you/they he/she/it	must / must not	speak / have

- "Elisa has lived in France for 10 years." "She **must speak** French very well." 그녀는 분명히 프랑스어를 잘 할 거야.
- Ken is still sleeping. He **must not have** class today. 그는 분명히 오늘 수업이 없을 것이다.
- Jay and Peter are always together. They **must be** close friends.
- Tim's room is always dirty. He **must not clean** it often.

PRACTICE

A. 주어진 동사와 must를 사용하여 대화를 완성하세요.

| ~~be~~ | be | hurt | like | miss | practice |

1. The diamond on that ring is so big! — It _must be_ very expensive.
2. Sara plays the piano beautifully. — She _____ a lot.
3. I haven't seen my mom for a year. — You _____ her.
4. Nick always listens to that band's album. — I le _____ their music.
5. I cut my finger. — It looks bad. It _____.
6. The children can't go on a picnic because of the rain. — They _____ sad.

B. 괄호 안에 주어진 동사와 must 또는 must not을 사용하여 문장을 완성하세요.

1. (be) Tommy _must be_ angry with me. He hasn't spoken to me since yesterday.
2. (feel) "We're leaving for Hong Kong tomorrow." "You _____ so excited!"
3. (sell) I don't see any hats in this store. It _____ them.
4. (cook) Sally eats out a lot. She _____ often.
5. (have) This tea isn't sweet. It _____ sugar in it.
6. (need) "My watch stopped." "It _____ a new battery."
7. (read) Mark _____ a lot. He has so many books.
8. (understand) The students look confused. They _____ the lecture.
9. (know) Those people are waving at you. They _____ you.
10. (allow) Nobody is smoking in here. This café _____ smoking.

UNIT 33

must와 have to (의무)

They must/have to stay in their seats.

They **must stay** in their seats. 또는
They **have to stay** in their seats.
그들은 반드시 자리에 앉아 있어야 한다.

1 must + 동사원형: (반드시) ~해야 한다
어떤 일을 반드시 해야 한다고 할 때 must를 쓴다.
- You **must arrive** on time for work. 회사에 제시간에 도착해야 한다.
- The concert isn't free. We **must buy** tickets. 반드시 티켓을 사야 한다.
- Travelers **must show** their passports before they get on the plane.

2 must와 같은 의미로 have to를 쓸 수도 있다.

I/we/you/they	have to	come
he/she/it	has to	hurry
		get

- We're having a party tonight. You **have to come**! 반드시 와야 해요!
- We **have to hurry**. The movie starts soon. 서둘러야 한다.
- Lily lost her credit card. She **has to get** a new one.

3 과거에 대해 말할 때 must를 쓸 수 없다. 이때는 had to를 쓴다.
- Clark **had to pay** for my lunch yesterday because I forgot my wallet. Clark가 어제 내 점심을 사야 했다.
- Mr. Smith had a lot of work last night, so he **had to stay** late. Smith씨는 어젯밤에 할 일이 많아서 늦게까지 있어야 했다.
- It started raining, so I **had to bring** the laundry inside.

PRACTICE

A. 주어진 동사와 have to/has to/had to를 사용하여 문장을 완성하세요.

| ask   attend   ~~stay~~   stop   use   wear |

1. Gina hurt her leg, so she _had to stay_ in the hospital last week.
2. "Can I leave work early today?" "You _____ Mr. Nelson first."
3. Terry _____ a suit tomorrow. He has a job interview.
4. The elevator isn't working again. We _____ the stairs.
5. We _____ at the gas station because we didn't have much gas.
6. "Is Melanie joining us for lunch on Saturday?" "No, she _____ a wedding."

B. must 또는 had to를 써넣으세요.

1. I _must_ leave now. My friends are waiting outside.
2. "Can I borrow your car tonight, Mom?" "OK, but you _____ be careful."
3. Brenda _____ quit the softball team. She was too busy at school.
4. We _____ finish the report by 3 o'clock tomorrow.
5. The restaurant was full last night, so we _____ wait.
6. You _____ return these DVDs before next Tuesday.
7. It was getting dark, so I _____ turn on the car lights.
8. Jim _____ close his store last year because he didn't make much money.

UNIT 34 People **must not** run near the pool.

1 must not + 동사원형: ~해서는 안 된다

어떤 일을 해서는 안 된다고 할 때 **must not**을 쓴다.

- People **must not run** near the pool. 수영장 근처에서 뛰어서는 안 된다.
- Visitors **must not bring** any food into the museum. 방문객들은 박물관에 음식을 가져와서는 안 된다.
- You **must not cross** the street when the light is red.

2 don't/doesn't have to + 동사원형: ~할 필요가 없다

I/we/you/they	don't	have to	worry
he/she/it	doesn't		see
			go

- You **don't have to worry**. Everything will be OK. 걱정할 필요가 없어.
- Scott canceled his appointment. He **doesn't have to see** the doctor today. 오늘 진찰을 받을 필요가 없다.
- We **don't have to go** to school this Friday. It's a national holiday.

과거에 대해 말할 때는 **didn't have to**를 쓴다.

- We **didn't have to cook** last night because we ordered pizza. 요리할 필요가 없었다.
- It was warm yesterday, so I **didn't have to wear** a jacket.

3 must와 have to는 의미가 같지만, must not과 don't have to는 의미가 다른 것에 주의한다.

- You **must be** quiet in the library. 또는 You **have to be** quiet in the library. 도서관에서는 조용히 해야 한다.
- Andy has had a lot of wine, so he **must not drive** tonight. 와인을 마셨기 때문에 운전해서는 안 된다.
- Daisy lives near her office, so she **doesn't have to drive** to work. 사무실 근처에 살기 때문에 운전할 필요가 없다.

PRACTICE

A. 주어진 동사와 must 또는 must not을 사용하여 각 표지의 의미에 대해 말하세요.

~~park~~   smoke   stop   take   turn off

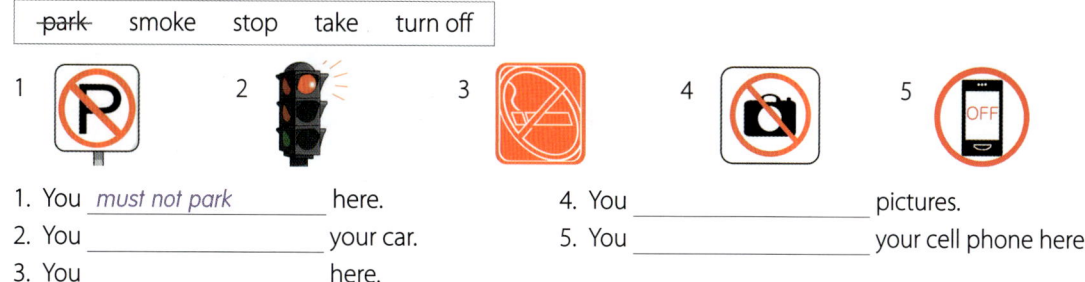

1. You _must not park_ here.
2. You _____ your car.
3. You _____ here.
4. You _____ pictures.
5. You _____ your cell phone here.

B. 주어진 동사와 must not 또는 don't have to를 사용하여 문장을 완성하세요.

bring   look   run   swim   throw   ~~write~~

1. I _don't have to write_ the essay today. I can do it tomorrow.
2. You _____ at the sun. It will hurt your eyes.
3. We _____. The bus isn't at the station yet.
4. You _____ anything to the party. We already have enough food.
5. You _____ in this river. It's too dangerous.
6. We _____ trash on the street. We have to keep our city clean.

UNIT 37 The newspaper **is delivered** every day.

수동태

능동태   Someone **delivers** the newspaper every day.

수동태   The newspaper **is delivered** every day.
신문이 매일 배달된다.

1 사람이나 사물이 '~되다'라고 말할 때 수동태를 쓴다. 수동태는 **am/is/are** + 과거분사로 쓴다.

긍정			부정		
am/is/are		spoken allowed	am/is/are	not	spoken allowed

- Spanish **is spoken** in Mexico. 멕시코에서는 스페인어가 사용된다.
- Children **are not allowed** in this pool. 어린이들은 이 수영장에 들어오는 것이 허락되지 않는다.
- Bananas **are grown** in tropical countries.
- You can sit here. This seat **isn't taken**.

2 수동태의 과거는 **was/were** + 과거분사로 쓴다.

능동태   Someone **sent** the invitations yesterday.

수동태   The invitations **were sent** yesterday. 초대장이 어제 발송되었다.

- Steak and fish **were served** at the dinner party. 스테이크와 생선이 저녁 파티에서 제공되었다.
- Vitamin C **wasn't discovered** until 1928.

PRACTICE

A. 괄호 안에 주어진 표현을 사용하여 수동태 문장을 완성하세요. 현재 시제로 쓰세요.

1. (lock) The office door _is locked_ at 7 o'clock.
2. (pack) Our bags _____. We're ready for our trip.
3. (not require) Tickets _____ to enter the museum. It's free.
4. (write) I can't read this book. It _____ in Italian.
5. (not use) Record players _____ very much these days.
6. (not collect) The trash _____ on weekends. It's picked up only on weekdays.

B. 괄호 안에 주어진 단어들을 사용하여 수동태 문장을 완성하세요. 현재 시제 또는 과거 시제를 사용하세요.

1. A: How old is the museum?
   B: (it, build) _It was built_ in 1910.

2. A: Is Tom a famous painter?
   B: (his paintings, display) Yes. _____ at many galleries.

3. A: Did you go to the concert last night?
   B: (it, cancel) No, _____.

4. A: (the road, block) Oh, no. _____.
   B: Then we have to take another road.

5. A: Where's the photocopier?
   B: (it, move) On the 3rd floor. _____ last week.

6. A: (these photos, take) _____ last year.
   B: Your hair has grown a lot since then.

UNIT 38 She **caught** a fish. A fish **was caught**.

능동태와 수동태 비교

She **caught** a fish.
그녀는 물고기를 잡았다.

A fish **was caught**.
물고기가 잡혔다.

1 능동태는 사람이나 사물이 '~하다'라는 의미이다. | 수동태는 사람이나 사물이 '~되다'라는 의미이다.

- Nate **washes** the floors on Saturdays.
  Nate는 토요일마다 바닥을 청소한다.
- Someone **stole** my bag yesterday.
  누군가가 어제 내 가방을 훔쳐갔다.
- Helen **didn't pay** the phone bill.

- The floors **are washed** on Saturdays.
  바닥이 토요일마다 청소된다.
- My bag **was stolen** yesterday.
  어제 내 가방이 도난당했다.
- The phone bill **wasn't paid**.

2 수동태 문장에서 누구 또는 무엇에 의해 일어난 일인지를 말할 때는 주로 **by**를 쓴다.

능동태 Jenny **cooked** this chicken.
수동태 This chicken **was cooked by** Jenny. 이 닭고기는 Jenny에 의해 요리되었다.

능동태
- Many people **learn** English these days.
- Mary **didn't paint** those pictures.
- John **fixed** the bicycle this morning.

수동태
- English **is learned by** many people these days.
- Those pictures **weren't painted by** Mary.
- The bicycle **was fixed by** John this morning.

PRACTICE

A. 그림을 보고 주어진 동사를 사용하여 능동태 또는 수동태 문장을 완성하세요. 과거 시제로 쓰세요.

| find | grow | hit | ~~make~~ | send |

1. The vase _was made_ in 1563.
2. The flowers _____ by John.
3. A ball _____ the girl.
4. The rice _____ in China.
5. They _____ a box under the bed.

B. 주어진 문장을 보고 **by**를 사용하여 수동태 문장을 완성하세요.

1. My husband wrote the letter. _The letter was written by my husband_.
2. Icy roads cause many accidents.
3. Professor Kim taught Sandra.
4. Many tourists visit this place.
5. Michael Smith designed those houses.
6. John Baird invented the television.

UNIT 39 She **is not** afraid.

부정문

긍정 He **is** afraid. 그는 무서워한다.

부정 She **is not** afraid. 그녀는 무서워하지 않는다.

1 be동사/현재완료 시제/조동사 부정문은 다음과 같이 쓴다.

주어	am/is/are was/were have has will can 등	not	... seen rained be play

- I **am not** interested in sports. 스포츠에 흥미가 없다.
- The movie was long, but it **wasn't** boring.
- We **haven't seen** Daniel since January. 1월 이후로 Daniel을 보지 못했다.
- It **hasn't rained** much this summer. It has been very dry.
- Ms. Jones **will not be** at work today. Jones씨는 오늘 출근하지 않을 것이다.
- Fred hurt his leg, so he **can't play** football.

2 일반동사 부정문에는 **don't/doesn't/didn't**를 쓴다.

주어	don't doesn't didn't	cook like stay

- I **don't cook** at home very often. 집에서 자주 요리하지 않는다.
- Sarah **doesn't like** skiing, but she likes snowboarding. 스키 타는 것을 좋아하지 않는다.
- We **didn't stay** at a hotel in Tokyo. We stayed at my friend's house.

일반동사 뒤에 **not**을 쓰거나, 일반동사 앞에 **be동사 + not**을 쓰지 않는 것에 주의한다.

- I **didn't go** to school yesterday. I had a cold. (I went not으로 쓸 수 없음)
- "These apples **don't look** fresh." "Let's buy some oranges, then." (These apples aren't look으로 쓸 수 없음)

PRACTICE

A. 괄호 안에 주어진 표현을 사용하여 예시와 같이 부정문을 완성하세요.

1. (healthy) French fries are tasty, but they _aren't healthy_____.
2. (to Venice) I have been to Rome, but I _____.
3. (French) My parents can speak German, but they _____.
4. (at 10 o'clock) Jane and I were studying at 8 o'clock, but we _____.
5. (in Vancouver) It has snowed a lot in Toronto, but it _____.
6. (pizza) We will make pasta, but we _____.
7. (on Sundays) The library opens on Saturdays, but it _____.
8. (any money) John had his wallet, but he _____ in it.

B. be동사, do, have를 적절한 형태로 써넣으세요. 부정문으로 쓰세요.

1. It's warm outside now, so you _don't_____ need a coat.
2. "Were you singing in the shower this morning?" "No. It _____ me."
3. I _____ get a haircut yesterday because I was too busy.
4. My brother _____ 20 years old. He's only 19.
5. David _____ eaten at that restaurant before. We should take him there.
6. Wendy _____ listen to rock music. She hates it.
7. I _____ going to clean the house today. I'm too tired.
8. Nathan and Rick _____ graduated yet. They still have one more year.

UNIT 40 Is the water too hot?

의문사가 없는 의문문

Is the water too hot?

긍정 The water **is** too hot. 물이 너무 뜨겁다.

의문 **Is** the water too hot? 물이 너무 뜨거운가요?

1 be동사/현재완료 시제/조동사 의문문은 다음과 같이 쓴다.

am/is/are was/were		... ?
have has	주어	tried ... ? arrived ... ?
will can 등		become ... ? open ... ?

- **Are you** from Canada? 당신은 캐나다 출신인가요?
- "**Was the weather** good in Miami?" "Yes, it was quite sunny."
- **Have you tried** Indian food before? 인도 음식을 먹어본 적 있나요?
- Carl hasn't arrived yet. **Has Dave arrived**?
- **Will Bob become** a famous actor? Bob은 유명한 배우가 될까?
- I can't open this jar. **Can you open** it?

2 일반동사 의문문은 주어 앞에 **do/does/did**를 쓴다.

do does did	주어	know ... ? live ... ? meet ... ?

- **Do you know** this song? 이 노래를 아나요?
- "Jenna lives in England." "**Does she live** in London?" 그녀는 런던에 사나요?
- "We met Mr. Jacobs last night." "**Did you meet** his wife too?"

일반동사 의문문에 **be**동사를 쓰지 않는 것에 주의한다.

- "**Do** you **have** a pen?" "No, but I have a pencil." (Are you have ~ ?로 쓸 수 없음)
- "**Did** Jerry **come** to your party?" "Yes, he did." (Was Jerry come ~ ?으로 쓸 수 없음)

PRACTICE

A. 괄호 안에 주어진 단어들을 적절히 배열하여 문장을 완성하세요.

1. (help / you / will) " _Will you help_ me?" "No problem."
2. (are / the cookies) " _____ in the oven." "They smell great!"
3. (Ted / done / has) " _____ his homework?" "He just finished."
4. (lives / Mitchell) " _____ with his parents." "I do too."
5. (you / did / pass) " _____ the math test?" "I think so."
6. (Julie / was / sleeping) " _____ when you called?" "Yes, I woke her up."
7. (should / take / we) " _____ a break." "OK."
8. (you / found / have) " _____ your keys yet?" "No. I'm still looking for them."

B. be동사, do, have를 적절한 형태로 써넣으세요.

1. _Are_ you going to the seminar next weekend? — I haven't decided yet.
2. _____ you talked to Jane lately? — Yes, I spoke to her yesterday.
3. _____ Tina work in China? — Yes, she's in Hong Kong.
4. _____ Debbie spend a lot of money last weekend? — Not too much.
5. _____ Kristin a nurse? — No, she's a doctor.
6. _____ Mr. Riley sold his car yet? — I'm not sure. I'll ask him.
7. _____ you wearing a new tie yesterday? — Yes, did you like it?

UNIT 41 Who is he? What is it?

Who is he? 그는 누구니?   **What** is it? 그것은 무엇이니?

1 who는 '누구'라는 의미로 사람에 대해 물을 때 쓴다.
- "**Who** are you going to meet tonight?" 오늘 밤에 누구를 만날 거니? "My girlfriend."
- "**Who** will you invite to dinner?" "Gwen and Brian."

2 what은 '무엇'이라는 의미로 사물에 대해 물을 때 쓴다.
- "**What** are you doing tomorrow?" 내일 뭐하니? "I don't have any plans yet."
- "**What** do you usually wear to work?" "A suit."

what + 명사: 무슨 ~, 몇 ~
- "**What sports** do you play?" 무슨 운동을 하세요? "I play basketball and soccer."
- "**What time** is your class today?" "It's at 5 o'clock."

3 의문문에서 who와 what (+ 명사)는 동사 앞에 쓴다.
- "**Who is** your best friend?" 너의 가장 친한 친구가 누구니? "Michelle."
- "**What did** you have for breakfast?" 아침에 무엇을 먹었니? "Bacon and eggs."
- "**What movie should** we watch?" "The comedy."

PRACTICE

A. 그림을 보고 괄호 안에 주어진 단어들과 who 또는 what을 사용하여 의문문을 완성하세요. 과거 시제로 쓰세요.

1. (she, pay) "_Who did she pay_____?" "Jill."
2. (John, send) "_____?" "A letter."
3. (they, visit) "_____?" "Larry."
4. (he, eat) "_____?" "The pizza."

B. 괄호 안에 주어진 단어들을 적절히 배열하여 문장을 완성하세요.

1. (magazine / what / you / reading / are) "_What magazine are you reading_____?" "Home Design."
2. (what / your major / was) "_____ in college?" "I studied art."
3. (who / Barry / call / did) "_____?" "His grandmother."
4. (see / who / you / did) "_____ at the mall?" "My friend Tom."
5. (that cake / is / what / flavor) "_____?" "Chocolate."
6. (should / who / I / contact) "_____ for reservations?" "Mr. Murphy."

UNIT 42 Which do you want?

Which do you want?
어떤 것을 원하나요?

1. **which**는 '어떤 것'이라는 의미로 사물에 대해 물을 때 쓴다.
   - **Which** should we take, the train or the bus? 기차와 버스 중 어떤 것을 타는 것이 좋을까요?
   - "**Which** does Joe want, cake, pie, or ice cream?" "He wants cake."

   which + 명사: 어떤 ~

   which + 명사는 사람과 사물 모두에 대해 물을 때 쓸 수 있다.
   - "**Which boy** is Jack?" 어떤 소년이 Jack인가요? "I'm not sure."
   - "**Which dress** do you like best?" "The black one."

2. 의문문에서 **which (+ 명사)**는 동사 앞에 쓴다.
   - **Which is** closer, Chicago or Dallas? 시카고와 댈러스 중 어디가 더 가까운가요?
   - "**Which channel do** you want to watch?" "Channel 9."

3. 제한적으로 주어진 몇 가지 사항 중에서 선택하는 경우에는 주로 **which**를 쓰지만, 선택할 사항이 제한적으로 주어지지 않은 경우에는 주로 **what**을 쓴다.
   - We have chicken and fish. **Which** would you like? (chicken과 fish로 선택할 사항이 제한적으로 주어졌으므로 Which를 썼음)
   - "**What** year were you born?" "1994." (선택할 연도가 제한적으로 주어지지 않았으므로 What을 썼음)

PRACTICE

A. 그림을 보고 주어진 명사와 which를 사용하여 의문문을 완성하세요.

| book | car | ~~restaurant~~ | shirt |

1. _Which restaurant_ should we go to?

2. _____ is more interesting?

3. _____ is cheaper?

4. _____ do you like?

B. who/what/which 중 가장 적절한 것을 써넣으세요.

1. _Who_ did you meet at Ken's wedding?
2. "_____ does Mr. Taylor teach?" "History."
3. There are two doors. _____ is the exit?
4. "_____ kind of drink would you like?" "Tea, please."
5. "_____ is the problem?" "Everything's fine."
6. "_____ is that woman?" "My neighbor."
7. _____ island did you like more, Fiji or Bali?
8. "_____ are those boys?" "They're my children."

UNIT 43 Where is the bathroom?

where, when, why

1. **where**은 '어디'라는 의미로 장소를 물을 때 쓴다.
   - "Excuse me, **where** is the bathroom?" 화장실이 어디인가요? "Over there."
   - **Where** did you get that necklace? It's so pretty. 그 목걸이를 어디에서 샀나요?
   - "**Where** can I find a bank machine?" "Across the street."

2. **when**은 '언제'라는 의미로 시간 또는 날짜를 물을 때 쓴다.
   - "**When** is your flight?" 비행기 출발 시간이 언제니? "It departs at 7 p.m."
   - "**When** does the new museum open?" 새 박물관이 언제 여나요? "Next month."
   - "**When** can you call me back?" "In the afternoon."

3. **why**는 '왜'라는 의미로 이유를 물을 때 쓴다.
   - "**Why** are you crying?" 왜 울고 있니? "I'm reading a sad story."
   - "**Why** did you take a taxi?" 왜 택시를 탔니? "Because I was late."
   - "**Why** has Terry been in her room all day?" "She isn't feeling well."

4. 의문문에서 **where, when, why**는 동사 앞에 쓴다.
   - "**Where are** you going to stay in California?" 캘리포니아에서 어디에 머물 거니? "At my uncle's house."
   - **When will** you be home tonight? 집에 언제 올 거예요?
   - "**Why does** Dana need more money?" "She has to pay her credit card bill."

PRACTICE

A. where/when/why를 써넣으세요.

1. When	does the next train for Chicago leave?	At 12 o'clock.
2. _____	is Sharon working these days?	At a hospital.
3. _____	did Simon get married?	Last month.
4. _____	are your hands so dirty?	I was fixing the car.
5. _____	can I return these shoes?	To the customer service counter.
6. _____	will the pizzas arrive?	They'll be here in 20 minutes.
7. _____	did you learn Italian?	I want to study in Italy.
8. _____	is Tom upset?	He lost his cell phone.

B. 괄호 안에 주어진 단어들을 적절히 배열하여 의문문을 완성하세요.

1. (quit / did / why / you) *Why did you quit* your job? I thought you liked it.
2. (be / will / your parents / when) "_____ home?" "I'm not sure."
3. (do / live / where / you) I live in Seattle. _____?
4. (when / buy / did / he) Fred's new camera is very nice. _____ it?
5. (why / wearing / you / are) _____ a coat? Are you going somewhere?
6. (Susan / where / is) "_____?" "She went to the store."
7. (closed / the mall / why / is) "_____ today?" "It closes every Monday."
8. (Ralph / leave / when / does) _____ for London? Is it next week?

UNIT 44 How can I help you?

1 how는 '어떻게'라는 의미로 방법을 물을 때 쓴다.

- **How** can I help you? 어떻게 도와드릴까요?
- **How** do you say "tree" in German? 독일어로 '나무'를 어떻게 말하나요?
- "**How** do I get to the library?" "Take bus 202."

2 how + be동사: ~은 어떤가요?

- **How is** the weather today? 오늘 날씨는 어떤가요?
- "**How was** your trip to Hong Kong?" 홍콩 여행은 어땠나요? "It was so much fun!"
- "**How are** your parents?" "They're fine."

3 how + 형용사/부사: 얼마나 ~

How	형용사/부사		
How	long	have you known Lucy?" (얼마나 오래)	"For six years."
How	fast	can a cheetah run?" (얼마나 빨리)	"I'm not sure."
How	much	is this skirt?"	"It's $90."
How	many	sisters do you have?"	"I have two sisters."
How	difficult	was the exam?"	"It wasn't too hard."

4 의문문에서 how (+ 형용사/부사)는 동사 앞에 쓴다.

- "**How was** the soup?" 수프가 어땠나요? "It was delicious."
- "**How often do** you exercise?" 얼마나 자주 운동하나요? "Twice a week."
- "**How close is** the post office?" "It's three blocks away."

PRACTICE

A. 괄호 안에 주어진 단어들과 how를 적절히 배열하여 의문문을 완성하세요.

1. (I / can / contact) _How can I contact_ _____ you?   — Here's my phone number.
2. (are / feeling / you) _____ today?   — A lot better. Thanks.
3. (you / make / do) _____ sushi?   — I'll show you.
4. (can / turn off / I) _____ the heat?   — Just push that button.
5. (the concert / was) _____ ? Was it good?   — Yes, it was great!
6. (is / doing / your son) _____ in college?   — He's doing well.

B. 주어진 형용사 또는 부사와 how를 사용하여 의문문을 완성하세요.

| far | ~~fast~~ | long | much | often | old |

1. "_How fast_ was Dan driving?" "I don't know, but it was really fast."
2. Your little brother is very cute. _____ is he?
3. "_____ do you check your e-mail?" "Once a day."
4. "These mangoes were on sale." "_____ were they?"
5. "Sorry, but you have to wait. The restaurant is full." "_____ do we have to wait?"
6. "_____ is your school from your house?" "Just a few kilometers."

UNIT 45 Do you know **where the station is**?

간접의문문

Where is the station?
Do you know where the station is?
역이 어디에 있는지 아시나요?

where the station is와 같이 문장 안에 포함되어 있는 의문문을 간접의문문이라고 한다.

1 의문사가 있는 의문문을 간접의문문으로 쓸 때 **의문사 + 주어 + 동사**로 쓴다.

be동사, 조동사, **have/has**(현재완료)를 포함하는 의문사 의문문을 간접의문문으로 말하는 경우

- **Who is Holly**? → I don't know **who Holly is**. (누가 Holly인지)
- **Where can we find** a gas station? → I don't know **where we can find** a gas station.
- **How has Peter been**? → I don't know **how Peter has been**.

do/does/did를 포함하는 의문사 의문문을 간접의문문으로 말하는 경우

- **What do you want** for Christmas? → Could you tell me **what you want** for Christmas? (네가 크리스마스 선물로 무엇을 원하는지)
- **When does the store close**? → Could you tell me **when the store closes**?
- **Why did Carol work** late? → Could you tell me **why Carol worked** late?

2 의문사가 없는 의문문을 간접의문문으로 쓸 때는 **if/whether + 주어 + 동사**로 쓴다. 이때, **if**와 **whether**는 '~인지 아닌지'라는 의미이다.

- **Does Sam speak** German? → I wonder **if/whether Sam speaks** German. (Sam이 독일어를 하는지 아닌지)
- **Is Jane coming** to the meeting? → I wonder **if/whether Jane is coming** to the meeting.

PRACTICE

A. 옆집에 Tony와 Sue 부부가 이사 왔습니다. Do you know를 사용하여 궁금한 점들을 질문하세요.

1. When can I meet them?
2. Where did they live before?
3. Why have they come here?
4. What does Tony do?
5. How many children do they have?
6. What are their hobbies?

1. *Do you know when I can meet them*?
2. _____?
3. _____?
4. _____?
5. _____?
6. _____?

B. 주어진 의문문을 보고 간접의문문을 사용하여 문장을 완성하세요. **if** 또는 **whether**를 함께 사용하세요.

1. Did Greg finish his report? — I don't know *if/whether Greg finished his report*.
2. Can Joey play the violin? — I wonder _____.
3. Is Annie going to visit us tomorrow? — Could you tell me _____?
4. Have you seen my brother? — I wonder _____.
5. Did many people come to the party? — I don't know _____.
6. Has Hannah gone home? — Could you tell me _____?

UNIT 46 Exercising is good for health.

-ing (1) 주어

Exercising is good for health.
운동을 하는 것은 건강에 좋다.

1 '~하는 것'이라는 의미로 **-ing**를 주어로 쓸 수 있다.
- **Painting** is fun. I really enjoy it. 그림을 그리는 것은 재미있다.
- **Traveling** can cost a lot of money. 여행하는 것은 돈이 많이 들 수 있다.
- "I'm still sleepy. I need to wake up." "**Drinking coffee** might help."
- **Planting trees** helps the environment.

2 다음과 같이 **-ing** 뒤에 여러 단어를 함께 쓸 수도 있다.
- **Learning a foreign language** takes a long time. (외국어를 배우는 것)
- **Washing your hands before meals** is important. (식사 전에 손을 씻는 것)
- **Riding a bicycle without a helmet** can be dangerous.

3 **to**+동사원형도 '~하는 것'이라는 의미로 주어로 쓸 수 있지만 자주 쓰지는 않는다. **to**+동사원형 보다 **-ing**를 주로 쓴다.
- **Smoking** is not allowed in this restaurant. 이 식당에서 담배를 피우는 것은 허용되지 않는다. (= To smoke)
- It's raining a lot. **Bringing an umbrella** was a good idea. 우산을 가져오는 것은 좋은 생각이었다. (= To bring an umbrella)
- **Walking in these old shoes** hurts my feet. I should get new ones.

PRACTICE

A. 주어진 동사를 -ing로 사용하여 문장을 완성하세요.

| drive | eat | lose | ~~read~~ | swim | wear |

1. I like comic books. _Reading_ them is one of my hobbies.
2. _____ in this lake is not safe. It's too deep.
3. _____ weight is hard. I exercise every day, but it doesn't help.
4. You should put on your sunglasses. _____ them protects your eyes.
5. Traffic is bad in the morning. _____ to work takes a long time.
6. _____ too much food can cause a stomachache.

B. 주어진 표현에 대해 자신의 생각과 가까운 것에 표시하고 -ing를 사용하여 예시와 같이 말해보세요.

make friends	☑ easy	☐ difficult
ride a roller coaster	☐ exciting	☐ scary
take a taxi	☐ cheap	☐ expensive
walk alone at night	☐ safe	☐ dangerous
play chess	☐ fun	☐ boring

1. _Making friends is easy_ .
2. _____.
3. _____.
4. _____.
5. _____.

UNIT 47 She **enjoys listening** to music.

-ing (2) 목적어

She enjoys listening to music.
그녀는 음악을 듣는 것을 즐긴다.

1 다음과 같은 동사 뒤에는 '~하는 것, ~하기'라는 의미로 말할 때 **-ing**를 쓴다.

enjoy	finish	keep	
avoid	mind	give up	**-ing**
suggest	practice		(writing, raining, waiting 등)

- "I **finished writing** my essay." 에세이 쓰는 것을 끝냈어. "Great. Can I read it?"
- It **kept raining** for three days. 삼일 동안 계속 비가 내렸다.
- "Do you **mind waiting** a moment?" "No problem."
- "My husband finally **gave up smoking**." "That's great!"
- We don't **suggest staying** at that hotel. The service isn't good.

PRACTICE

A. 주어진 동사를 -ing로 사용하여 문장을 완성하세요.

| drive | read | take | ~~talk~~ |

1. I think Bill likes Diane. He keeps _talking_ about her.
2. Julie avoids _____ during rush hour because of the traffic.
3. I finished _____ that book last night. It was very good.
4. Jody enjoys _____ photos. It's her hobby.

| hit | open | solve | wear |

5. Do you mind _____ the window? It's hot in here.
6. "We gave up _____ this puzzle. It's too difficult." "Really? Let me see it."
7. Our baseball team practices _____ the ball every day.
8. I suggest _____ that blue dress to the party. You look great in it.

B. 괄호 안에 주어진 동사들을 적절히 배열하여 문장을 완성하세요. 필요한 경우 동사를 -ing로 쓰세요.

1. (enjoy / play) I _enjoy playing_ the piano.
2. (pack / finish) "Did you _____ for your trip?" "Yes."
3. (keep / lose) Have you seen my keys? I _____ them.
4. (share / mind) "Do you _____ a taxi?" "No, that's a good idea."
5. (avoid / drink) I _____ wine. It gives me a headache.
6. (speak / practice) Jane and I take a Chinese class together. We _____ Chinese every day.
7. (teach / give up) Ken might _____ and go to law school.
8. (get / suggest) "My flight is at 9 p.m." "Then I _____ to the airport by 7 p.m."

UNIT 48 He **wants to open** a restaurant.

to + 동사원형

He **wants to open** a restaurant.
그는 식당을 열기를 원한다.

1 다음과 같은 동사 뒤에는 '~하는 것, ~하기'라는 의미로 말할 때 **to** + 동사원형을 쓴다.

want	need	hope	expect	**to** + 동사원형
decide	choose	plan	promise	(to worry, to work, to take 등)
offer	ask	learn	refuse	

- You don't **need to worry** about me. I'm fine. 나에 대해 걱정할 필요 없어.
- We **hope to work** with you again soon. 곧 당신과 함께 다시 일하기를 바랍니다.
- "Have you **decided to take** the job?" "Yes, I start next week."
- Megan is **planning to travel** around Europe this summer.
- Jackie and Allison **offered to bring** a cake to the party.

PRACTICE

A. 주어진 동사들을 사용하여 예시와 같이 문장을 완성하세요.

| become | find | ride | ~~spend~~ | wash | watch |

1. (expect) I didn't _expect to spend_ so much money at the mall today.
2. (hope) We are looking for a sofa. We _____ a cheap one.
3. (choose) "Why did you _____ a writer?" "I love writing short stories."
4. (want) "Have you seen that new movie yet?" "No, but I _____ it."
5. (learn) "When did you _____ a motorcycle?" "Last year."
6. (promise) I'm busy right now, but I _____ the dishes later.

B. 주어진 표현을 사용하여 문장을 완성하세요. -ing 또는 to + 동사원형으로 쓰세요.

| buy this house | clean the bathroom | ~~get some gas~~ |
| look at me | open the door | play the flute |

1. We need _to get some gas_ _____.

2. Do you mind _____ for me?

3. I finished _____.

4. We decided _____.

5. I plan _____ at a concert.

6. He keeps _____.

UNIT 49 They **like visiting/to visit** art museums.

-ing와 to+동사원형 모두 뒤에 올 수 있는 동사

They **like visiting** art museums. 또는

They **like to visit** art museums.
그들은 미술관을 방문하는 것을 좋아한다.

1 다음과 같은 동사 뒤에는 **-ing**와 **to+동사원형**을 둘 다 쓸 수 있다.

| like | love | prefer | hate | **-ing** (hiking, doing 등) |
| start | begin | continue | | **to+동사원형** (to hike, to do 등) |

- Polly **loves hiking** in the mountains. 또는 Polly **loves to hike** in the mountains. Polly는 하이킹하는 것을 좋아한다.
- I **hate doing** the dishes. 또는 I **hate to do** the dishes. 설거지하는 것을 싫어한다.
- When did you **start studying** French? 또는 When did you **start to study** French?
- Harry will **continue working** at the bank. 또는 Harry will **continue to work** at the bank.

2 **stop** 뒤에는 **-ing**를 쓸 수도 있고 **to+동사원형**을 쓸 수도 있지만, 다음과 같은 의미 차이가 있다.

stop + -ing : ~하는 것을 멈추다

- Please **stop making** noise. I can't sleep. 소음 내는 것을 멈춰주세요.
- Paula **stopped listening** to the radio and turned on the TV.

stop + to+동사원형 : ~하기 위해 (하던 일을) 멈추다

- I met Katie on the street, so I **stopped to talk** to her. 그녀와 이야기하기 위해 멈췄다.
- "Can we **stop to eat** something?" "Sure. What do you want?"

PRACTICE

A. 괄호 안에 주어진 동사를 -ing 또는 to+동사원형으로 사용하여 문장을 완성하세요.

1. (find) We expected _to find_ Mr. Miller in his office, but he wasn't there.
2. (go) We avoid _____ to the mall on Saturdays. It's too crowded.
3. (feel) "When did you begin _____ sick?" "This morning."
4. (join) Greg and I refused _____ the golf club because it costs too much.
5. (paint) "Did Jake finish _____ the fence?" "Not yet."
6. (fix) Jonathan gave up _____ his bicycle and took it to the repair shop.
7. (use) My grandmother learned _____ the computer two years ago.
8. (drive) I don't like _____ in the snow.

B. 주어진 동사와 stop을 사용하여 문장을 완성하세요.

| ask | buy | laugh | take | ~~walk~~ | worry |

1. Can we _stop walking_ now? My feet hurt.
2. The movie was so funny. I couldn't _____.
3. "I think we're lost." "We should _____ for directions."
4. "I'm so nervous about my speech." "_____ about it so much."
5. Can we _____ some milk at the store? We don't have any at home.
6. Let's _____ a picture here. The view from this mountain is beautiful.

UNIT **50** She **wants him to finish** the report.

동사 + 사람 + to + 동사원형

She **wants him to finish** the report.
그녀는 그가 보고서를 끝내기를 원한다.

1 **want + 사람 + to + 동사원형**: ~가 …하기를 원하다
- I'm really tired, so I **want you to drive**. 당신이 차를 운전해주기를 원해요.
- Jennifer didn't **want Albert to buy** the TV. It was too expensive. Jennifer는 Albert가 그 TV를 사는 것을 원하지 않았다.
- I'm going to the store. Do you **want me to get** anything for you?

want 뒤에 **to** + 동사원형만 쓸 수도 있다. 다음과 같은 차이에 주의한다.
- I **want to help** him. 나는 그를 돕기를 원해요.
  I **want you to help** him. 당신이 그를 돕기를 원해요.

2 다음과 같은 동사 뒤에도 사람 + **to** + 동사원형을 쓸 수 있다.

| advise | allow | ask | expect | teach | tell |

동사	사람	to + 동사원형
The doctor	advised	Judy	to exercise more.	의사는 Judy에게 운동을 더 하라고 조언했다.
We didn't	expect	Fred	to win the race.	우리는 Fred가 경주를 이길 것이라고 기대하지 않았다.
Can you	teach	me	to dance?	

P R A C T I C E

A. 괄호 안에 주어진 단어들과 **want**를 사용하여 대화를 완성하세요.

1. A: (you, come) I _want you to come_ to my wedding.
   B: Of course! I'll be there.

2. A: Let's stay home tonight.
   B: (us, have) Actually, Leo and Marcy _____ dinner with them.

3. A: (me, move) Do you _____ those boxes upstairs?
   B: Thanks, but I can do it.

4. A: Mom, can I go to the party?
   B: (you, clean) OK, but I _____ your room first.

B. 각 사람의 말을 보고 괄호 안에 주어진 동사를 사용하여 예시와 같이 문장을 완성하세요. 과거 시제로 쓰세요.

 JOE ⟨Bill, can you close the window?⟩
1. (ask) Joe _asked Bill to close the window_.

 DIANA ⟨David will call back soon.⟩
4. (expect) Diana _____.

 ANDY ⟨Jamie, you can use the camera.⟩
2. (allow) Andy _____.

 TIM ⟨Nick, please speak louder.⟩
5. (want) Tim _____.

 LYNN ⟨Brian, could you answer the phone?⟩
3. (tell) Lynn _____.

ANNA ⟨Nancy, you should go to bed.⟩
6. (advise) Anna _____.

UNIT 51 He made her scream.

make/have/let + 사람 + 동사원형

He **made her scream.**
그는 그녀가 소리 지르게 했다.

1 make/have/let + 사람 + 동사원형: ~가 …하게 하다

	make/have/let	사람	동사원형	
• Bob and Helen	made	me	wait	for an hour. Bob과 Helen은 내가 한 시간 동안 기다리게 했다.
• Erin	had	Jake	move	some furniture. Erin은 Jake가 가구를 옮기게 했다.
•	Let	me	introduce	myself.

이때, 동사원형 대신 **to** + 동사원형을 쓰지 않도록 주의한다.
- Exercising **makes me feel** healthy. (makes me to feel로 쓸 수 없음)
- Becky **had Jay fix** her printer. (had Jay to fix로 쓸 수 없음)

2 help + 사람 + 동사원형: ~가 …하는 것을 돕다

	help	사람	동사원형	
• Can you	help	me	find	the post office? 제가 우체국을 찾는 것을 도와주시겠어요?
• I	helped	Sean	finish	his homework.

이때, 동사원형 대신 **to** + 동사원형을 쓸 수도 있다.
- I'll **help you hang** that picture. 또는 I'll **help you to hang** that picture. 네가 그 그림을 거는 것을 도와줄게.

PRACTICE

A. 주어진 동사를 사용하여 예시와 같이 문장을 완성하세요.

| bake | buy | drive | pay | ~~run~~ | stay |

1. My wife wants me to lose weight. She makes _me run_ every morning now.
2. "Where is Larry?" "I had _____ some eggs at the store."
3. I want to use Dad's car but he won't let _____ it.
4. "Did you and Lucy find a hotel?" "No, but my friend let _____ at her house."
5. Jim and Troy broke a vase in the store, so the clerk made _____ for it.
6. Gina makes delicious cookies, so I had _____ some for me.

B. 주어진 동사와 **help**를 사용하여 예시와 같이 도와주겠다고 제안하세요.

| answer | carry | find | ~~prepare~~ | wash |

1. I have to make dinner.   I can _help you prepare_ OR _help you to prepare_ it.
2. I lost my passport.   I will _____ it.
3. These bags are so heavy.   I can _____ them.
4. I don't understand this question.   I can _____ it.
5. My dog is so dirty.   I will _____ him.

UNIT 52 They're running **to catch** the bus.

목적을 나타내는 to + 동사원형과 명사 + to + 동사원형

Oh, no! We have to catch the bus!

They're running **to catch** the bus.
그들은 버스를 타기 위해 뛰어가고 있다.

1 '~하기 위해'라는 의미로 말할 때 **to** + 동사원형을 쓸 수 있다.

- I must study hard **to pass** the exam. 시험에 합격하기 위해 열심히 공부해야 한다.
- "How can I help you?" "I'm here **to meet** Mr. Johnson." Johnson씨를 만나기 위해 왔어요.
- We usually go to a bar **to drink** some wine on Friday nights.
- "Where's Fred?" "He went out **to play** baseball."

2 '~할 …'이라는 의미로 말할 때 다음과 같이 명사 뒤에 **to** + 동사원형을 쓸 수 있다.

time	to go	갈 시간
work	to do	할 일
things	to tell	말할 것
place	to stay	머무를 장소
money	to spend	쓸 돈

- Hurry up! It's **time to go.** 갈 시간이야.
- Mary can't come for dinner. She has a lot of **work to do** tonight. 오늘 밤에 할 일이 많다.
- I have so many **things to tell** you. Let's go for coffee.
- Are there any hotels nearby? I need a **place to stay**.

PRACTICE

A. 그림을 보고 주어진 표현을 사용하여 예시와 같이 문장을 완성하세요.

| ~~get a haircut~~ | return a book | see the pandas | send a package | visit his friend |

1. She went to the _hair salon to get a haircut_ .
2. He went to the _____ .
3. He went to the _____ .
4. She went to the _____ .
5. They went to the _____ .

B. 괄호 안에 주어진 단어들을 적절히 배열하여 문장을 완성하세요. to를 함께 쓰세요.

1. (spend / money) I can't go shopping. I have no _money to spend_ .
2. (place / sit) All of the seats are taken. There's no _____ .
3. (time / visit) I don't have _____ my grandparents these days.
4. (ask / questions) Can we meet this afternoon? I have some _____ you.
5. (book / read) It'll be a long trip. You should take a _____ .

UNIT 53 a girl, snow

셀 수 있는 명사와 셀 수 없는 명사

1 명사에는 셀 수 있는 명사와 셀 수 없는 명사가 있다.

셀 수 있는 명사	셀 수 없는 명사

a girl   four hats

snow   sugar

girl	hat	dog	apple		snow	sugar	air	time
brother	pen	bird	flower		water	rice	money	news

◈ 셀 수 없는 명사: 부록 p. 174 참고

2 셀 수 있는 명사는 단수 또는 복수로 쓸 수 있다.

단수	a **boy**	an **egg**	one **cat**	this **bag**
복수	two **boys**	many **eggs**	some **cats**	these **bags**

단수는 하나의 사람이나 사물을 말할 때 쓴다. 이때, 앞에 **a** 또는 **an**을 함께 쓸 수 있다.

- **A boy** is standing by the window. 한 소년이 창문 가에 서 있다.
- I'm going to have **an egg** for breakfast.

복수는 둘 이상의 사람이나 사물을 말할 때 쓴다. 이때, 명사 끝에 주로 **-s**를 붙인다.

- There are **30 students** in my class. 우리 반에는 서른 명의 학생이 있다.
- I picked **some flowers** from my mother's garden.

3 셀 수 없는 명사에는 단수와 복수의 개념이 없다. 따라서 앞에 **a** 또는 **an**을 쓰거나 끝에 **-s**를 붙일 수 없다.

- There will be **rain** this evening. (a rain 또는 rains로 쓸 수 없음)
- Can you give me some **advice**? (an advice 또는 advices로 쓸 수 없음)

PRACTICE

A. 괄호 안에 주어진 명사를 사용하여 문장을 완성하세요. 필요한 경우 **a**를 함께 쓰세요.

1. (taxi) Let's take _a taxi_ to the airport.
2. (rice) I'd like _____ with my steak, please.
3. (music) Do you enjoy listening to _____ ?
4. (postcard) There's _____ for you from Derek.
5. (computer) I'm saving money to buy _____ .
6. (pen) I need _____ . Can I use yours?
7. (salt) Could you bring me some _____ ?
8. (man) I saw _____ with brown hair.
9. (milk) "This _____ smells bad." "Don't drink it. I bought it three weeks ago."
10. (snow) Many schools are closed because of _____ .

B. 둘 중 맞는 것을 고르세요.

1. Jane has four (sister /(sisters)) but no brothers.
2. We need some (butter / butters) for the cake.
3. Do you want to see a (movie / movies)?
4. Could you lend me some (money / moneys)?
5. There are many (apple / apples) on the tree.
6. I don't have a lot of (time / times) now.
7. Marcus visited Italy two (year / years) ago.
8. Molly, could you sing a (song / songs) for us?
9. We own a (house / houses) in the country.
10. This city has clean (air / airs).

UNIT 54 a dog, two dogs

단수와 복수

1
자음으로 시작하는 단수명사 앞에는 **a**를 함께 쓰고, 모음으로 시작하는 단수명사 앞에는 **an**을 함께 쓴다.
- "Do you own any pets?"   "I have **a dog**." 개 한 마리가 있어.
- I think I lost **an earring**.

이때, 단어의 첫 번째 철자가 아니라 발음에 따라서 **a** 또는 **an**을 쓰는 것에 주의한다.
- Joseph teaches biology at **a university**. (university의 첫 음이 [ju]로 발음되므로 a를 썼음)
- Mr. Roberts is out, but he will return in **an hour**. (hour의 첫 음이 [a]로 발음되므로 an을 썼음)

2
복수명사 끝에는 **-s**를 붙인다.
- I live with **two roommates**. They're very nice. 나는 두 명의 룸메이트와 함께 산다.
- Many **stores** are not open on Christmas Day.

단, 다음과 같이 -s를 붙일 때 주의해야 할 명사가 있다.

-sh, -ch, -s, -x, -z, -o + es	church → chur**ches**	potato → potat**oes**	예외) photo → photo**s**
-y → -ies	city → cit**ies**	baby → bab**ies**	예외) day → day**s**
-f/-fe → -ves	knife → kni**ves**	wife → wi**ves**	shelf → shel**ves**
불규칙	person → **people**	man → **men**	child → **children**

◆ 명사의 복수형: 부록 p. 171 참고

- There are many old **churches** in Rome. 로마에는 오래된 교회들이 많다.
- We'll visit some famous **cities** in China during our trip. 여행 동안 중국의 몇몇 유명한 도시들을 방문할 거야.
- "Can you put these **knives** in the drawer?"   "Sure."
- Some **people** can write with both hands.

3
단수명사는 **a** 또는 **an** 등 없이 단독으로 쓸 수 없지만 복수명사는 단독으로 쓸 수 있다.
- We saw **a lion** at the zoo. (saw lion으로 쓸 수 없음)
- We saw **lions** at the zoo. (saw lions로 쓸 수 있음)

PRACTICE

A. 주어진 명사를 복수로 쓰세요.

1. doctor → *doctors*
2. foot → _____
3. day → _____
4. photo → _____
5. child → _____
6. shelf → _____
7. brush → _____
8. ticket → _____
9. potato → _____
10. bedroom → _____
11. party → _____
12. wife → _____

B. 그림을 보고 주어진 명사를 사용하여 문장을 완성하세요. **a** 또는 **an**을 함께 쓰거나 복수로 쓰세요.

| baby   book   ~~cat~~   tomato   umbrella |

1    2    3    4    5

1. Some *cats* _____ are in the basket.
2. He is carrying _____.
3. The _____ are crying.
4. She is buying some _____.
5. There is _____ by the door.

UNIT 55 a fish, some fish

단수, 복수에 주의해야 할 명사

1 다음과 같은 명사들은 단수와 복수를 같은 형태로 쓴다.

단수	a fish	a sheep	a deer
복수	some fish	eight sheep	many deer

- Look! **Some fish** are swimming in the water. 몇몇 물고기들이 물속에서 헤엄치고 있어.
- Mr. Anderson has **eight sheep** and a horse on his farm. Anderson씨의 농장에는 양 여덟 마리와 말 한 마리가 있다.
- We saw **many deer** during our camping trip.

2 다음과 같이 두 개의 부분이 모여 하나의 사물을 이루는 경우에는 항상 복수로 쓴다.

| pajamas | scissors | jeans | pants | glasses |

- I like my **pajamas**. They're very comfortable. 내 잠옷을 좋아한다.
- Can I borrow your **scissors** for a minute? 가위를 잠깐 빌릴 수 있을까요?
- "Do you wear **jeans** often?" "No, I don't."

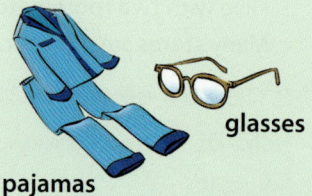
glasses
pajamas

위의 명사들을 셀 때는 **a pair of/two pairs of** 등을 함께 쓴다.

- I got **a pair of pants** for my birthday. 내 생일에 바지 한 벌을 받았다.
- I have **two pairs of glasses**. I use one pair at home and the other pair at work.

PRACTICE

A. 괄호 안에 주어진 명사를 사용하여 문장을 완성하세요. a 또는 an을 함께 쓰거나 복수로 쓰세요.

1. (deer) We saw _a deer_ in the woods. It was beautiful.
2. (cookie) "Would you like some _____? I just baked them." "Thanks!"
3. (fish) "I went fishing last weekend." "How many _____ did you catch?"
4. (key) "I found _____ on the floor." "Oh, it's mine."
5. (sheep) Some _____ are sleeping on the grass. They look peaceful.
6. (baby) Look at those _____. They're twins!

B. 둘 중 맞는 것을 고르세요.

1. I'd like to buy these (pant /(pants)) in a larger size.
2. "I don't have any ((money)/ moneys) for the taxi." "I can pay."
3. I bought new (pajama / pajamas), but they're too small for me. I should return them.
4. Be careful. Those (scissor / scissors) are very sharp.
5. Cindy has worn (glass / glasses) for many years.
6. George has eaten two (sandwich / sandwiches), but he's still hungry.

C. Tara의 상점에 남아 있는 상품의 목록을 보고 one/two 등 또는 a pair of/two pairs of 등을 함께 사용하여 말하세요.

INVENTORY LIST
TARA

We have...
1. (sunglasses) _two pairs of sunglasses_ .
2. (caps) _____ .
3. (jeans) _____ .
4. (skirts) _____ .
5. (pajamas) _____ .

UNIT 56 a glass of water, two cans of soda

1 다음과 같은 셀 수 없는 명사들은 단위를 나타내는 표현을 사용하여 수나 양을 말할 수 있다.

a glass of water   two cans of soda   three bottles of juice

a glass of water 물 한 잔	**a can of** soda 탄산음료 한 캔	**a bottle of** juice 주스 한 병
a cup of coffee 커피 한 컵	**a loaf of** bread 빵 한 덩어리	**a piece of** cake/paper 케이크 한 조각/종이 한 장
a carton of milk 우유 한 통	**a box of** cereal 시리얼 한 박스	**a slice of** pizza 피자 한 조각

- Can I have **a glass of water**? 물 한 잔 마실 수 있을까요?
- I need **two loaves of bread** and **a box of cereal**. 빵 두 덩어리와 시리얼 한 박스가 필요해요.
- "What did you have for lunch?" "I ate **two slices of pizza**."

2 soda나 coffee 등과 같은 음료를 주문하는 상황에서는 다음과 같이 쓸 수도 있다.

- Would you like **a soda**? 또는 Would you like **a can of soda**? 탄산음료 한 캔 마실래?
- **Two coffees**, please. 또는 **Two cups of coffee**, please.

PRACTICE

A. Katherine은 슈퍼마켓에서 장을 봤습니다. 그림을 보고 a glass of, two bottles of 등의 표현을 사용하여 문장을 완성하세요.

KATHERINE

I am buying…
1. (wine) _two bottles of wine_ .
2. (milk) _____ .
3. (cake) _____ .
4. (soda) _____ .
5. (bread) _____ .

B. 다음 문장을 읽고 틀린 부분이 있으면 바르게 고치세요. 틀린 부분이 없으면 O로 표시하세요.

1. There is a lot of snows on the street.   _snows → snow_
2. I'd like to have an orange juice, please.
3. Julia bought two box of cereals for her kids.
4. The market on Hill Street sells many fresh fish and vegetables.
5. When I went hiking last weekend, I saw three deers.
6. "Can I see a jean and a shirt, please?" "Sure."
7. Ms. Graham needs to buy 10 scissors for her hair shop.
8. "I need two sheets of paper." "OK. Here you go."
9. We got table and four chairs for the dining room.
10. "Would you like some coffee?" "Yes, with some sugars, please."

UNIT 57 a lamp, the lamp

We need **a lamp**. 램프가 하나 필요해요.

The lamp is too bright. 램프가 너무 밝아요.

1 특별히 정해지지 않은 막연한 사람 또는 사물 하나에 대해 말할 때 **a** 또는 **an**을 쓴다.

- "Do you have **a car**?" "Yes, but it's old."
 (막연한 차 하나를 의미하므로 a를 썼음)
- Brenda is looking for **an apartment** in the downtown area. (막연한 아파트 하나를 의미하므로 an을 썼음)
- We're going to buy **a cake** for Tim's birthday.

특정한 사람 또는 사물에 대해 말할 때나, 어떤 사람 또는 사물을 가리키는지 명확할 때 **the**를 쓴다.

- **The car** in front of the store is Jane's.
 (상점 앞의 특정한 차를 의미하므로 the를 썼음)
- **The apartments** in this city are very old.
 (이 도시의 아파트를 가리키는 것이 명확하므로 the를 썼음)
- Did you make **the cake**? It looks delicious!

2 어떤 대상에 대해 처음 말할 때는 **a** 또는 **an**을 쓰고, 그 대상을 다시 말할 때는 **the**를 쓴다.

- Ms. Young has **a son** and **a daughter**. **The son** is eight years old, and **the daughter** is six years old.
 (son과 daughter를 앞에서 언급했으므로 The son과 the daughter로 썼음)
- I ate **a sandwich** and **a salad** for lunch. **The sandwich** was very delicious, but I didn't like **the salad**.
 (sandwich와 salad를 앞에서 언급했으므로 The sandwich와 the salad로 썼음)

PRACTICE

A. a/an 또는 the를 써넣으세요.

1. Look out <u>the</u> window. It's snowing!
2. "Do we have _____ exam tomorrow?" "No, we don't. We have one next Friday."
3. "I heard _____ funny joke today." "I want to hear it."
4. "What happened?" "There was _____ accident on Main Street."
5. Can you answer _____ phone? I'm busy right now.
6. _____ students in our school are very smart.
7. "Is there a bank machine nearby?" "There is one across _____ road."
8. _____ new mall just opened on Maple Street. Let's go there next weekend.

B. 괄호 안에 주어진 명사와 a/an 또는 the를 함께 사용하여 문장을 완성하세요.

1. (gloves) Nancy sent me some nice gloves. <u>The gloves</u> are very warm.
2. (question) "I have _____ for you." "OK. What is it?"
3. (water) _____ in this river is very clear.
4. (problem) There is _____ with my computer. I should take it to the repair shop.
5. (keys) I need to open the office. Where are _____?
6. (good restaurant) I know _____. Do you want to go there tonight?
7. (umbrella) It's raining outside. Do you have _____?
8. (mountains) Colorado has beautiful mountains. In the winter, _____ are covered in snow.

UNIT 58 I want to travel around **the world**.

the를 쓰는 경우와 쓰지 않는 경우 (1)

1 다음과 같은 경우 명사 앞에 주로 **the**를 쓴다.

the	세상에 하나밖에 없는 것	the world	the sun	the moon	the earth
	자연환경	the sky	the sea	the ocean	
	국가/도시 등에 하나밖에 없는 것	the army	the police	the government	
	방송, 매체	the radio	the Internet		

- I want to travel around **the world**. 세계를 여행하고 싶다.
- Look at the color of **the sky**. It is beautiful. 하늘 색깔 좀 봐.
- John was in **the army** 20 years ago.
- I always listen to the news on **the radio** in the morning.

악기를 연주한다고 할 때 악기 이름 앞에 **the**를 쓴다.
- "Can you play **the guitar**?" 기타를 칠 수 있나요? "Not very well."

2 다음과 같은 경우는 명사 앞에 **the**를 쓰지 않는다.

~~the~~	운동	tennis	football	basketball
	학과목	English	history	biology
	식사	breakfast	lunch	dinner

- Ted and Mike play **basketball** every Sunday. Ted와 Mike는 일요일마다 농구를 한다.
- My son is studying **biology** at college. 내 아들은 대학에서 생물학을 공부한다.
- "Have you eaten **dinner** yet?" "Yes, I have."

PRACTICE

A. 그림을 보고 주어진 명사를 사용하여 문장을 완성하세요. 필요한 경우 **the**를 함께 쓰세요.

golf   math   moon   ~~piano~~   radio

1  2  3  4  5

1. She is playing _the piano_____.
2. She is listening to _____.
3. He is playing _____.
4. They are looking at _____.
5. He's studying _____ at school.

B. 괄호 안에 주어진 명사를 사용하여 문장을 완성하세요. 필요한 경우 **the**를 함께 쓰세요.

1. (lunch) I had _lunch_____ with Eric today. We went to a Mexican restaurant.
2. (ocean) Muriel likes to go surfing in _____.
3. (history) "Are you taking _____ this year?" "No, I'm not."
4. (Internet) "What time does the flight arrive?" "Let me check on _____."
5. (government) _____ is going to build a new road in my hometown.
6. (baseball) I like watching _____. It's very exciting.
7. (breakfast) I usually eat pancakes for _____.
8. (world) "How many countries are there in _____?" "196."

UNIT 59 They went to the movies.

the를 쓰는 경우와 쓰지 않는 경우 (2) 장소

They **went to the movies**.
그들은 영화관에 갔다

They are **at home**.
그들은 집에 있다.

1 다음과 같은 장소에 간다고 할 때는 **the**를 쓴다.

| go to the movies | go to the station | go to the bank |
| go to the theater | go to the airport | go to the post office |

- "Do you want to **go to the theater** tomorrow?" 내일 극장에 갈래? "Sure."
- "Which subway line **goes to the airport**?" 어느 지하철 노선이 공항으로 가나요? "The blue line."
- Dad **went to the bank** to pay the bill.
- Are you **going to the post office**? Could you send this package for me?

2 집/직장에 가거나 있다고 할 때는 **the**를 쓰지 않는다.

| go home | go to work | at home | at work |

- Joanne **went home** early because she had a cold. Joanne은 감기에 걸려서 집에 일찍 갔다.
- We always have coffee in the morning before we **go to work**. 직장에 가기 전에 항상 커피를 마신다.
- "What are you doing for your birthday?" "I'm going to have a small party **at home**."
- "How do you know Jonathan?" "We met **at work**."

◇ 주의해야 할 the 용법: 부록 p. 174 참고

PRACTICE

A. 괄호 안에 주어진 명사를 사용하여 문장을 완성하세요. 필요한 경우 **the**를 함께 쓰세요.

1. (movies) "Let's go to _the movies_ this evening." "Sorry, but I have other plans."
2. (work) "Where were you last night?" "I was at _____."
3. (station) I need to go to _____. Can you give me a ride?
4. (home) We usually don't stay at _____ during the summer. We like to travel.
5. (bank) "Is Mr. Harris in his office?" "No, he went to _____."
6. (theater) "Did you go to _____ yesterday?" "Yes. I saw a funny play."

B. 주어진 명사와 **go (to)**를 사용하여 문장을 완성하세요. 필요한 경우 **the**를 함께 쓰세요.

| airport   bank   home   movies   ~~post office~~   work |

1. "We don't have any stamps." "I'll _go to the post office_ to buy some."
2. I must _____ right now. My parents are coming, and I need to clean the house.
3. "What time do you _____ in the mornings?" "I have to be in the office by 8:30."
4. "Would you like to _____ tonight?" "Sure. I haven't seen any films recently."
5. We should _____ in 10 minutes. I don't want to miss our flight.
6. "I have to _____ to get some money." "It closes at 5, so you should hurry."

UNIT 60 She is my friend.

사람과 사물을 가리키는 대명사

This is Kate. She's my friend. I met her in high school.

This is Kate.

She is my friend. 그녀는 내 친구야.

I met her in high school. 고등학교 때 그녀를 만났어.

She와 her는 Kate를 가리키는 대명사이다.

1 앞서 언급한 사람이나 사물을 반복해서 말하지 않기 위해 대명사를 쓴다. 대명사는 다음과 같이 쓴다.

	주격			목적격	
(나는)	I			me.	(나를, 나에게)
(우리는)	We			us.	(우리를, 우리에게)
(너는, 너희들은)	You	saw Danny.	Danny saw	you.	(너를/너희를, 너에게/너희에게)
(그는)	He			him.	(그를, 그에게)
(그녀는)	She			her.	(그녀를, 그녀에게)
(그들은)	They			them.	(그들을, 그들에게)
(그것은)	It	looked beautiful.	I bought	it.	(그것을, 그것에게)
(그것들은)	They			them.	(그것들을, 그것들에게)

- **Can you** take **me** to the airport? 네가 나를 공항에 데려다 줄 수 있니?
- This hat is for Rob. **I** bought **it** in Sweden. 나는 그것을 스웨덴에서 샀어.
- "Have **you** met your new neighbors?" "Yes, **they**'re very nice."
- "Elisa is moving tomorrow." "I know. **She** told **me**. **We** should help **her**."
- "**I** sent **you** two postcards. Did **you** get **them**?" "Yes, **they** arrived yesterday."

PRACTICE

A. 그림을 보고 상황에 맞게 알맞은 대명사를 써넣으세요.

1. _I_ am Sam. People call _____ Sammy.

2. I know _____ very well. _____ is my neighbor.

3. _____ is my uncle. I don't see _____ very often.

4. _____ are my grandparents. I love _____ very much.

B. 적절한 대명사를 써넣으세요.

1. Do you enjoy movies? Yes, but I don't watch _them_ often.
2. What are they building over there? _____ is a new hotel.
3. You should call Mr. Green now. I'm busy right now. I'll contact _____ later.
4. Are we going to the party? Yes. Bruce invited _____.
5. I'll be in the hospital for a week! Don't worry. I'll visit _____ every day.
6. Did you and Shane go to the museum yesterday? Yes. _____ saw many beautiful paintings.

UNIT 61 It is Monday.

비인칭 주어 it

It is Monday.
월요일이다.

It is snowing.
눈이 오고 있다.

1 다음과 같은 경우에 **it**을 주어로 쓸 수 있다.

시간을 말할 때
- "What time is **it** now?" "**It's** 5 o'clock." 5시예요.
- **It's** noon. Let's go to lunch.

날짜를 말할 때
- "When is your birthday?" "**It's** July 29th." 7월 29일이야.
- "**It's** October 31st today." "Really? I can't believe **it's** already Halloween."

요일을 말할 때
- "What day is **it** today?" "**It's** Friday." 금요일이에요.
- **It's** Saturday. What should we do?

날씨를 말할 때
- Let's go on a picnic. **It's** very sunny today. 오늘 아주 화창해.
- **It's** raining outside. Did you bring an umbrella?

거리를 말할 때
- **It's** two miles to the airport from my house. 우리집에서 공항까지 2마일 떨어져 있다.
- "From here, **it's** 10 kilometers to the park." "Let's take the bus."

이때, **it**은 '그것'이라는 의미가 아니다.
- **It's** 1:50 right now. The meeting will start soon. 지금 1시 50분이다. ('그것은 1시 50분이다'라는 의미가 아님)
- "What's in the box?" "A sweater. It's a gift for my dad." 그것은 아빠 선물이야.

PRACTICE

A. 주어진 표현과 **it**을 사용하여 예시와 같이 문장을 완성하세요.

| 12:30 | close | December 1st | ~~Thursday~~ | warm |

1. Is today Wednesday?
2. What time is it?
3. How is the weather today?
4. Is it far from here to the hospital?
5. What is today's date?

No, _it's Thursday_ .
_____.
_____.
No, _____.
_____.

B. 적절한 대명사를 써넣으세요.

1. "Where is Peter?" " _He_ is in his bedroom."
2. I can't open the door. _____ is locked.
3. I got these earrings on sale, so _____ weren't very expensive.
4. "I called you this morning, but _____ didn't answer." "I didn't have my phone with me."
5. _____ is almost midnight. You should go to bed.
6. "Kevin and I have great news. _____ are getting married!" "Congratulations!"
7. _____ was snowing this morning. We went outside and made a snowman.

UNIT 62 This is **my** camera.

소유를 나타내는 표현

1 '(누구)의'라는 의미로 소유를 나타낼 때, 명사 앞에 **my/your/his** 등을 쓴다.

주격	I	we	you	he	she	they	it
소유격	my	our	your	his	her	their	its

- This is **my camera**. I bought it yesterday. 내 카메라야.
- I can't find Mr. Tyler. He's not in **his office**. 그의 사무실에 없다.
- "Why are you returning that jacket?" "**Its zipper** is broken."

2 mine/yours/his 등: (누구)의 것

주격	I	we	you	he	she	they
소유격	my	our	your	his	her	their
소유대명사	mine	ours	yours	his	hers	theirs

- "I found a camera in the doghouse." "That's **mine**!" 내 것이야!
- That's my cup. **Yours** is on the table. 네 것은 식탁 위에 있어.
- The farm over there is **ours**. We have horses and pigs.

  mine/yours/his 등과 같은 대명사 뒤에는 명사를 쓰지 않는 것에 주의한다.
  - I lent Diane my laptop because **hers** was not working. (hers laptop으로 쓸 수 없음)
  - My neighbors have a son. My son often plays with **theirs**. (theirs son으로 쓸 수 없음)

3 Whose + 명사 ~ ?: 누구의 ~인가요?

- "**Whose scissors** are these?" 누구의 가위인가요? "Sophie was just here. Maybe they're her scissors."
- "**Whose newspaper** is this?" "It's mine. Do you want to read it?"

P R A C T I C E

A. 그림을 보고 괄호 안에 주어진 명사와 my/your 등 소유격을 사용하여 상황에 맞게 문장을 완성하세요.

1. (house) This is _our house_.
2. (bag) This is _____.
3. (key) It's _____.
4. (dog) This is _____.
5. (ball) It's _____.

B. 괄호 안에 주어진 단어를 사용하여 예시와 같이 대화를 완성하세요. 질문을 할 때는 whose를 함께 쓰세요.

1. A: (car) _Whose car_ can I borrow?
   B: (we) You can take _ours_.

2. A: (glasses) _____ are these?
   B: (he) Jim wears glasses. Maybe they're _____.

3. A: (sandwich) _____ is in the fridge? It looks good.
   B: (I) It's _____, but you can have it.

4. A: (pen) _____ is this?
   B: (you) Oh, I thought it was _____.

5. A: (scarf) _____ is on the chair?
   B: (she) Jan was wearing it. It must be _____.

6. A: (kids) _____ are those?
   B: (they) They look just like Sue and Eric. They might be _____.

UNIT 63 It's Amy's book.

명사의 소유격

It's **Amy's** book.
이것은 Amy의 책이다.

1 '(누구)의'라는 의미로 사람의 소유를 나타낼 때 **-'s**를 쓴다.

Mr. Wright's	job
Karen's	room
the children's	toys

- "What's **Mr. Wright's job**?" Wright씨의 직업이 무엇인가요? "He's a lawyer."
- Where is **Karen's room**? Karen의 방은 어딘가요?
- "Where are **the children's toys**?" "I put them in the closet."

그러나 **-s**로 끝나는 복수명사의 끝에는 **'**만 쓴다.

| my parents' | anniversary |
| the Grays' | house |

- Today is **my parents' anniversary**. 오늘은 부모님의 결혼 기념일이다.
- "Is this **the Grays' house**?" "No, theirs is next door."

'(누구)의 것'이라는 의미로 명사 없이 **-'s**만 쓸 수도 있다.
- "I like your hat." "Thanks. It's **my brother's**." (my brother's = my brother's hat)
- This isn't my cup. It's **Tom's**. (Tom's = Tom's cup)

2 사물에 대해 말할 때는 **-'s** 대신 **of**를 주로 쓴다.
- "Can you play chess?" "No. I don't know **the rules of the game**." 게임의 규칙을 몰라.
- **The time of the flight** has changed. It will leave at 7:40.

PRACTICE

A. 주어진 단어들과 -'(s)를 사용하여 문장을 완성하세요.

| boat | garden | husband | ~~name~~ | paintings | voice |

1. (dentist) "What's _your dentist's name_ ?" "Jack Williams."
2. (Laura) "What does _____ do?" "He works for her father."
3. (our neighbor) _____ is so beautiful. It has so many flowers.
4. (your brother) "Is that _____ ?" "Yes. He sometimes goes fishing on it."
5. (Richard) _____ is amazing. He's a great singer.
6. (artists) There are many famous _____ in this museum.

B. 그림을 보고 상황에 맞게 문장을 완성하세요.

1. "I found a key." "It's _Emma's_ ."
2. "Is this your coat?" "No, it might be _____."
3. "Whose cat is that?" "I think it's _____."
4. "These gloves were on the floor." "They're _____."
5. "Whose phone is this?" "It's _____."

UNIT 64 **How much is this/that?**

this/these와 that/those

How much is **this**? 이것은 얼마예요?
How much are **these**? 이것들은 얼마예요?

How much is **that**? 저것은 얼마예요?
How much are **those**? 저것들은 얼마예요?

1. '(여기) 이 사람, 이것'이라는 의미로 가까이에 있는 대상을 가리켜서 말할 때 **this**를 쓴다.
   - "**This** is my cousin, Alex." 이 사람은 내 사촌 Alex야.
     "It's nice to meet you."

   둘 이상의 대상을 가리켜서 말할 때는 **these**를 쓴다.
   - "Which jeans should I buy?"
     "**These** are nice." 이것들이 괜찮네요.

   '(저기) 저 사람, 저것'이라는 의미로 멀리 있는 대상을 가리켜서 말할 때는 **that**을 쓴다.
   - **That**'s my car. My father gave it to me.
     저것은 내 차야.

   둘 이상의 대상을 가리켜서 말할 때는 **those**를 쓴다.
   - "Are **those** your kids?" 저 아이들이 당신의 아이들인가요?
     "Yes, they are."

2. **this/these, that/those** 뒤에 명사를 함께 쓸 수도 있다.

   this + 단수명사 또는 셀 수 없는 명사
   - It feels cold in **this room**. 이 방 안은 춥게 느껴진다.

   that + 단수명사 또는 셀 수 없는 명사
   - Is **that luggage** yours? 저 짐이 네 것이니?

   these + 복수명사
   - I took **these photos** at my friend's wedding.
     친구의 결혼식에서 이 사진들을 찍었다.

   those + 복수명사
   - Julie made **those sandwiches** for lunch.
     Julie는 점심으로 저 샌드위치들을 만들었다.

PRACTICE

A. this/these 또는 that/those를 써넣으세요.

1. "These scissors aren't sharp." "Here, try _these_____."
2. "What is _____ on the wall over there?" "It looks like a spider!"
3. _____ are my brother's friends. Let's go and say hello.
4. "Are you wearing a new suit?" "Yes, _____ is new."
5. "What are you holding in your hand?" "_____ are the invitations for the party."

B. 그림을 보고 괄호 안에 주어진 명사와 this/these 또는 that/those를 사용하여 예시와 같이 가격을 물으세요.

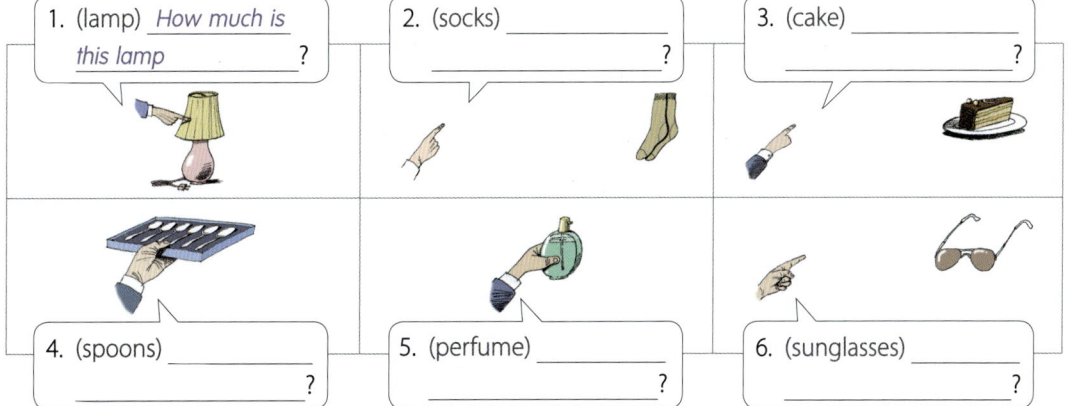

1. (lamp) How much is this lamp ?
2. (socks) _____ ?
3. (cake) _____ ?
4. (spoons) _____ ?
5. (perfume) _____ ?
6. (sunglasses) _____ ?

UNIT 65 How about this **one**?

one과 ones

How about this one?
이것은 어떤가요?

How about these big ones?
이 큰 것들은 어떤가요?

1 앞서 말한 명사를 다시 말할 때 명사 대신 **one** 또는 **ones**를 쓸 수 있다.

한 사람 또는 한 개의 사물을 말할 때는 **one**을 쓴다.
- "Which **boy** is your son?" "The **one** in a white shirt." (one = a boy)
- "You should take **a taxi**." "Where can I catch **one**?" (one = a taxi)
- There are so many **dogs**. Which **one** is yours?

둘 이상의 사람 또는 사물을 말할 때는 **ones**를 쓴다.
- Can you bring me my **glasses**? They are the **ones** on the desk. (ones = glasses)
- "Adam can speak four **languages**." "Really? Which **ones**?" (ones = languages)
- I want to be **a cheerleader**. The **ones** at my school are very popular.

2 **one**과 **ones** 앞에 형용사를 함께 쓸 수 있다.

a(n)/the + 형용사 + **one**
- "That is a famous building."
  "It looks like **an old one**." 오래된 것처럼 보여요.
- All of these ties are nice, but I think I'll buy **the blue one**.

some/the + 형용사 + **ones**
- Let's go see a movie. There are **some good ones** in the theater. 몇몇 좋은 것들이 상영되고 있다.
- The small envelopes are $2, and **the large ones** are $3.

PRACTICE

A. one 또는 ones를 써넣으세요.

1. Does anyone have an eraser?   I have _one_ . Here you go.
2. What do you think of these pants? I prefer the black _____.
3. Can you hand me my bag?   Which _____ is yours?
4. What type of table are you looking for? A round _____.
5. Let's sell some of our old DVDs.   Which _____?

B. 주어진 형용사와 one 또는 ones를 사용하여 문장을 완성하세요. a/an 또는 some을 함께 쓰세요.

| bigger   black   cheap   chocolate   ~~exciting~~   important |

1. Do you want to play a video game? I have _an exciting one_ .
2. "Do you have any brown boots?" "No, we don't. But we have _____."
3. "I can't put all these clothes in this suitcase." "I have _____. You can borrow it."
4. I have a meeting tomorrow. It's _____.
5. "What kind of muffins did you bake?" "I made _____."
6. These earrings are expensive. Do you have _____?

some과 any

UNIT 66 There are **some** children on the bus.

There are **some children** on the bus.
버스에 몇 명의 아이들이 있다.

There aren't **any children** on the bus.
버스에 아이들이 한 명도 없다.

1 '몇몇의, 약간의'라는 의미로 사람 또는 사물의 불특정한 수나 양에 대해 말할 때 **some** 또는 **any**를 쓴다.

some은 주로 긍정문에 쓴다.
- **Some students** ask a lot of questions during class. 몇몇 학생들은 수업 시간에 많은 질문을 한다.
- We spent **some time** in the mountains last weekend. 주말에 산에서 약간의 시간을 보냈다.
- "What did you buy at the market?" "I got **some flowers**."

any는 주로 부정문과 의문문에 쓴다.
- There weren't **any people** at the beach. The weather was too cold. 바닷가에 사람들이 하나도 없었다.
- I'm tired today because I didn't get **any sleep** last night. 어젯밤에 잠을 하나도 못 자서 피곤하다.
- "Do you have **any plans** for Saturday?" "Yes, I'm visiting my parents."

  그러나 권유나 요청을 할 경우에는 의문문에 **any**가 아니라 **some**을 쓴다.
  - "Can I offer you **some advice**?" 조언을 해드려도 될까요? "Of course."

2 명사 없이 **some** 또는 **any**만 쓸 수도 있다.
- We have ice cream. Do you want **some**? (some = some ice cream)
- "Did you see any dolphins at the zoo?" "No, there weren't **any**." (any = any dolphins)

PRACTICE

A. 주어진 명사와 some 또는 any를 사용하여 문장을 완성하세요.

| friends | ~~pancakes~~ | paper | snow | sports | trains |

1. "What are you cooking?" "I'm making *some pancakes* for breakfast."
2. It was warm last winter, so there wasn't _____.
3. We need to buy _____ for the printer.
4. "Does Sandra play _____?" "I think she plays hockey."
5. "Are there _____ to London tonight?" "Yes, there is one at 8 o'clock."
6. Jenna used to live in Australia, so she has _____ there.

B. some 또는 any를 써넣으세요.

1. I haven't eaten today. I'm hungry.
2. Have you seen any movies lately?
3. I made this cake myself.
4. The weather is very clear today.
5. Do we have any eggs?
6. Can I have a steak?

Let's order *some* Chinese food.
No, I haven't watched _____.
It looks delicious. Can I have _____?
Yes. There aren't _____ clouds in the sky!
No, we don't have _____.
Sure. Would you like _____ wine with it?

UNIT 67 There are **no** rooms.

no와 none

There are no rooms.
방이 없다.

1 '~이 없다'라는 의미로 말할 때 **no** + 명사를 쓴다.
- Mrs. White has three sons but **no daughters**. 아들은 셋이지만 딸은 없다.
- That sofa is too big for our apartment. There's **no space** for it.

no + 명사는 **not**과 함께 쓸 수 없는 것에 주의한다.
- We couldn't eat at that restaurant. There were **no empty tables**. (There weren't no empty tables로 쓸 수 없음)
- I want to meet you today, but I have **no time**. (I don't have no time으로 쓸 수 없음)

2 **no** + 명사 대신에 **not ~ any** + 명사를 쓸 수도 있다.
- We got **no mail** today. 또는 We **didn't** get **any mail** today. 오늘 아무 편지도 받지 않았다.
- There are **no girls** in my class. 또는 There **aren't any girls** in my class.

3 **no** + 명사 대신에 **none**을 쓸 수도 있다.
- "How much pizza is left?" "**None**. Jeff ate it all." (None = No pizza)
- "Did you buy an umbrella?" "No. The store had **none**." (none = no umbrellas)

no는 명사와 함께 쓰지만 **none**은 명사와 함께 쓰지 않는 것에 주의한다.
- I checked for messages, but there were **none**. (there were none messages로 쓸 수 없음)
- "How many cousins do you have?" "**None**." (None cousins로 쓸 수 없음)

PRACTICE

A. 주어진 명사와 no를 사용하여 문장을 완성하세요.

| bread | money | plans | ~~seats~~ | students | tickets |

1. There were _no seats_ on the bus, so I had to stand.
2. "What are you doing tonight?" "I have _____ yet. How about you?"
3. "I want to make some sandwiches, but there's _____." "I'll go to the store."
4. _____ are at school today because it's a holiday.
5. There's _____ in my wallet. I spent it all.
6. I want to go to the concert, but there are _____.

B. no/any/none을 써넣으세요.

1. "How many people are coming today?" "_None_. The meeting was canceled."
2. I couldn't take any pictures in the museum. _____ cameras were allowed.
3. Mike bought two suits at the mall, but I bought _____.
4. There weren't _____ buildings here 10 years ago. Those are all new.
5. The library was very quiet. There was _____ noise.
6. There aren't _____ cups on the table. Could you get some?

UNIT **68** **Someone** left this briefcase in the lobby.

someone/anything/nowhere…

1 '누군가, 무언가, 어딘가'라는 의미로 정확히 알 수 없는 사람, 사물, 장소에 대해 말할 때 다음과 같은 표현을 쓴다.

사람	someone/somebody	anyone/anybody
사물	something	anything
장소	somewhere	anywhere

- "**Someone** left this briefcase in the lobby." 누군가 로비에 이 서류 가방을 두고 갔어요. "Oh. That's mine."
- I'm going to the supermarket. Do you need **anything**? 무언가 필요하니?
- "Where is Jen's office?" "It's **somewhere** on Washington Avenue."

2 **someone, something** 등은 주로 긍정문에 쓰고, **anyone, anything** 등은 주로 부정문과 의문문에 쓴다.

- "**Something** smells great!" 무언가 좋은 냄새가 나! "I'm baking a pie."
- We haven't traveled **anywhere** lately. 최근에 아무 곳도 여행하지 않았다.
- "Is **anybody** sitting here?" "No. Have a seat."

단, 권유나 요청을 하는 의문문에는 **anyone, anything** 등이 아니라 **someone, something** 등을 쓴다.
- "Can you bring **something** to drink to the party?" 마실 무언가를 파티에 가져올 수 있니? "Sure."

3 '아무 ~도 …않다'라는 의미로 말할 때 다음과 같은 표현을 쓴다.

사람	no one/nobody
사물	nothing
장소	nowhere

- "Who is that girl?" "She must be new to this school. **No one** knows her." 아무도 그녀를 몰라.
- We need to go to the grocery store. We have **nothing** to eat. 먹을 것이 아무 것도 없다.
- "Where did you go last weekend?" "**Nowhere**. I stayed at home."

no one, nothing 등은 **not**과 함께 쓸 수 없는 것에 주의한다.
- Claire told a joke, but **nobody** laughed. (nobody didn't laugh로 쓸 수 없음)

PRACTICE

A. 그림을 보고 someone (또는 somebody)/something/somewhere를 써넣으세요.

Where is my umbrella?

I'm hungry.

Who is it?

Where are they going?

1. _Someone_ OR _Somebody_ took his umbrella.
2. He wants _____ to eat.
3. _____ is at the door.
4. They're going _____.

B. someone, anything, nowhere 등을 써넣으세요.

1. "I don't want to cook tonight." "Let's go out _somewhere_ for dinner, then."
2. I looked for my dog, but she was _____ in the house.
3. William is angry because _____ parked a car in front of his house again.
4. "Are you busy?" "No, I'm not doing _____ right now."
5. "I haven't seen Ben _____ today." "He went to his brother's wedding."
6. "_____ was hurt in the accident." "That's good news."
7. I need to go shopping. I have _____ to wear to the party.

UNIT 69 many cars, much sugar

many와 much

There are **many cars** on the road.
차가 많이 있다.

There isn't **much sugar** in the spoon.
설탕이 많이 없다.

1 **many** + 복수명사: 많은 ~
- I invited **many friends** to my house.
  많은 친구들을 집으로 초대했다.
- **Many people** were standing in line at the bank.

much + 셀 수 없는 명사: 많은 ~
- I won't have **much time** tomorrow.
  내일 시간이 많지 않을 것이다.
- Do you use **much oil** in your cooking?

2 **many**는 긍정문, 부정문, 의문문 모두에 쓴다.
- Ted can speak **many different languages**.
  Ted는 많은 다른 언어를 할 줄 안다.
- **Many stores** don't open on holidays.
  많은 상점들이 휴일에는 문을 열지 않는다.
- "Do you have **many children**?" "Yes, I have four."

much는 주로 부정문과 의문문에 쓴다.
- I don't have **much work** to do today.
  오늘 할 일이 많지 않다.
- Did you get **much sleep** last night?
  어젯밤에 많이 잤나요?
- Will I need **much money** for my trip?

3 명사 없이 **many** 또는 **much**만 쓸 수도 있다.
- Maria likes flowers. She grows **many** in her garden. (many = many flowers)
- "Do we have any cheese for the burgers?" "Yes, but there isn't **much**." (much = much cheese)

PRACTICE

A. 그림을 보고 괄호 안에 주어진 명사와 **many** 또는 **much**를 사용하여 문장을 완성하세요. **There are** 또는 **There isn't**를 함께 쓰세요.

  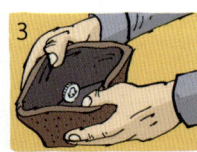  

1. (books) _There are many books_ on the bookshelf.
2. (space) _____ in the fridge.
3. (money) _____ in the wallet.
4. (students) _____ on the playground.
5. (bread) _____ in the basket.

B. 괄호 안에 주어진 명사와 **many** 또는 **much**를 사용하여 문장을 완성하세요. 필요한 경우 명사를 복수로 쓰세요.

1. (orange) _Many oranges_ are grown in Florida.
2. (interest) "Do you like playing basketball?" "No. I don't have _____ in sports."
3. (furniture) We don't have _____ in our house. We're going to buy some this weekend.
4. (cup) "How _____ do we need?" "Well, there are 12 guests."
5. (dog) There are _____ in my neighborhood. They bark too much at night.
6. (information) "Did you find _____ for your trip?" "No, not yet."

UNIT 70 She received **a lot of** letters.

She received **a lot of** letters.
많은 편지를 받았다.

1 **a lot of ~**: 많은 ~

a lot of는 복수명사와 셀 수 없는 명사 앞에 모두 쓸 수 있다.
- **A lot of children** are playing at the park. 많은 아이들이 공원에서 놀고 있다.
- My mom gives me **a lot of advice** about life.

  a lot of 대신 **lots of**를 쓸 수도 있다.
  - **A lot of tourists** were at the art museum. 또는 **Lots of tourists** were at the art museum.

2 **a lot of**는 긍정문, 부정문, 의문문 모두에 쓴다.
- I'm so full! I ate **a lot of food** for dinner. 많은 음식을 먹었다.
- Jane likes music, but she doesn't attend **a lot of concerts**. 콘서트에 많이 참석하지 않는다.
- "Did you visit **a lot of places** in New Zealand?" "Yes, I did."

3 명사 없이 **a lot**만 쓸 수도 있다.
- "I want to buy these shoes. They're so pretty!" "But you already have **a lot**." (a lot = a lot of shoes)
- "Did you take any pictures at the zoo?" "Yes, **a lot**." (a lot = a lot of pictures)

PRACTICE

A. 주어진 명사와 **a lot of**를 사용하여 문장을 완성하세요.

| ~~books~~ difficulty fun money people |

1. "Do you have to read _a lot of books_ for your history class?" "Yes. The class is very hard."
2. Jennifer doesn't make _____, but she enjoys her job.
3. "How was your camping trip? Did you have _____?" "Yes, it was great."
4. I'm having _____ with this homework. Could you help me?
5. There are _____ on the sidewalk. It's hard to walk.

B. much 또는 a lot of 중 더 적절한 것을 써넣으세요.

1. "Let's go to the movies tonight!" "I can't. I have _a lot of_ things to do."
2. It's raining a lot, but there isn't _____ wind.
3. My roommates were making _____ noise last night, so I couldn't sleep.
4. "Do you eat _____ vegetables?" "Yes. I especially like carrots."
5. This lamp doesn't use _____ electricity.
6. "Is there _____ traffic in the city?" "Only during the morning."
7. I spend _____ time with my family on weekends.
8. "Was there _____ fog this morning?" "Yes, many flights were delayed."

UNIT 71 a few cookies, a little milk

There are **a few cookies**.
약간의 쿠키가 있다.

There is **a little milk**.
약간의 우유가 있다.

1 '약간의'라는 의미로 **a few** 또는 **a little**을 쓸 수 있다.

a few + 복수명사
- Can I talk to you for **a few minutes**?
  몇 분간 이야기할 수 있나요?
- Sue bought **a few magazines** at the store.
  Sue는 가게에서 약간의 잡지를 샀다.
- It's late, but **a few restaurants** might be open.
- Tim is out of the office. He'll be back in **a few hours**.

a little + 셀 수 없는 명사
- Nick had **a little wine** at dinner.
  Nick은 저녁 식사 때 약간의 와인을 마셨다.
- I have saved **a little money** since last year.
  작년부터 약간의 돈을 모았다.
- Can I have **a little salt** in my soup?
- There is **a little ice** on the road this morning. Drive carefully.

2 명사 없이 **a few** 또는 **a little**만 쓸 수도 있다.
- "Let's make omelets for breakfast. Do we have any eggs?" "Yes, **a few**." (a few = a few eggs)
- "Is there any paper in the printer?" "There's **a little**." (a little = a little paper)
- "Are there any banks nearby?" "**A few**."
- "Did you lose any weight?" "Yes, **a little**."

PRACTICE

A. 그림을 보고 주어진 명사와 **a few** 또는 **a little**을 사용하여 문장을 완성하세요. 필요한 경우 명사를 복수로 쓰세요.

~~hair~~   rose   ticket   water

1 2  3  4

1. He has _a little hair_____.
2. There is _____ in the cup.
3. There are _____ in the vase.
4. She has _____.

B. **a few** 또는 **a little**을 써넣으세요.

1. Did your baseball team win any games this year?
2. Would you like some cheese on your pasta?
3. How many people are you inviting to the party?
4. Can you recommend a good movie?
5. Do you want some ice cream with your cake?
6. Do we have time before the meeting starts?

Yes, _a few_____.
_____, please.
Just _____.
Yes, I know _____.
Sure, I'll have _____.
Yes, _____.

UNIT 72 few cookies, little milk

There are **few cookies**.
쿠키가 거의 없다.

There is **little milk**.
우유가 거의 없다.

1 '거의 없는'이라는 의미로 few 또는 little을 쓸 수 있다.

few + 복수명사
- We see **few stars** in the sky these days.
  요즘에는 하늘에서 별을 거의 볼 수 없다.
- The store just opened, so it has **few customers**.

little + 셀 수 없는 명사
- Eric spends **little money** on clothes. He always wears the same ones. Eric은 옷에 돈을 거의 쓰지 않는다.
- I have **little knowledge** about physics. I've never studied it.

명사 없이 **few** 또는 **little**만 쓸 수도 있다.
- My brother reads many books, but I read **few**. (few = few books)
- "Do you have much homework today?" "No, very **little**." (little = little homework)

2 a few는 '약간 있다'라는 긍정적인 의미이고, few는 '거의 없다'라는 부정적인 의미이다.

- The party was fun. **A few people** came.
  약간의 사람들이 왔다.
- The party was boring. **Few people** came.
  사람들이 거의 오지 않았다.

a little은 '약간 있다'라는 긍정적인 의미이고, little은 '거의 없다'라는 부정적인 의미이다.

- I got **a little sleep** on the plane, so I feel fine.
  잠을 약간 잤다.
- I got **little sleep** on the plane, so I'm very tired now. 잠을 거의 자지 못했다.

PRACTICE

A. 주어진 명사와 few 또는 little을 사용하여 문장을 완성하세요. 필요한 경우 명사를 복수로 쓰세요.

| car information letter space ~~student~~ sugar |

1. The test was very difficult. *Few students* passed it.
2. The police are still looking for the thief. They have very _____ about him.
3. _____ were on the road after midnight. It was almost empty.
4. There is _____ in this pie, so it's not very sweet.
5. I can't put this sofa in the garage. There is _____.
6. People write _____ these days. They usually use e-mail.

B. a few/few 또는 a little/little을 써넣으세요.

1. "How's your life in Spain?" "Good. I've made *a few* friends here."
2. My sister has _____ interest in cooking. She always eats out.
3. "Could you give me _____ help? I don't understand this question." "Sure."
4. "Would you like some grapes?" "Yes, I'll have _____."
5. I found _____ errors in your report. You did a good job.
6. I had _____ time to prepare for my speech, so I was very nervous.

UNIT 73 All dogs have tails.

All dogs have tails.
모든 개들은 꼬리가 있다.

1 all + 복수명사/셀 수 없는 명사

'모든'이라는 의미로 말할 때, **all**을 쓸 수 있다.

- Nancy often goes to the zoo. She loves **all animals**. 그녀는 모든 동물을 사랑한다.
- "Is **all wine** made from grapes?" "No. There are many different kind**s**."

all + 복수명사를 주어로 쓸 때 복수동사를 쓴다.

- **All banks close** on Sundays. 모든 은행들은 일요일에 문을 닫는다.

all + 셀 수 없는 명사를 주어로 쓸 때는 단수동사를 쓰는 것에 주의한다.

- "**All fruit is** on sale today." "Let's buy some then!" (All fruit are로 쓸 수 없음)

2 all + day/week/month 등: ~ 종일, ~ 내내

이때, **all**은 복수명사가 아닌 단수명사와 함께 쓴다.

- I'm hungry. I haven't eaten anything **all day**. 하루 종일 아무것도 먹지 않았다.
- "Why didn't you call me?" "Sorry. I've been busy **all week**."

PRACTICE

A. 주어진 명사와 **all**을 사용하여 문장을 완성하세요. 필요한 경우 명사를 복수로 쓰세요.

| day | ~~driver~~ | floor | luggage | month | seafood |

1. _All drivers_ must wear seat belts.
2. I like _____, but fish is my favorite.
3. There are restrooms on _____ of the building.
4. Tanya went to London in June and stayed there _____.
5. _____ must be checked before you get on the plane.
6. I have to work _____ tomorrow, so I can't go to the picnic.

B. 괄호 안에 주어진 단어들과 **all**을 사용하여 현재 시제 문장을 완성하세요. 필요한 경우 명사를 복수로 쓰세요.

1. (furniture, be) _All furniture_ in the store _is_ made of wood.
2. (language, have) _____ grammar.
3. (rain, come) _____ from clouds.
4. (flight, be) _____ canceled today because of the bad weather.
5. (baby, need) _____ a lot of sleep.
6. (advice, be) We need ideas for the project. _____ welcome.

UNIT

every

Every house has a roof.

1 every + 단수명사

'모든'이라는 의미로 말할 때, **every**를 쓸 수 있다.
- **Every house** has a roof. 모든 집에는 지붕이 있다.
- **Every book** in this library is in English. 이 도서관에 있는 모든 책은 영어로 되어 있다.
- I open **every window** when I get up.

every + 단수명사를 주어로 쓸 때 단수동사를 쓴다.
- In my school, **every class has** 30 students. (every class have로 쓸 수 없음)
- I couldn't get into the office because **every door was** locked. (every door were로 쓸 수 없음)

2 '모든 ~'이라는 의미로 사람, 사물, 장소에 대해 말할 때 다음과 같은 표현을 쓴다.

사람	everyone/everybody
사물	everything
장소	everywhere

- The concert was amazing. **Everyone** enjoyed it. 모든 사람이 즐겼다.
- "Did you have a nice vacation?" "Yes. **Everything** was perfect." 모든 것이 완벽했다.
- You need to clean your room. Your clothes are **everywhere**.

3 every + day/week/year 등: ~마다, 매~
- I take a shower **every day**. 날마다 샤워를 한다.
- "Do you visit your parents often?" "Yes, I visit them **every week**." 매주 부모님을 찾아 뵙는다.
- We have turkey **every year** on Thanksgiving Day.

PRACTICE

A. 그림을 보고 주어진 명사와 every를 사용하여 문장을 완성하세요.

| ~~cat~~ | flower | man | seat | student |

1 2 3 4 5

1. _Every cat_ _____ is white.
2. _____ is wearing a uniform.
3. _____ is red.
4. _____ is taken.
5. _____ is wearing glasses.

B. everyone (또는 everybody)/everything/everywhere를 써넣으세요.
1. Thank you for the meal. _Everything_ _____ was so good!
2. Mr. and Mrs. Adams traveled _____ in Asia after they retired.
3. _____ in my family loves to hike. We go hiking every weekend.
4. I've tried _____, but the computer is still not working.
5. "Has _____ arrived?" "No. Ken isn't here yet."
6. "Look! It snowed last night. There is snow _____." "Let's make a snowman!"

UNIT 75 all of the pie, some of the pie

all/most/some/none of ~

all of the pie
파이 전부

most of the pie
파이 대부분

some of the pie
파이 약간

none of the pie
파이가 없음

1 특정한 사람 또는 사물을 가리킬 때 **all/most/some/none** 뒤에 **of ~**를 쓸 수 있다.

| all
most
some
none | of | the/my/these 등 + 명사 |
| | | it/us/you/them |

- **All of my friends** like playing football. 내 친구들 전부는 축구하는 것을 좋아한다.
- **Some of the clothes** in the store are on sale. 상점의 옷 몇몇은 세일 중이다.
- On weekends, I spend **most of my time** with my family.
- We took a taxi to the airport because **none of us** could drive.

2 all of ~와 all + 명사

all/some of ~ 등은 특정한 대상에 대해 말할 때 쓴다.
- I've met **all of the people** in our company.
  (우리 회사에 있는 사람들 전부)
- **Most of these cars** are expensive.
  (이 차들 중 대부분)

all/some 등 + 명사는 일반적인 대상에 대해 말할 때 쓴다.
- **All people** have secrets.
  (일반적인 사람들 전부)
- **Most cars** use gas.
  (일반적인 차들 대부분)

PRACTICE

A. 그림을 보고 all/most/some/none을 사용하여 예시와 같이 문장을 완성하세요.

1-3

4-6

1. _All of them_ are in the kitchen.
2. _____ are sitting at the table.
3. _____ are wearing yellow shirts.
4. _____ have red ribbons.
5. _____ have green ribbons.
6. _____ are under the Christmas tree.

B. 괄호 안에 주어진 단어들을 사용하여 문장을 완성하세요. 필요한 경우 of를 함께 쓰세요.

1. (most, the work) "Do you need help fixing the roof?" "No. _Most of the work_ is done."
2. (some, animals) _____ sleep all winter.
3. (none, my children) The movie was boring. _____ liked it.
4. (most, trees) _____ lose their leaves in the winter.
5. (all, them) I've tried on these sweaters, and I want to buy _____ .

UNIT 76 He enjoys playing **both**.

both/either/neither

1 both (+ 복수명사): 둘 다, 두 ~ 모두

- Alan likes baseball and basketball. He enjoys playing **both**.
  그는 둘 다 하는 것을 좋아한다.
- Look **both ways** before you cross the street. 길을 건너기 전에 양쪽을 모두 봐라.
- "Does Karen speak English or Spanish?" "She can speak **both**."

both

2 either (+ 단수명사): 둘 중 아무 것이나 하나, 두 ~ 중 아무 것이나 하나

- "Do you want chicken or fish?" "**Either** is fine." 둘 중 아무거나 괜찮아요.
- We can stay at **either hotel**. Both seem nice. 두 호텔 중 아무 곳에서나 묵어도 괜찮아요.
- "Do you want to go to the beach or the lake?" "I'm OK with **either**."

either

3 neither (+ 단수명사): 둘 다 아닌, 두 ~ 모두 아닌

- I'm not buying these dresses. **Neither** looks good on me.
  둘 다 나에게 어울리지 않는다.
- "Which house has a garage?" "**Neither house** has one." 두 집 모두 없어.
- Our office has two printers, but **neither** is working.

neither

4 both/either/neither of ~

both either neither	of	the/my/these 등 + 복수명사 us/you/them

- **Both of my parents** are teachers. (부모님 두 분 모두)
- "Should I wear a red tie or a blue one?" "**Either of those colors** matches your suit." (두 가지 색깔 중 아무거나)
- "Have Brad and Andy arrived?" "No, **neither of them** is here yet."

PRACTICE

A. both/either/neither를 써넣으세요.

1. "Do you like horror movies or action movies?" " _Neither_ . I like comedies."
2. "Which bag is yours?" "_____ are mine. I brought two."
3. "Should I leave the box here or on your desk?" "It doesn't matter. Just leave it _____ place."
4. _____ plays start at 8 o'clock. Which would you like to see?
5. "How were your math and science exams?" "Terrible. _____ was easy."
6. Our company always uses _____ sides of the paper to save money.
7. "Could we meet on Friday or Saturday?" "Sure. I can see you _____ day."
8. We went to two different bakeries, but _____ bakery was open.

B. 괄호 안에 주어진 표현과 both/either/neither of를 사용하여 문장을 완성하세요.

1. (them) "Which table do you want to sit at?" " _Either of them_ is OK."
2. (our cars) Mandy and I can't drive right now. _____ are in the repair shop.
3. (my dogs) _____ likes staying at home, so I take them to the park every day.
4. (the restaurants) I'm fine with _____. You can choose.
5. (us) My friend and I like singing, but _____ likes dancing.
6. (my legs) I jogged for too long, so _____ hurt.

UNIT 77 He's wearing a **black** jacket.

형용사

He's wearing a **black** jacket.
그는 검은 재킷을 입고 있다.

He's **tall**.
그는 키가 크다.

black과 tall은 형용사이다.

1 사람이나 사물의 상태 또는 특징을 말할 때 형용사를 쓸 수 있다.

형용사 + 명사
- We bought a house with a **pretty garden**. 예쁜 정원이 있는 집을 샀다.
- "Have you met Dr. Morris?" "Yes, he's a **nice man**. I really like him." 그는 좋은 사람이다.
- My sister has **blonde hair**, but I have **brown hair**.
- "What is your **favorite sport**?" "Hockey."
- Frank is writing a **short story** about his family.

be동사 + 형용사
- "I**'m thirsty**. Can I have a glass of water?" 목이 말라요. "Of course."
- Don't touch that pan. It**'s hot**. 그것은 뜨겁다.
- Let's go home. It'll **be dark** soon.
- "**Are** those cookies **good**?" "Yes, they**'re delicious**."
- Charlie's old apartment **wasn't big**, but it **was expensive**.

PRACTICE

A. 주어진 단어들을 사용하여 문장을 완성하세요.

cold empty important ~~new~~ pink

1. (suit) "Is that a _new suit_?" "No, it's an old one. I've had it for years."
2. (meeting) Jennifer can't join us for lunch. She has an _____ at work.
3. (weather) I don't like _____, so I hate winter.
4. (roses) I ordered some _____ for my wife, but they sent red ones!
5. (seats) We had to stand at the concert because there were no _____.

B. 그림을 보고 주어진 형용사와 be동사를 사용하여 문장을 완성하세요.

~~full~~ heavy long small tall

1. I _'m full_ .
2. It _____ .
3. These bags _____ .
4. The line _____ .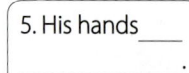
5. His hands _____ .

UNIT 78 They are walking **carefully**.

부사

They are walking **carefully**.
그들은 조심스럽게 걷고 있다.

carefully는 부사이다.

1. 행동이나 일이 '어떻게' 일어나는지를 말할 때 부사를 쓸 수 있다. 부사는 일반적으로 형용사 끝에 **-ly**를 붙인다.

형용사	clear	quiet	slow
부사	clear**ly**	quiet**ly**	slow**ly**

- I bought new glasses, so now I can see **clearly**. 선명하게 볼 수 있다.
- Please shut the door **quietly**. The baby is sleeping. 문을 조용하게 닫아주세요.
- The cars are moving **slowly** today because of the traffic.

2. -ly를 붙일 때 주의해야 할 부사가 있다.

-y → -ily	busy → bus**ily**
-le → -ly	gentle → gent**ly**
불규칙	good → well

- I worked **busily** all night to finish a report. 밤새 바쁘게 일했다.
- Please handle the vase **gently**. 꽃병을 조심히 다루어 주세요.
- Our computer is very old, but it still runs **well**.

◇ 형용사에 -ly 붙이는 방법: 부록 p. 171 참고

PRACTICE

A. 그림을 보고 주어진 형용사를 부사로 사용하여 문장을 완성하세요.

| bright | comfortable | nervous | quick | ~~sudden~~ |

The interview is in 5 minutes.

1. _Suddenly_ the door closed.
2. He is running _____ across the road.
3. They are waiting _____.
4. He is sitting _____.
5. The sun is shining _____.

B. 적절한 부사를 사용하여 예시와 같이 문장을 완성하세요.

1. Your paintings are wonderful. You paint pictures _wonderfully_.
2. The test was easy. The students passed it _____.
3. Susan is a terrible dancer. She dances _____.
4. Our wedding was perfect. Everything was planned _____.
5. My neighbor's dogs are so noisy. They bark _____.
6. The Tigers and the Eagles are good teams. They always play _____.

UNIT 79

형용사와 부사 비교

Jake is a **nice** guy. Jake always dresses **nicely**.

1 형용사와 부사는 다음과 같은 차이가 있다.

형용사는 사람이나 사물이 어떠한지를 나타낼 때 쓴다.

- Jake is a **nice** guy. Everyone likes him.
  Jake는 좋은 사람이다.
- Our new bed is **comfortable**.
  우리 새 침대는 편안하다.
- This book has a **happy** ending.
- My neighborhood is very **safe**.

부사는 행동이나 일이 어떻게 일어나는지를 나타낼 때 쓴다.

- Jake always dresses **nicely**.
  Jake는 항상 옷을 멋지게 입는다.
- We slept **comfortably** last night.
  우리는 어젯밤에 편안하게 잤다
- The story ends **happily**.
- Did Rita arrive in Canada **safely**?

2 다음과 같이 **look/smell/sound** 등의 뒤에 형용사를 자주 쓴다.

look smell sound taste feel	형용사	~해 보이다 ~한 냄새가 나다 ~하게 들리다 ~한 맛이 나다 ~함을 느끼다

- You **look sad**. What happened? 슬퍼 보여.
- What is this? It **smells strange**. 이상한 냄새가 나요.
- "Let's go to the beach this weekend." "That **sounds good**!"
- This pizza **tastes delicious**. Try some.
- Jason **felt angry** when he heard the news.

이때, **look/smell/sound** 등의 뒤에 부사를 쓸 수 없는 것에 주의한다.

- "Your hair **looks different** today." "I got a haircut." (looks differently로 쓸 수 없음)
- "Can you hear the violin?" "Yes, it **sounds beautiful**." (sounds beautifully로 쓸 수 없음)

PRACTICE

A. 둘 중 맞는 것을 고르세요.

1. I'm not going to stay at this hotel again. The service is (**terrible**/ terribly).
2. Lisa is a very (smart / smartly) student. She knows everything.
3. The children shouted (excited / excitedly) when they saw their new cat.
4. I don't like history. It is not (interesting / interestingly) to me.
5. "Today is Jack's birthday." "Oh no! I (complete / completely) forgot."
6. Josh did (bad / badly) in the race. He came in last.
7. I heard a (strange / strangely) noise last night. Did you hear anything?
8. You should exercise (regular / regularly) to stay healthy.

B. 그림을 보고 괄호 안에 주어진 형용사와 look/smell/sound/taste/feel을 사용하여 문장을 완성하세요.

1. (nice) You _look nice_ .

2. (delicious) It _____ .

3. (scared) I _____ .

4. (good) It _____ .

5. (great) It _____ .

6. (happy) They _____ .

UNIT 80 It's **late**. I got home **late**.

주의해야 할 형용사와 부사

1 다음과 같이 형용사와 부사 두 가지 모두로 쓸 수 있는 단어가 있다.

	형용사	부사
late	It's **late**. It's almost midnight. 늦었어.	I got home **late** last night. Everyone was asleep. 어젯밤 늦게 집에 왔다.
long	Sarah has **long** hair. Sarah는 긴 머리를 가졌다.	Let's walk to the park. It doesn't take **long**. 오래 걸리지 않는다.
hard	My father is a **hard** worker. 우리 아버지는 열심히 일하시는 분이다.	The soccer team is practicing **hard**. 축구팀이 열심히 연습하고 있다.
fast	Nicole's car is **fast**. Nicole의 차는 빠르다.	Nicole speaks **fast**. Nicole은 빠르게 말한다.
early	I had an **early** breakfast. 이른 아침 식사를 했다.	Mr. Jenkins arrived **early** for his interview. Jenkins씨는 면접에 일찍 도착했다.

2 다음과 같이 -ly로 끝나지만 부사가 아니라 형용사인 단어도 있다.

friendly (친절한) **lovely** (사랑스러운) **silly** (어리석은) **ugly** (못생긴) **lonely** (외로운)

- My new neighbors are **friendly**. I really like them. 나의 새 이웃들은 친절하다.
- "Where did you get that **lovely** dress?" 어디에서 그 사랑스러운 드레스를 샀나요? "At the mall."
- "Sorry. I made a **silly** mistake." "That's OK."

PRACTICE

A. 괄호 안에 주어진 단어를 형용사나 부사로 사용하여 문장을 완성하세요.

1. (late) The library opens _late_ on Mondays.
2. (fast) We need to get to the theater _____. The show starts in 10 minutes.
3. (beautiful) The concert was great. The singer sang _____.
4. (hard) We finally finished the project! Thank you for your _____ work.
5. (early) "Why did you leave the party _____ last night?" "I wasn't feeling well."
6. (happy) Anne and Mike got married two years ago. They are living _____.
7. (long) I haven't spoken to Judy for a _____ time. I hope she's well.
8. (exciting) Did you watch the baseball game last night? It was so _____.
9. (nervous) "You look _____. Is something wrong?" "I'm waiting for my test results."
10. (careful) "Did you read this article?" "Yes, but I didn't read it _____."

B. 다음 문장을 읽고 틀린 부분이 있으면 바르게 고치세요. 틀린 부분이 없으면 ○로 표시하세요.

1. Max got up lately this morning. → _lately → late_
2. This painting is lovely! We should buy it.
3. "Do you visit the dentist regular?" "Yes, I go once a month."
4. "Which sofa do you like?" "That one. It feels comfortably."
5. The children are playing noisy on the playground.
6. Please walk slowly. We don't need to hurry.
7. My aunt is a good cook. Her pasta is amazingly.
8. Ron has tried hardly, but his grades are not good.
9. Golf isn't an easily sport. You must practice often.
10. I'm taking an early flight to Boston tomorrow.

UNIT 81　He **always** eats cereal for breakfast.

always, often, never …

He always eats cereal for breakfast.
그는 항상 아침으로 시리얼을 먹는다.

1 어떤 일을 얼마나 자주 하는지를 말할 때 다음과 같은 부사를 쓴다.

always	usually	often	sometimes	rarely	never
(항상)	(보통)	(자주)	(가끔)	(좀처럼 ~하지 않는)	(전혀 ~하지 않는)

- My parents **often** give me advice. It helps a lot. 내 부모님은 자주 나에게 조언을 해주신다.
- We **sometimes** invite friends to our house on weekends.

2 **always**, **usually**, **never** 등은 다음과 같이 쓴다.

일반동사 앞
- Mark **always** cleans his room on Sunday mornings. Mark는 항상 일요일 아침에 방 청소를 한다.
- We **rarely** cook dinner these days. We **usually** eat out.

be동사 뒤, will/can 등의 뒤
- This hotel is **usually** full during the summer. 이 호텔은 보통 여름 동안에 꽉 찬다.
- I will **never** take a taxi to the airport again. It cost over $50!

PRACTICE

A. 다음의 활동들을 얼마나 자주 하는지 always/often/never 등을 사용하여 자신에 대해 답하세요.

How often do you… ?

1. wear jeans
2. exercise
3. watch movies
4. travel
5. go shopping
6. listen to music

1. _I always wear jeans_ OR _I rarely wear jeans_____.
2. _____.
3. _____.
4. _____.
5. _____.
6. _____.

B. 주어진 단어들을 적절히 배열하여 문장을 완성하세요.

1. (read / rarely / I) _I rarely read_____ the newspaper during the week.
2. (always / smiling / is / she) Julia seems happy all the time. _____.
3. (often / plays / Nick) _____ chess with his sister.
4. (I / free / am / usually) _____ on Sundays.
5. (should / never / you / leave) _____ a baby alone.
6. (Danny / meets / sometimes / his cousins) _____ on weekends.
7. (always / can / you / call) _____ me when you need help.
8. (finish / rarely / we) _____ work before 8 o'clock.

UNIT 82 The bag is **too** small.

The bag is **too** small.
가방이 너무 작다.

1 too + 형용사/부사

'(필요 이상으로) 너무 ~한/~하게'라는 의미로 말할 때 **too**를 쓴다.
- Our washing machine is **too old**. We need a new one. 우리 세탁기는 너무 낡았다.
- "I lost my wallet again!" "You lose things **too easily**." 넌 물건을 너무 쉽게 잃어버려.
- My neighbors are sometimes **too noisy** at night. I can't go to sleep.

2 too ~ 뒤에 for + 사람 또는 to + 동사원형을 함께 쓸 수도 있다.

too + 형용사 + for + 사람: (사람)에게 너무 ~한
- Do you want half of my burger? It's **too big for me**. 그것은 나에게 너무 크다.
- This movie is **too scary for kids**.

too + 형용사 + to + 동사원형: …하기에 너무 ~한
- Stephen is **too young to drive**. Stephen은 운전을 하기엔 너무 어려.
- The bakery is already closed. It's **too late to buy** bread.

PRACTICE

A. 그림을 보고 주어진 형용사와 too를 사용하여 문장을 완성하세요.

| dark   fast   high   long   ~~small~~ |

1. This bag is _too small_.
2. It's _____.
3. It's _____. I can't see you.
4. They are _____.
5. It's _____.

B. 주어진 단어들과 too를 사용하여 문장을 완성하세요. for 또는 to를 함께 쓰세요

| busy   difficult   ~~heavy~~   sick   spicy   warm |

1. (me) This suitcase is _too heavy for me_. Can you carry it?
2. (go) I've got a bad cold. I'm _____ to class today.
3. (answer) "How was your exam?" "Some of the questions were _____."
4. (us) The chicken wings had a lot of red pepper. They were _____.
5. (me) Can I turn off the heater? The room is _____.
6. (take) I'm so tired, but I'm _____ a break.

UNIT 83 They aren't big enough.

형용사/부사 + enough

His pants don't fit.
They aren't **big enough**.
바지가 충분히 크지 않다.

1 형용사/부사 + enough

'충분히 ~한/~하게'라는 의미로 말할 때 **enough**를 쓴다.

- Mike can get into law school. He's **smart enough**. 그는 충분히 똑똑하다.
- Tina was late for work. She didn't wake up **early enough**. 그녀는 충분히 일찍 일어나지 않았다.
- You didn't write the report **carefully enough**. There are many errors.
- The necklace wasn't **cheap enough**, so I didn't buy it.

2 enough 뒤에 for + 사람 또는 to + 동사원형을 함께 쓸 수도 있다.

형용사 + enough + for + 사람: (사람)에게 충분히 ~한

- This book is **easy enough for children**. 이 책은 아이들에게 충분히 쉽다.
- "Is the soup **hot enough for you**?" "Yes, it's fine. Thanks."

형용사 + enough + to + 동사원형: …하기에 충분히 ~한

- The weather isn't **cold enough to wear** a coat today. 날씨가 코트를 입기에 충분히 춥지 않다.
- I broke Mom's favorite dish, but I wasn't **brave enough to tell** her.

PRACTICE

A. 그림을 보고 주어진 형용사와 enough를 사용하여 문장을 완성하세요.

| large | long | ~~loud~~ | tall |

1. Her voice isn't _loud enough_ .
2. The space is _____ .
3. The boy is _____ .
4. His arm isn't _____ .

B. 괄호 안에 주어진 단어들과 enough를 사용하여 문장을 완성하세요. **for** 또는 **to**를 함께 쓰세요.

1. (good, sell) Ralph's paintings are _good enough to sell_ . He's a really good painter.
2. (clear, see) The sky was _____ the stars.
3. (big, two people) The hotel room had a very small bed. It wasn't _____ .
4. (sweet, me) I don't like this cheesecake. It isn't _____ .
5. (old, drink) My daughter isn't _____ beer. She's only 15.
6. (lucky, meet) During my trip to LA, I was _____ my favorite actor.

UNIT 84 There aren't **enough** seats on the bus.

enough + 명사

There aren't **enough seats** on the bus.
버스에 충분한 자리가 없다.

1 enough + 명사

'충분한 ~'이라는 의미로 말할 때 **enough** + 명사를 쓴다.

- We can't go skiing. There's not **enough snow**. 충분한 눈이 없다.
- I brought a bottle of wine for the guests. Are there **enough glasses**?

enough + 명사 + **for** + 사람: (사람)에게 충분한 ~

- We didn't make **enough food for everyone**. We should cook some more. 모두에게 충분한 음식을 만들지 않았다.
- Jane doesn't have **enough tickets for all of us**.

enough + 명사 + **to** + 동사원형: …하기에 충분한 ~

- Do we have **enough money to pay** the rent? 우리가 집세를 내기에 충분한 돈이 있나요?
- I don't have **enough time to finish** my homework.

2 명사 없이 **enough**만 쓸 수도 있다.

- "Do we need to stop for gas?" "No, we have **enough**." (enough = enough gas)
- "I'd like some cream for my coffee." "Here you go. Is that **enough**?" (enough = enough cream)

PRACTICE

A. 괄호 안에 주어진 단어와 enough를 사용하여 문장을 완성하세요.

1. (comfortable) "Was your flight _comfortable enough_, sir?" "Yes, it was fine."
2. (jobs) The new company will provide _____ for 500 people.
3. (close) "What does that sign say?" "I can't read it. It's not _____."
4. (long) I think we've walked _____. Let's rest for a minute.
5. (light) There isn't _____ in here. Can you open the curtains?
6. (hard) Ray tried to score a goal, but he didn't kick the ball _____.
7. (paper) I have to print 100 pages. Is there _____?
8. (energy) I'm not going to the gym today. I don't have _____.

B. 주어진 단어들을 하나씩 사용하여 문장을 완성하세요. enough와 for 또는 to를 함께 사용하세요.

bedrooms	biology books	exercise	+	~~cook~~	get	lose
~~potatoes~~	time			the students	your family	

1. I'm going to the grocery store. I don't have _enough potatoes to cook_ for dinner.
2. Our school library doesn't have _____.
3. "We're going to miss our train!" "Don't worry. There's _____ to the station."
4. Roger should jog more. He doesn't get _____ weight.
5. You and your children can stay at my house. There are _____.

UNIT 85 An airplane is **faster**.

비교급

A car is fast.

An airplane is **faster**.
비행기가 더 빠르다.

faster는 비교급이다.

fast (빠른)   faster (더 빠른)

1
'더 ~한/~하게'라는 의미로 말할 때 비교급을 쓴다. 비교급은 일반적으로 형용사/부사 끝에 **-er**을 붙인다.

| hard → hard**er** | high → high**er** | cold → cold**er** | quiet → quiet**er** |

- "Japanese is hard to learn." "I think Russian is **harder**." 러시아어가 더 어려운 것 같아.
- This roller coaster goes high, but that one goes **higher**. 이 롤러코스터는 높이 올라가지만, 저것이 더 높이 올라간다.
- Take your jacket. It might get **colder** tonight.
- This café is noisy. Do you know a **quieter** place?

2
비교급 + than ~: ~보다 더 …한/…하게

'~보다'라는 의미로 비교의 대상을 말할 때 비교급 뒤에 **than ~**을 쓴다.

- Silver is **cheaper than** gold. 은이 금보다 더 싸다.
- Sound travels **slower than** light. 소리는 빛보다 더 느리게 이동한다.
- I used to be **taller than** Kevin, but now I'm shorter.
- This tennis racket is **lighter than** that one. Let's get this one.

P R A C T I C E

A. 주어진 단어의 비교급을 사용하여 문장을 완성하세요.

| dark   loud   old   ~~quick~~   small |

1. The subway is _quicker_ than a taxi during rush hour.
2. This dress is too big. Do you have a _____ size?
3. Can you speak _____? I can't hear you.
4. The sky is getting _____. It might rain soon.
5. Larry is my brother. He's one year _____ than me.

B. 그림을 보고 주어진 단어의 비교급과 than을 사용하여 문장을 완성하세요.

| long   short   warm   ~~young~~ |

1. Peter is _younger than Nicole_.
2. Mike is _____.
3. Miami is _____.
4. The Nile is _____.

UNIT 86 I'm looking for a **larger** one.

주의해야 할 비교급 형태

1 -er을 붙일 때 주의해야 할 단어들이 있다.

| large → larger | hot → hotter | early → earlier |
| nice → nicer | big → bigger | dry → drier |

- I like this desk, but I'm looking for a **larger** one. 이 책상이 좋지만, 더 큰 것을 찾고 있어요.
- Summer is almost here. It's getting **hotter**. 더 더워지고 있다.
- "Does the movie start at 8:30?" "No, it's **earlier** than that. I think it starts at 7:45."

◇ 비교급 만드는 방법: 부록 p. 172 참고

2 다음과 같이 긴 단어(2음절 이상)는 앞에 **more**를 쓴다.

| beautiful → **more** beautiful | comfortable → **more** comfortable |
| carefully → **more** carefully | expensive → **more** expensive |

- I think roses are **more beautiful** than lilies. 장미가 백합보다 더 아름다운 것 같아.
- "I fell off my bike again." "You should ride **more carefully**."

-er로 끝나는 비교급 앞에 **more**를 쓰지 않는 것에 주의한다.
- I moved into a new apartment. It's **closer** to my school. (more closer로 쓸 수 없음)

3 다음과 같이 형태가 불규칙적으로 변하는 단어들이 있다.

| good → **better** | bad → **worse** | far → **farther** |

- Both of these paintings are good, but that one is **better**. 이 그림 둘 다 좋지만, 저것이 더 낫다.
- I put some salt in this soup, and now it tastes **worse**!

PRACTICE

A. 주어진 단어의 비교급을 쓰세요.

1. long → *longer*
2. thin → _____
3. bad → _____
4. nice → _____
5. dangerous → _____
6. low → _____
7. busy → _____
8. big → _____
9. easy → _____
10. far → _____
11. interesting → _____
12. close → _____
13. good → _____
14. cheap → _____
15. comfortable → _____

B. 그림을 보고 비교급을 사용하여 예시와 같이 문장을 완성하세요.

| expensive | far | fast | heavy | ~~high~~ |

1. (Mt. Fuji) Mt. Everest is *higher than Mt. Fuji* .
2. (the brown cap) The blue cap is _____ .
3. (Seattle) Vancouver is _____ .
4. (the man) The horse is _____ .
5. (the white box) The black box is _____ .

UNIT 87 Chris is **the tallest** person.

최상급

Amy is taller than Justin. Chris is taller than Amy.

Chris is **the tallest** person.
Chris가 가장 키가 큰 사람이다.

tallest는 최상급이다.

1 '가장 ~한'이라는 의미로 말할 때 최상급을 쓴다. 최상급은 일반적으로 형용사/부사 끝에 **-est**를 붙인다.

deep → deep**est**   new → new**est**   long → long**est**

- Lake Baikal is **the deepest** lake in Russia. 바이칼호는 러시아에서 가장 깊은 호수이다.
- That gym just opened. It's **the newest** gym in the city. 시내에서 가장 새로운 체육관이다.
- Emily has worked here **the longest**. She started 20 years ago.

최상급은 **the**와 함께 쓴다.

- My room is **the cleanest** room in our house. 내 방은 우리 집에서 가장 깨끗한 방이다.
- Sirius is **the brightest** star in the night sky.

2 다음과 같이 명사 없이 최상급만 쓸 수도 있다.

- I'm **the youngest** in my family. 나는 우리 가족 중에서 가장 어리다.
- "Do you have a cheaper computer?" "No, that's **the cheapest** in the store."

PRACTICE

A. 주어진 단어를 사용하여 문장을 완성하세요. 최상급으로 쓰세요.

| fresh | ~~hard~~ | high | kind | quiet | strong |

1. (decision) Choosing a college was _the hardest decision_ of my life.
2. (man) Mr. Miller is _____ in our office. He is always nice to everyone.
3. (animals) Elephants can lift heavy things. They're one of _____.
4. (score) I received _____ on the math exam. I was very happy.
5. (vegetables) That market sells _____ in town. I always shop there.
6. (girl) Cindy doesn't talk much. She's _____ in our school.

B. 다음 육상 선수들에 대한 정보를 보고 괄호 안에 주어진 단어의 최상급을 사용하여 예시와 같이 문장을 완성하세요.

	JASON	DAVID	BOB
Height	177cm	175cm	180cm
Age	23	25	19
Ranking	1st	3rd	2nd

1. (tall) _Bob is the tallest_.
2. (old) _____.
3. (fast) _____.
4. (young) _____.
5. (short) _____.

UNIT 88

주의해야 할 최상급 형태

Where is **the closest** café from here?

1 -est를 붙일 때 주의해야 할 단어들이 있다.

| close → the closest | big → the biggest | easy → the easiest |
| large → the largest | hot → the hottest | happy → the happiest |

- "Where is **the closest** café from here?" 여기에서 가장 가까운 카페가 어디에 있나요? "Just around the corner."
- That hotel has **the biggest** swimming pool in town. 저 호텔은 시내에서 가장 큰 수영장을 가지고 있다.
- Let's do this report first. It's **the easiest**.

◇ 최상급 만드는 방법: 부록 p. 172 참고

2 다음과 같이 긴 단어(2음절 이상)는 앞에 **most**를 쓴다.

popular → the **most** popular   crowded → the **most** crowded   widely → the **most** widely

- This is **the most popular** song on the radio these days. 이것이 요즘 라디오에서 가장 인기 있는 노래이다.
- Victoria Station is **the most crowded** station in London.

-est로 끝나는 최상급 앞에 **most**를 쓰지 않는 것에 주의한다.
- The library is **the largest** building on campus. (the most largest로 쓸 수 없음)

3 다음과 같이 형태가 불규칙적으로 변하는 단어들이 있다.

good → the **best**   bad → the **worst**   far → the **farthest**

- I had **the best** birthday! It was so fun. 최고의 생일을 보냈어!
- Gary lives **the farthest** from work, but he's never late.

PRACTICE

A. 주어진 단어의 비교급과 최상급을 쓰세요.

1. low   - *lower*   - *lowest*
2. beautiful - _____   - _____
3. good   - _____   - _____
4. high   - _____   - _____
5. nice   - _____   - _____
6. hot   - _____   - _____
7. happy   - _____   - _____
8. important - _____   - _____
9. bad   - _____   - _____
10. cold   - _____   - _____

B. 그림을 보고 주어진 단어의 비교급과 최상급을 사용하여 예시와 같이 문장을 완성하세요.

| expensive   ~~fast~~   good   young |

1. Victor is *the fastest* _____ runner.
   He is *faster than* _____ Smith.
2. A is _____ B.
   It is _____ dress.
3. Tina is _____ child.
   She is _____ Lucy.
4. Ronny's grade is _____ Martin's.
   His grade is _____.

UNIT 89 Chris is **as heavy as** Paul.

Chris is **as heavy as** Paul.
Chris는 Paul만큼 무겁다. (즉, 둘의 몸무게가 같음)

1 as + 형용사/부사 + as

'~만큼 …한/…하게'라는 의미로 말할 때 **as ~ as**를 쓸 수 있다.
- I know Julie's sister. She's **as beautiful as** Julie. 그녀는 Julie만큼 아름답다.
- Mary speaks French **as well as** a native speaker. Mary는 원어민만큼 불어를 잘한다.
- I thought the film was **as interesting as** the book.

2 as ~ as possible: 가능한 한 ~한/하게

as soon as possible	가능한 한 빨리
as long as possible	가능한 한 오래
as early as possible	가능한 한 일찍

- Please come home **as soon as possible**. 가능한 한 빨리 집으로 와주세요.
- We'll wait for you **as long as possible**. 우리는 가능한 한 오래 기다릴 거예요.
- "Let's leave **as early as possible** to avoid traffic." "Good idea."

PRACTICE

A. 그림을 보고 주어진 단어와 as ~ as를 사용하여 문장을 완성하세요.

| expensive   fast   heavy   ~~long~~   old   tall |

1. I've lived in Seoul for two years. (JENNY) / I've lived in Seoul for two years. (TED)
2. I'm 175cm tall. (ROBERT) / I'm 175cm tall. (FRED)
3. My luggage is 30kg. (HELEN) / My luggage is 30kg. (SARAH)
4. My shoes cost $100. (JASON) / My shoes cost $100. (JOY)
5. I can run 100 meters in 13 seconds. (JIM) / I can run 100 meters in 13 seconds. (ANNA)
6. My dog is nine years old. (NICK) / My dog is nine years old. (PAULA)

1. Ted has lived in Seoul _as long as_ Jenny.
2. Robert is _____ Fred.
3. Helen's luggage is _____ Sarah's.
4. Jason's shoes are _____ Joy's.
5. Anna can run _____ Jim.
6. Paula's dog is _____ Nick's.

B. 주어진 형용사/부사와 as ~ as possible을 사용하여 문장을 완성하세요.

| carefully   loud   often   short   ~~soon~~ |

1. I have to go now, but I'll call you back _as soon as possible_.
2. There are glasses in those boxes, so carry them _____.
3. This is our favorite restaurant. We come here _____.
4. I still can't hear the music. Turn up the volume _____.
5. The meeting won't take long. We'll keep it _____.

UNIT 90 She isn't as old as him.

not as ~ as

She isn't as old as him.
그녀는 그만큼 나이가 많지 않다. (즉, 그의 나이가 더 많음)

1 not as + 형용사/부사 + as ~: ~만큼 …하지 않은/…하지 않게

- These cookies are **not as good as** Laura's. 이 쿠키들은 Laura의 것만큼 맛있지 않다.
- I don't read the newspaper **as often as** my dad. 나는 아빠만큼 신문을 자주 보지 않는다.
- "It's very hot this summer." "Yes, but it's **not as hot as** last year."

2 not as ~ as와 같은 의미로 비교급 + than도 쓸 수 있다.

- This lamp is **not as bright as** that one. 이 램프는 저것만큼 밝지 않다.
  또는 That lamp is **brighter than** this one. 저 램프는 이것보다 더 밝다.
- Terry doesn't eat **as quickly as** his brother.
  또는 Terry's brother eats **more quickly than** Terry.

PRACTICE

A. 그림을 보고 괄호 안에 주어진 형용사와 as ~ as를 사용하여 문장을 완성하세요. 필요한 경우 부정문으로 쓰세요.

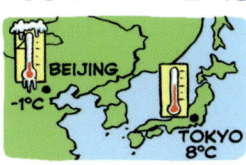

1. (expensive) A _is as expensive as_ B.
2. (cold) Tokyo _____ Beijing.
3. (new) Liz's car _____ Selena's.
4. (strong) Billy _____ Bob.

B. 주어진 문장을 보고 not as ~ as를 사용하여 문장을 완성하세요. 현재 시제로 쓰세요.

| early   far   long   ~~often~~   old |

1. Tom exercises every day. I exercise twice a week.   (exercise) I _don't exercise as often as Tom_.
2. Katie was born in 1990. Eric was born in 1992.   (be) Eric _____.
3. The park is 5km away. The mall is 10km away.   (be) The park _____.
4. Sally goes to work at 9:30. Judy goes to work at 8:30.   (go) Sally _____.
5. The bus tour is two hours. The train tour is an hour.   (last) The train tour _____.

C. 위의 문장을 비교급 + than을 사용하여 다시 말하세요.

1. Tom _exercises more often than me_.
2. Katie _____.
3. The mall _____.
4. Judy _____.
5. The bus tour _____.

UNIT 91 at the bus stop, in the living room, on the floor

장소 전치사 at, in, on (1)

at the bus stop
버스 정류장에

in the living room
거실 안에

on the floor
바닥 위에

1 어떤 지점에 있다고 말할 때 **at**을 쓴다.

| at the bus stop | at the door/window | at the desk | at the corner | at the traffic light |

- "Who's **at the door**?" (문 앞에) "It might be Ted."
- Go straight and turn right **at the corner**. Then you'll see the bookstore. (모퉁이에서)

2 어떤 공간 안에 있다고 말할 때는 **in**을 쓴다.

| in the room | in the box | in the forest | in Paris | in Canada |

- Please put these letters **in the box**. (상자 안에)
- Michelle will spend this summer **in Paris**. (파리에서)

3 어떤 표면 위에 있거나 어떤 표면에 붙어 있다고 말할 때는 **on**을 쓴다.

| on the floor | on the wall | on the ceiling | on the table | on the bench |

- The clock **on the wall** isn't working. It needs new batteries. (벽 위에)
- "Have you seen my bag?" "Yes, it's **on the table**." (테이블 위에)

PRACTICE

A. 그림을 보고 at/in/on을 사용하여 문장을 완성하세요.

1. There are three people _in_ the room.
2. A picture is hanging _____ the wall.
3. A man is sitting _____ the desk.
4. There are flowers _____ the vase.
5. A woman is standing _____ the window.
6. There are toys _____ the box.
7. A dog is _____ the floor.

B. at/in/on을 써넣으세요.

1. I studied English _in_ Canada four years ago.
2. "What is Nora doing _____ the kitchen?" "She's washing the dishes."
3. "Where did you see Nick?" "_____ the bus stop."
4. Let's go skiing. There's lots of snow _____ the mountain.
5. Some people are eating sandwiches _____ the bench.
6. All cars must stop _____ the traffic light when the light is red.
7. "What's that _____ the ceiling?" "It's a fire alarm."
8. "Is there any juice _____ the fridge?" "No, there's only water."

UNIT 92 I don't have to wear a suit **at** work.

장소 전치사 at, in, on (2)

1 **at**을 사용한 다음과 같은 표현이 있다.

직장·학교 등 일상적으로 다니는 장소	**at** work	**at** home	**at** school	**at** church
	at the doctor's (office)	**at** somebody's (house)		
역·공항	**at** the station	**at** the airport		
공연·행사·경기	**at** a concert	**at** a party	**at** a baseball game	

- I don't have to wear a suit **at work**. (회사에서)
- "Did you enjoy yourself **at the concert**?" "Yes, I had a great time." (콘서트에서)

2 **in**을 사용한 다음과 같은 표현이 있다.

하늘·대양 등 자연환경	**in** the world	**in** the sky	**in** the ocean
책·사진 등 인쇄물	**in** a book	**in** a picture	**in** a newspaper
(어떤 장소에서) ~하는 중인	**in** bed (잠자는 중인)	**in** the hospital (입원 중인)	**in** prison/jail (수감 중인)

- Mount Everest is the highest mountain **in the world**. (세계에서)
- "Have you ever heard of Issac Newton?" "Yes. I read about him **in a book**." (책에서)

3 **on**을 사용한 다음과 같은 표현이 있다.

거리	**on** 2nd Avenue	**on** Main Street	
층	**on** the first floor	**on** the 3rd floor	
교통수단	**on** the train	**on** the bus	**on** the plane
예외)	**in** the car	**in** the taxi	

- "Excuse me. I'm looking for the restroom." "It's **on the first floor**." (1층에)
- I bought a newspaper to read **on the train**. (기차에서)

PRACTICE

A. 그림을 보고 주어진 장소와 at/in/on을 사용하여 문장을 완성하세요.

| ~~2nd Avenue~~ | a birthday party | the bus | the sky |

1. The bookstore is _on 2nd Avenue_ .
2. They are _____.
3. There are birds _____.
4. They are _____.

B. at/in/on을 써넣으세요.

1. "I can't see you _in_ the picture." "I'm there, at the back."
2. "Are you going out tonight?" "I might just watch TV _____ home."
3. Mr. Brown's apartment is _____ Main Street.
4. Could you pick me up _____ the airport? I'll arrive at 12 p.m.
5. "Is the cafeteria _____ the 2nd floor?" "No, the 3rd floor."
6. "Where is your brother?" "He's already _____ the car."

UNIT 93 The bus stops **in front of** my house.

위치 전치사 (1) in front of, behind, by, next to

1

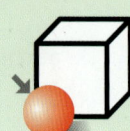

in front of: ~ 앞에
- The bus stops **in front of my house**. (내 집 앞에)
- Daniel is waiting for you **in front of the station**. (역 앞에서)
- Jessica can speak well **in front of people**.

behind: ~ 뒤에
- "Where is my scarf?" "It's **behind the chair**." (의자 뒤에)
- I sit **behind Monica** in history class. (Monica 뒤에)
- "Can I park my car **behind the building**?" "Sorry, but you can't."

2

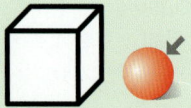

by, next to: ~ 옆에
- We had a picnic **by the lake** last weekend. (호수 옆에서)
- "I'll meet you **by the elevator**." (엘리베이터 옆에서) "OK. Sounds good."
- "Who's the girl **next to Jake**?" "Ching. She's from China."

PRACTICE

A. 그림을 보고 in front of/behind/by/next to를 써넣으세요.

1. Sarah is _in front of_ Ben.
2. Tom is standing _____ Mary.
3. Someone is standing _____ the curtain.
4. The kids are walking _____ the woman.
5. Nicolas is sitting _____ Nancy.

B. 둘 중 맞는 것을 고르세요.

1. Kathy is sitting ((on) / next to) the floor. She is doing yoga.
2. Janet is my neighbor. Her house is (next to / on) mine.
3. "Where's the train?" "It isn't (at / behind) the station yet."
4. "Where should I sit?" "You can sit (at / by) me."
5. The sun went (behind / by) the clouds. I can't see it now.
6. Kim and I sat (next to / at) each other on the bench and held hands.
7. The salad is ready. Would you put it (at / on) the table, please?
8. I spent all day (in front of / on) the TV last weekend.
9. I can't see the professor. The man (behind / in front of) me is too tall.
10. "Where is Thomas?" "He's sleeping (in / in front of) his bedroom."
11. Frank's desk is (by / in) mine, so we can easily talk to each other.
12. "Where's the fountain?" "It's (behind / in front of) you. You have to turn around to see it."

UNIT 94 She is standing **between** Emily and Lynn.

위치 전치사 (2) between, among, over, under

1

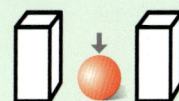

between: (명확히 구분된 둘 이상의 사람·사물) 사이에
- That's my sister. She is standing **between Emily and Lynn**. (Emily와 Lynn 사이에)
- I can't decide **between the cake, the donut, or the cookie** for dessert.
  (케이크와 도넛과 쿠키 사이에)

among: (명확히 구분되어 있지 않은 셋 이상의 그룹·집단) 중에
- Joan is the tallest girl **among the students** in her class. (학생들 중에)
- Who is the best player **among the team members**? (팀 선수들 중에)

2

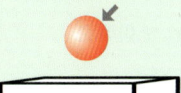

over: ~ 위에
- A lamp is hanging **over the table**. (탁자 위에)
- It started raining, so Diane held an umbrella **over her head**. (머리 위에)

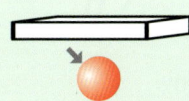

under: ~ 아래에
- I found a coin **under the sofa**. (소파 아래에서)
- When we went to Paris, we took a picture **under the Eiffel Tower**. (에펠탑 아래에서)

PRACTICE

A. 그림을 보고 between/among/over/under를 써넣으세요.

1. The bench is _between_ two large trees.
2. There are clouds _____ the mountains.
3. There is a cat _____ several dogs.
4. A man is sleeping _____ the tree.
5. Mike is sitting _____ the two men.

B. 둘 중 맞는 것을 고르세요.

1. "Who is Mr. Nelson?" "The man (**between** / among) Mr. Smith and Mr. Miller."
2. "Can I sit (next to / over) you?" "Sorry, this seat is taken."
3. The mall is (between / among) Main Street and Park Avenue.
4. There is a police car (in front of / behind) us. Why is it following us?
5. In China, the Great Wall is the most popular place (by / among) tourists.
6. There is a park (by / between) my house. I often play there.
7. Put the printer (between / under) the desk. There's not enough room on the desk.
8. There's a new exit sign (over / among) the door. We put it there yesterday.
9. People are waiting (in front of / over) the store. There must be a sale.
10. "Who is the oldest (among / over) your brothers?" "Harry. He's 21."
11. I woke up on Christmas morning and found many presents (under / over) the Christmas tree.
12. Tower Bridge is (over / under) the Thames River in London.

UNIT 95 Where is this letter **from**?

방향 전치사 (1)

1

from: ~으로부터   **to**: ~으로   **up**: ~ 위로   **down**: ~ 아래로

   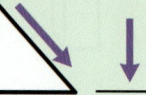

- Where is this letter **from**? (어디로부터)
- Susie's family came **from Europe**.
- I'm traveling **to Vietnam** next week. (베트남으로)
- We went **to the museum** last weekend.

- Jim went **up the ladder** to fix the roof. (사다리 위로)
- Look! A spider is climbing **up the wall**.
- A rock is rolling **down the hill**. (언덕 아래로)
- It's getting dark. Let's walk **down the mountain**.

2

into: ~ 안으로   **out of**: ~ 밖으로   **over**: ~을 넘어서   **under**: ~ 아래로

- Please knock before you come **into my office**. (내 사무실 안으로)
- George poured soda **into the glasses**.
- Mark took his wallet **out of his pocket**. (주머니 밖으로)
- Can you take the bread **out of the oven**?

- A cat jumped **over the balcony**. (발코니를 넘어서)
- Are we flying **over the Grand Canyon**?
- I dropped my keys **under the seat**. (의자 아래로)
- Sam put the suitcases **under the bed**.

PRACTICE

A. 그림을 보고 괄호 안에 주어진 동사와 적절한 전치사를 사용하여 문장을 완성하세요. 현재진행 시제로 쓰세요.

1. (walk) She _'s walking up_ the stairs.
2. (get) They _____ school.
3. (dive) She _____ the pool.
4. (go) The car _____ the bridge.
5. (walk) She _____ the stairs.

B. 적절한 전치사를 써넣으세요.

| down | ~~from~~ | into | out of | over | to | under | up |

1. My neighbors moved here _from_ Chicago last year.
2. My kite is in the tree, but I'm afraid to climb _____ there.
3. You should get _____ the bed! You're late for school.
4. The bridge is very low, so large trucks can't pass _____ it.
5. Jimmy hit the ball _____ the fence! It's a home run!
6. "Did you spend your vacation in Hawaii?" "No, I went _____ Bali."
7. "The elevator is broken. We have to walk _____ the stairs." "Oh, no! We're on the top floor."
8. "I'll help you pack." "Great! Could you put these clothes _____ that box?"

UNIT 96 The Nile River flows **through** Egypt.

방향 전치사 (2)

1

through: ~을 통과해서   **across**: ~을 가로질러   **along**: ~을 따라서   **around**: ~을 돌아서

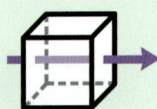 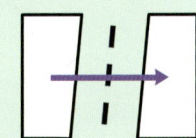  

- The Nile River flows **through** Egypt. (이집트를 통과해서)
- We carried the piano **through the door**.
- Don't walk **across the road**. It's dangerous. (길을 가로질러)
- The actors danced **across the stage**.
- I jogged **along the beach** for an hour. (해변을 따라)
- The flowers are growing **along the lake**.
- The boats are sailing **around the island**. (섬을 돌아서)
- Jane rode her bicycle **around the track**.

2

on: ~ 위로   **off**: ~에서 (떨어져)   **past**: ~을 지나서   **toward**: ~쪽으로

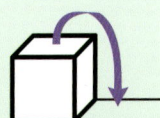 

- Can you put the bags **on the sofa**? (소파 위에)
- Excuse me. You dropped your gloves **on the floor**.
- We need to get **off the train** soon. (기차에서)
- Maria fell **off the bed** and woke up.
- I drive **past the mall** every day. (쇼핑몰을 지나서)
- We went **past the bus stop** by mistake.
- The bird flew **toward the tree**. (나무 쪽으로)
- The children ran **toward their parents**.

PRACTICE

A. 그림을 보고 괄호 안에 주어진 동사와 적절한 전치사를 사용하여 문장을 완성하세요. 현재진행 시제로 쓰세요.

 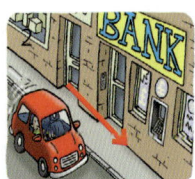   

1. (run) The train _is running through_ the tunnel.
2. (go) The car _____ the bank.
3. (fall) He _____ the table.
4. (walk) She _____ the street.
5. (drive) The car _____ the fountain.

B. 주어진 전치사를 써넣으세요.

| around | into | off | on | out of | through | ~~toward~~ | under |

1. John is running _toward_ the school. He must be late for class.
2. "Can you tell me where the zoo is?" "Go _____ that corner, and you'll find it on the left."
3. Ted read the letters and threw them _____ the trash can.
4. I found Andy. He was hiding _____ his desk!
5. During the meeting, Mr. Miller walked _____ the room angrily and never came back.
6. "Ouch! You stepped _____ my foot." "Oh, I'm sorry."
7. Becky didn't like the picture, so she took it _____ the wall.
8. A storm passed _____ the city last night. Many houses were damaged.

UNIT 97 It arrives at 5:30.

시간 전치사 (1) at, on, in

1 at

시각	at 5:30	at noon	at 3 o'clock
식사	at breakfast	at lunch	at dinner

- "What time does the plane arrive?" "It arrives **at 5:30**." (5시 30분에)
- We can talk about our business trip **at dinner**. (저녁 식사 때)

2 on

요일	on Monday/Tuesday	on Friday night/Sunday morning
평일·주말	on weekdays/a weekday	on weekends/the weekend
날짜·기념일	on May 21 on my birthday	on our anniversary

- Do you want to go hiking **on Monday**? (월요일에)
- I usually get up late **on weekends**. (주말에)

3 in

월·계절	in January/April/July	in (the) spring/summer/fall/winter
연도·세기	in 2008	in the 18th century
오전·오후·저녁	in the morning/afternoon/evening	예외) at night

- Angela is moving to Sydney **in July**. (7월에)
- Cars were invented **in the 18th century**. (18세기에)

PRACTICE

A. 그림을 보고 적절한 명사와 at/on/in을 사용하여 문장을 완성하세요.

1. Patrick's birthday is *on Friday* .
2. Carol got the message _____ .
3. The building was built _____ .
4. He often exercises _____ .
5. Gina is having lunch with Greg _____ .

B. 괄호 안에 주어진 표현과 at/on/in을 사용하여 문장을 완성하세요.

1. (our anniversary) My husband gave me a necklace *on our anniversary* .
2. (February) The new mall will open _____ . Let's go shopping then.
3. (breakfast) "Do you read the newspaper _____ ?" "No, not usually."
4. (10 a.m.) The meeting is _____ tomorrow morning.
5. (Sunday) "I'm going to play baseball _____ ." "That will be fun."
6. (2005) My brother graduated _____ . Now he works at a library.
7. (the morning) Amanda walks her dog _____ .
8. (weekdays) I can't watch TV _____ . I'm too busy.

UNIT 98 Bats sleep **during** the day.

시간 전치사 (2) during, for, in, within

1 during과 for

during + the day, the basketball game 등: ~ 동안에

- Bats sleep **during the day**. (낮 동안에)
- Terry got hurt **during the basketball game**. (농구 경기 동안에)

for + a second, three years 등: ~ 동안 (내내)

- "Can I talk to you **for a second**?" (잠시 동안) "Sure."
- Holly has studied French **for three years**. (3년 동안)

for와 **during** 모두 '~ 동안'이라는 뜻이지만, 특정 기간을 나타내는 명사 앞에는 **during**을 쓰는 것에 비해, 숫자를 포함한 기간 앞에는 **for**를 쓰는 것에 주의한다.

- We are going to travel in Asia **during the summer**. ('여름 동안'이라는 의미로 특정 기간을 나타내는 명사 앞에 during을 썼음)
  We are going to travel in Asia **for two months**. ('두 달 동안'이라는 의미로 숫자를 포함한 기간 앞에 for를 썼음)

2 in과 within

in + 10 minutes, two hours 등 (기간): ~ 후에

- "Are you ready?" "Not yet. I will be ready **in 10 minutes**." (10분 후에)
- The store will close **in two hours**. (두 시간 후에)

within + 15 minutes, four days 등 (기간): ~ 이내에

- I can get there **within 15 minutes**, so please wait for me. (15분 이내에)
- Please pay this bill **within four days**. (4일 이내에)

PRACTICE

A. 괄호 안에 주어진 표현과 **for** 또는 **during**을 사용하여 대화를 완성하세요.

1. How long has Jimmy been asleep?
2. When did you get your hair cut?
3. How long have you collected stamps?
4. When did Amber leave the office?
5. When were these pictures taken?
6. How long should I cook this sauce?
7. How long have you worked here?
8. When will you see your parents?

(about 10 hours) _For about 10 hours_ .
(the weekend) _____.
(eight years) _____.
(lunchtime) _____.
(winter) _____.
(five minutes) _____.
(about four months) _____.
(the holidays) _____.

B. 둘 중 맞는 것을 고르세요.

1. The race lasted 50 minutes. All runners finished (during / (within)) an hour.
2. "It's noon right now. Let's meet here at 12:30." "OK. I'll see you (in / during) 30 minutes."
3. People cannot smoke (during / for) the flight.
4. I have played the flute (in / for) three years, but I can't play very well.
5. Frank usually listens to music (for / during) dinner.
6. I'm returning from LA (within / for) a week. I'm only staying there for four days.
7. We cleaned the house (during / for) two hours, but it's still dirty.
8. The lecture will begin (in / during) exactly 45 minutes. Please don't be late.

UNIT 99 Dr. Kim sees his patients **from** 9 a.m. **to** 6 p.m.

시간 전치사 (3) from ~ to, by, until

1 from ~ to ...: ~부터 ...까지
- Dr. Kim sees his patients **from 9 a.m. to 6 p.m.** (오전 9시부터 오후 6시까지)
- Our Spanish class lasts **from August to December**. (8월부터 12월까지)

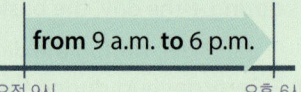

from ~ to ...와 같은 의미로 **from ~ until ...**을 쓸 수 있다.
- Mr. Chan was the president **from 2008 until last year**. (2008년부터 작년까지)
- It usually rains a lot here **from April until May**. (4월부터 5월까지)

이때, **to** ...없이 **from** ~만 쓸 수도 있다.
- Call me in the afternoon. I'll be in my office **from 12 p.m.** (12시부터)

2 by: (늦어도) ~까지
by는 늦어도 정해진 시점까지 어떤 행동이나 상황이 끝난다고 할 때 쓴다.
- You must pay $120 **by October 3**. (늦어도 10월 3일까지)
- I'm going to be late. I can't get there **by 8**. (8시까지)
- "Have our guests arrived yet?" "No, but they will arrive **by noon**."

3 until: ~까지 계속
until은 특정 시점까지 어떤 행동이나 상황이 계속된다고 할 때 쓴다.
- The art exhibit will continue **until June 17**. (6월 17일까지 계속)
- "Can I keep this book **until Saturday**?" "Yes, that's fine." (토요일까지 계속)
- I won't be home **until 9 p.m.** tonight.

PRACTICE

A. 그림을 보고 from ~ to ...를 사용하여 문장을 완성하세요.

1. The class is _from 9 a.m. to 11 a.m._ .
2. The road is closed _____.
3. The store is open _____.
4. Drivers cannot park here _____.
5. The tickets will be on sale _____.

B. by 또는 until을 써넣으세요.

1. I studied _until_ 11 o'clock last night. I have an important test today.
2. This coupon must be used _____ August 3. You can't use it after that.
3. Some of my friends are coming to visit. They will stay with me _____ Friday.
4. "Can you finish this work _____ next Monday?" "Sure. I can do it."
5. The plane leaves at 3:30 p.m. We should arrive at the airport _____ 2:00 p.m.
6. The football game lasted _____ midnight.

UNIT 100 The house **with** the yellow roof is ours.

기타 전치사 with, without, by

1 with: ~을 가진, ~와 함께

- The house **with the yellow roof** is ours. 노란 지붕을 가진 집이 우리 집이다.
- "Should I wait here?" "No. Come **with me**, please."

'(신체적 특징)을 가진'이라는 의미로 말할 때도 **with**를 쓴다.

- Tom is the only boy **with green eyes** in his class. 녹색 눈을 가진 유일한 소년이다.
- The elephant is an animal **with a long nose**.

'(도구)를 사용하여'라는 의미로 말할 때도 **with**를 쓴다.

- The fisherman caught the fish **with a net**. 어부는 그물을 사용하여 물고기를 잡았다.
- I took these photos **with my new camera**.

with the yellow roof

2 without: ~ 없는/없이

- I can't imagine life **without the Internet**. 인터넷이 없는 삶을 상상할 수 없다.
- You must not drive **without a license**. 면허증 없이 운전해서는 안 된다.
- We have to start the meeting **without Jenny**. She's going to be late.

3 by + taxi, train 등 (교통수단): ~을 타고

- "How did you get here?" "We came **by taxi**." 택시를 타고 왔어.
- "Are you driving to Chicago?" "No, I'm going **by train**."

'걸어서'라는 의미로 말할 때는 **on foot**을 쓴다.

- I go to work **on foot**. It takes 30 minutes from my house. 걸어서 회사에 간다.

PRACTICE

A. 그림을 보고 주어진 표현과 with 또는 without을 사용하여 문장을 완성하세요.

| a helmet | ~~a knife~~ | a swimming pool | his dog | his glasses |

My house.

1. He is cutting the bread _with a knife_ .
2. He is reading _____ .
3. He is running _____ .
4. She has a house _____ .
5. She is riding a motorcycle _____ .

B. 괄호 안에 주어진 표현과 with/without/by/on을 사용하여 문장을 완성하세요.

1. (my brother) "Do you live alone?" "No, I live _with my brother_ ."
2. (subway) The best way to get to city hall is _____ .
3. (brown hair) "Who is Teresa?" "She's the girl _____ over there."
4. (a ticket) The concert is free. You can get in _____ .
5. (plane) We're going to Las Vegas _____ . The tickets were on sale.
6. (foot) "How far is the mall from here?" "It's close enough to go _____ ."
7. (my wallet) Can I borrow a few dollars? I left home _____ this morning.

UNIT 101 They are talking **about visiting** Susan.

전치사 + -ing

They are talking **about visiting** Susan.
그들은 Susan을 방문하는 것에 대해 이야기하고 있다.

1 전치사 뒤에 **-ing**를 쓸 수 있다.
- "How **about having** a cup of coffee?" 커피 한 잔 마시는 게 어때? "That sounds great."
- I need to finish this report **before going** home tonight. 오늘 밤 집에 가기 전에 이 보고서를 끝낼 필요가 있어요.
- I never go to bed **without brushing** my teeth.
- Michelle is very good **at singing**.

이때, 전치사 뒤에 동사원형을 쓰지 않는 것에 주의한다.
- **After eating** our dinner, we had chocolate cake for dessert. (After eat으로 쓸 수 없음)
- Kyle is thinking **of moving** to Seattle. He wants to be closer to his family. (of move로 쓸 수 없음)

PRACTICE

A. 괄호 안에 주어진 전치사를 사용하여 예시와 같이 문장을 완성하세요.

1. I can't skate. I'm terrible at it.
   → (at) I'm terrible _at skating_ .

2. We drove for 10 hours. We didn't stop.
   → (without) We drove for 10 hours _____ .

3. Please close all windows and then leave.
   → (before) Please close all windows _____ .

4. Jenny watched the movie. Then she had dinner.
   → (after) Jenny had dinner _____ .

5. Paula is going to get a promotion. She's happy.
   → (about) Paula is happy _____ .

6. You visited me at the hospital. Thanks.
   → (for) Thanks _____ .

B. 주어진 동사를 사용하여 문장을 완성하세요.

| break | fall | look | read | ~~travel~~ | wake |

1. We're excited about _traveling_ to Thailand next month.
2. I don't want to ride the horse. I'm scared of _____ off.
3. After _____ up in the morning, I always take a shower.
4. Don't cross the street without _____ in both directions.
5. Robert had to pay $5 for _____ a glass at a store.
6. I recommended a good book to Gina, and she's interested in _____ it.

UNIT 102 Are you **sure about** that?

형용사 + 전치사

1 다음과 같이 형용사와 전치사를 함께 쓸 수 있다.

about	excited about ~에 대해 흥분한	sorry about ~에 대해 미안한	sure about ~에 대해 확신하는
at	angry/mad at ~에게 화가 난	good at ~을 잘하는	surprised at ~에 놀란
of	afraid of ~을 무서워하는 proud of ~을 자랑스러워 하는	full of ~으로 가득 찬 short of ~이 부족한	tired of ~에 질린
to	married to ~와 결혼한	similar to ~와 비슷한	
with	busy with ~으로 바쁜	careful with ~에 주의하는	familiar with ~에 익숙한
for·from·in	famous for ~으로 유명한	different from ~와 다른	interested in ~에 관심 있는

- "Sally failed her science test." "Are you **sure about** that?" 그것에 대해 확신하니?
- "Why is Lisa **angry at** you?" 왜 Lisa가 너에게 화가 났니? "I forgot her birthday."
- When I was young, I was **afraid of** spiders.
- Laura got **married to** Greg last month.
- You have to be **careful with** that knife. It's very sharp.
- "Have you heard this song?" "No, I'm not **familiar with** it."
- The bakery across the street is **famous for** its apple pies.
- How is this computer **different from** that one over there?
- Jay is **interested in** fashion. He likes to read fashion magazines.

◎ 더 많은 형용사 + 전치사 표현: 부록 p. 176 참고

PRACTICE

A. 적절한 전치사를 써넣으세요.

1. Frank is excited _about_ the football game today.
2. "Emily quit her job." "Yes. I was surprised _____ the news."
3. "You shouldn't bring food into the library." "I'm sorry _____ that. I didn't know."
4. I'm tired _____ pizza. Let's get Japanese food tonight.
5. Your shirt is similar _____ mine. Where did you buy it?
6. I'm very busy _____ work today, so I can't meet you.
7. Jack doesn't want to come to the gallery with us. He's not interested _____ art.
8. Fifth Avenue in New York City is famous _____ its shops.
9. Jake is afraid _____ the water, so he doesn't swim.
10. Please be careful _____ the vase. It's very expensive.

B. 그림을 보고 주어진 형용사와 적절한 전치사를 사용하여 문장을 완성하세요.

| different | full | ~~good~~ | proud | sure |

1. Mike is _good at_ _____ basketball.
2. Jim's hair color is _____ his brothers'.
3. She is _____ herself.
4. The cup is _____ coffee.
5. He is not _____ the answer.

UNIT 103 Look at that baby.

동사 + 전치사

1 다음과 같이 동사와 전치사를 함께 쓸 수 있다.

at	look at ~을 보다		shout at ~에게 소리치다		work at ~에서 일하다
for	wait for ~을 기다리다 ask for ~을 요청하다		search for ~을 찾다 look for ~을 찾다		apply for ~에 지원하다
on	spend ··· on ~에 (돈/시간 등) ···을 쓰다		depend on ~에 의지하다, ~에 달렸다		
to	talk to ~에게 말하다 happen to ~에게 일어나다		listen to ~을 듣다 write to ~에게 편지를 쓰다		belong to ~의 것이다, ~에 속하다

- **Look at** that baby. He's so cute. 저 아기 좀 봐.
- "Who are you **waiting for**?" 누구를 기다리는 중인가요? "Mr. Johnson."
- You shouldn't **spend** so much money **on** clothes. You need to save more.
- "Can I **talk to** you for a few minutes?" "Sure."
- "How long have you **worked at** this company?" "For three years."
- "Did you order already?" "No, I just **asked for** the menu."
- "What **happened to** Samuel?" "He was injured during the baseball game."

◇ 더 많은 동사 + 전치사 표현: 부록 p. 178 참고

2 다음과 같은 동사 뒤에는 전치사를 쓰지 않는 것에 주의한다.

call ~에게 전화하다	answer ~에 답하다	discuss ~에 관해 논의하다	reach ~에 도착하다, ~에 닿다

- Will you **call** me when you get home? (call to me 등으로 쓸 수 없음)
- We'll **discuss** the schedule tomorrow. (discuss about the schedule 등으로 쓸 수 없음)
- You can **reach** the airport easily from the train station.

PRACTICE

A. 그림을 보고 주어진 동사와 at/for/to를 사용하여 문장을 완성하세요. 현재진행 시제로 쓰세요.

| ask | look | ~~talk~~ | write |

1. He 's talking to a police officer.
2. They _____ the stars.
3. She _____ a salad.
4. She _____ a friend.

B. 괄호 안에 주어진 동사를 사용하여 문장을 완성하세요. 필요한 경우 at/for/on/to를 함께 쓰세요.

1. (listen) Students must listen to the teacher carefully during the class.
2. (apply) "Did you _____ the job?" "Yes, but I didn't get it."
3. (answer) Betty didn't _____ the phone. Maybe she's busy.
4. (depend) Charlie is my best friend. I can always _____ him.
5. (belong) This car doesn't _____ me. It's Mr. Jackson's.
6. (reach) "Can you help me? I can't _____ the top shelf." "Sure."
7. (shout) You don't have to _____ me. I can hear you.
8. (discuss) We're going to _____ the history of America.

UNIT 104 She is **trying on** a hat.

She is trying on a hat.
그녀는 모자를 써보고 있다.

try on은 구동사이다.

1 동사와 **on, in, down** 등을 함께 써서 하나의 의미를 갖는 구동사를 쓸 수 있다.
- Let's **go in**. It's getting cold outside. 들어가자.
- Can you **slow down**? You're driving too fast. 속도를 줄여줄래?
- I don't want to cook dinner tonight. Can we **eat out**?

◈ 더 많은 구동사 표현: 부록 p. 178 참고

2 구동사와 목적어를 함께 쓰는 경우 다음과 같이 두 가지 형태로 쓸 수 있다.
- Cathy **put on** the socks. 또는 Cathy **put** the socks **on**.
- Please **turn off** your phone. 또는 Please **turn** your phone **off**.

단, **me/them** 등의 대명사를 목적어로 쓰는 경우에는 동사와 **up, away** 등의 사이에 쓰는 것에 주의한다.
- "Can you **wake me up** at 6 tomorrow morning?" "OK." (wake up me로 쓸 수 없음)
- These shoes are really old. I'll **throw them away**. (throw away them으로 쓸 수 없음)

PRACTICE

A. 주어진 구동사를 사용하여 문장을 완성하세요.

| come back | get off | go out | ~~grow up~~ | turn up | work on |

1. "Where did you _grow up_?" "I was raised in Florida."
2. Janet can't come to the party. She has to _____ her essay.
3. I'll _____ with Amanda this weekend. We might watch a movie together.
4. "I can't hear the TV. Can you _____ the volume?" "Sure."
5. "Should we _____ the subway now?" "No, this isn't our stop."
6. My parents are traveling in Europe now. They will _____ home next Saturday.

B. 주어진 단어들을 적절한 순서로 배열하여 문장을 완성하세요.

1. (pick / up / it) "There is a package for you at the front desk." "I'll _pick it up_ later."
2. (this report / in / hand) "When should I _____?" "By Friday."
3. (up / it / clean) "Billy, your room is so dirty!" "I'll _____ today."
4. (away / take / them) I've finished reading these magazines. You can _____.
5. (off / turn / the heater) "Can you _____, please?" "Of course."
6. (down / the address / write) You should _____ before you forget it.

UNIT 105 The door opened, **and** he came in.

and, but, or

The door opened. He came in.
The door opened, **and** he came in.
문이 열렸고, 그가 들어왔다.

1. 두 문장을 하나로 연결하기 위해 **and**, **but**, **or**를 쓸 수 있다.

   and (그리고, ~이고)
   - I met Tony, **and** we had dinner. 나는 Tony를 만났고, 저녁을 먹었다.
   - Ms. Morris is a teacher, **and** her two sons are also teachers.

   but (그러나, ~이지만)
   - It was cloudy this morning, **but** the sky is clear now. 오늘 아침에는 흐렸지만, 지금은 하늘이 맑다.
   - Michael can speak Spanish very well, **but** he can't speak French.

   or (또는, 아니면)
   - Are you using this chair, **or** can I use it? 이 의자를 사용하시나요, 아니면 제가 사용해도 될까요?
   - Shall we go home now, **or** do you want to stay longer?

2. **and**, **but**, **or** 뒤에서 반복되는 내용은 생략하고 말할 수 있다. 이때, **콤마(,)**는 쓰지 않는다.
   - I start work at 9 **and** finish at 6. (= , and I finish work at 6)
   - We can watch a comedy **or** an action movie. (= , or we can watch an action movie)

PRACTICE

A. and/but/or를 써넣으세요.

1. I bought my motorbike last year, _and_ now I ride it every day.
2. We want to go to the concert with Tina, _____ she already has other plans.
3. Do I have to cook, _____ are we going to eat out?
4. I called my dentist this morning _____ canceled my appointment.
5. Have you been to Greece before, _____ is it your first time?
6. We can go to the mall, _____ I need to go to the library first.
7. I went to the zoo last weekend _____ took a lot of pictures.
8. Lori applied for the job, _____ she didn't get it.

B. 주어진 문장과 and/but/or를 사용하여 문장을 완성하세요.

| do you need more time | do you want to drive yours | he couldn't attend |
| it hurt a lot | it tasted terrible | ~~they won the game~~ |

1. The soccer team played well, _and they won the game_.
2. Are you ready to order, _____?
3. I cut my finger, _____.
4. Wendy invited John to the wedding, _____.
5. The soup smelled delicious, _____.
6. Shall we take my car, _____?

UNIT 106 The movie was boring, so they didn't enjoy it.

so와 because

The movie was boring.   They didn't enjoy it.

The movie was boring, **so** they didn't enjoy it.

영화가 지루해서, 그들은 영화를 즐기지 않았다.

1 so (그래서, ~해서)
- Adam is shy, **so** he doesn't talk much. (그래서 말을 많이 하지 않음)
- My car needed gas, **so** I stopped at a gas station. (그래서 주유소에 들렀음)

2 because (왜냐하면, ~이기 때문에)
- We missed the train **because** we woke up late. (늦게 일어났기 때문에)
- Nicole got wet **because** she didn't have an umbrella. (우산이 없었기 때문에)

because는 다음과 같이 문장의 맨 앞에 쓸 수도 있다. 이때, 뒤에 **콤마(,)**를 쓴다.
- **Because** I lived in Paris for 10 years, I know the city well. 파리에 10년 동안 살았기 때문에 그 도시를 잘 안다.

because of도 이유를 말할 때 쓸 수 있다. **because**는 문장을 연결할 때 쓰지만, **because of** 뒤에는 명사를 쓴다.
- The flight was canceled **because there was a storm**. (because of there was a storm으로 쓸 수 없음)
- The flight was canceled **because of the storm**. (because the storm으로 쓸 수 없음)

PRACTICE

A. 그림을 보고 주어진 문장과 so, because를 각각 한 번씩 사용하여 예시와 같이 문장을 완성하세요.

| he got very tired | ~~she bought a new one~~ | she had a headache |

1. Her TV wasn't working, _so she bought a new one_ .
   → 2. _She bought a new TV because her TV wasn't working_ .
3. He ran for an hour, _____ .
   → 4. _____ .
5. She took some medicine _____ .
   → 6. _____ .

B. because 또는 because of를 써넣으세요.
1. I like swimming _because_ it's fun and good for my health.
2. Leo has no time to meet his friends _____ his busy schedule.
3. Ben couldn't go to school _____ he was sick.
4. I need to leave now _____ I have a class in 30 minutes.
5. We couldn't sleep last night _____ the baby. She cried all night.
6. Megan is moving to China _____ her new job.

UNIT 107 She was watching TV **when** he came in.

She was watching TV when he came in.
그가 들어왔을 때, 그녀는 TV를 보고 있었다.

He fell asleep **while his boss was talking**.
상사가 말하는 동안, 그는 잠이 들었다.

1 when: ~할 때
- My family moved to LA **when I was six years old**. 내가 여섯 살 때 우리 가족은 LA로 이사했다.
- I was driving to work **when I saw an accident**.

while: ~하는 동안
- Carol usually listens to music **while she's jogging**. Carol은 조깅하는 동안 보통 음악을 듣는다.
- Can you turn off the TV **while I'm on the phone**?

when과 while은 다음과 같이 문장의 맨 앞에 쓸 수도 있다. 이때, 뒤에 **콤마(,)**를 쓴다.
- **When I was six years old**, my family moved to LA. 내가 여섯 살 때 우리 가족은 LA로 이사했다.
- **While Carol is jogging**, she usually listens to music.

2 when과 while 다음에 미래의 일을 말할 때는 미래 시제가 아니라 현재 시제를 쓰는 것에 주의한다.
- **When** Bill **saves** enough money, he'll buy a house. (돈을 모으는 것은 미래의 일이지만 When Bill will save로 쓸 수 없음)
- It'll be warm and sunny **while** we **are** on vacation. (휴가를 가는 것은 미래의 일이지만 while we will be로 쓸 수 없음)

PRACTICE

A. 그림을 보고 주어진 문장과 when 또는 while을 사용하여 문장을 완성하세요.

| ~~he saw Daniel and Kelly~~ | he was sitting on the chair | he woke up | the movie was playing |

1  2  3 4

1. (when) _When he saw Daniel and Kelly_____, they were going to play tennis.
2. (while) _____, it broke.
3. (while) They arrived at the theater _____.
4. (when) It was already afternoon _____.

B. 괄호 안에 주어진 동사들을 사용하여 문장을 완성하세요. 현재 시제로 쓰거나 will을 함께 사용하세요.

1. (grow) What do you want to be when you _grow_ up?
2. (get) I _____ a shopping cart while you find a parking space.
3. (see) Have a safe flight. I _____ you when you come back.
4. (make) Will you set the table while I _____ dinner?
5. (buy) When I go to the post office, I _____ some stamps.
6. (clean) While Sam _____ the kitchen, Laura will do the laundry.

UNIT 108 The restaurant closed **before** they arrived.

The restaurant closed before they arrived.
그들이 도착하기 전에 식당이 닫았다.

They arrived after the restaurant closed.
식당이 닫은 후에 그들이 도착했다.

1 **before**: ~하기 전에

- Please come to my office **before you leave.** 떠나기 전에 제 사무실로 와주세요.
- "Shall we get some drinks **before the concert starts?**" "Sure."

after: ~한 후에

- Let's go out to eat **after we do the cleaning.** 청소를 한 후에 외식하러 나가자.
- I'll finish the report **after I come back from lunch.**

before와 **after**는 다음과 같이 문장의 맨 앞에 쓸 수도 있다. 이때, 뒤에 **콤마(,)**를 쓴다.

- **Before you leave,** please come to my office. 떠나기 전에 제 사무실로 와주세요.
- **After we do the cleaning,** let's go out to eat.

2 **before, after** 다음에 명사 또는 **-ing**를 쓸 수도 있다.

- You should be home **before midnight.** 자정 전에 집에 와야 한다.
- Everyone was excited **after hearing** about the picnic.

PRACTICE

A. 주어진 문장을 보고 **before** 또는 **after**를 사용하여 문장을 완성하세요.

1. Diane entered the room. Then she turned on the light.
   → *After Diane entered the room*_____, she turned on the light.
2. I took a shower. Then I put on my clothes.
   → I put on my clothes _____.
3. Andy goes to the library. Then he goes home.
   → _____, he goes to the library.
4. I had to wait in line. Then I ordered a cup of coffee.
   → I had to wait in line _____.
5. The visitors checked out of the hotel. Then they went to the art museum.
   → _____, they went to the art museum.

B. 주어진 표현과 **before** 또는 **after**를 사용하여 문장을 완성하세요.

| drive | ~~go~~ | our wedding | read | the exam | the show |

1. Brush your teeth *before going* _____ to bed.
2. I cried _____ the book. The ending was so sad.
3. I studied a lot _____, so I was prepared for it.
4. People should not drink alcohol _____ a car.
5. Dave is watching TV right now. He'll help me with my homework _____.
6. We're going to Hawaii _____. It will be a fun honeymoon.

UNIT 109 The city has changed a lot **since** I moved here.

1 since: ~한 이후로 지금까지

- The city has changed a lot **since I moved here**.
  여기로 이사한 이후로 지금까지 도시가 많이 변했다.
- Many people have visited the zoo **since it opened**.

과거   지금

since는 현재완료 시제와 주로 함께 쓴다. 이때, **since** 뒤에는 과거 시제를 쓴다.

- How have you been? It**'s been** a while **since** we **saw** each other.
  우리가 서로를 본지 한참 되었다.
- "Do you know Alice?" "Yes, I**'ve known** her **since** she **was** very young."

2 until: ~할 때까지 (계속)

- They didn't eat dinner **until he came home**.
  그가 집에 올 때까지 그들은 저녁을 먹지 않았다.
- We stayed at the beach **until it started raining**.

until 다음에 미래의 일을 말할 때는 미래 시제가 아니라 현재 시제를 쓰는 것에 주의한다.

- "When should I put the eggs in the water?" "Wait **until** it **boils**."
  (물이 끓는 것은 미래의 일이지만 until it will boil로 쓸 수 없음)
- Please do not leave your seat **until** the bus **stops**.
  (버스가 멈추는 것은 미래의 일이지만 until the bus will stop으로 쓸 수 없음)

3 since, until 다음에 명사를 쓸 수도 있다.

- I haven't seen Mike and Julie **since their wedding**. 결혼식 이후로 Mike와 Julie를 보지 못했다.
- Mr. Brooks is on vacation now. He won't be back in the office **until next Thursday**.

PRACTICE

A. 주어진 그래프를 보고 since 또는 until을 사용하여 문장을 완성하세요.

1-2 lost his camera / now
[enjoy his trip | not enjoy his trip]

1. Todd enjoyed his trip _until he lost his camera_ .
2. Todd hasn't enjoyed his trip _since he lost his camera_ .

3-4 moved to Seoul / now
[work at a bar | work at a hotel]

3. Jason worked at a bar _____.
4. Jason has worked at a hotel _____.

5-6 bought a car / now
[take the bus | not take the bus]

5. Sandra took the bus _____.
6. Sandra hasn't taken the bus _____.

B. 둘 중 맞는 것을 고르세요.

1. Please turn off your cell phones (**until** / since) the opera is over.
2. (Until / After) Alison worked all night, she went to bed.
3. (After / Since) Shelly was a child, she has played the piano.
4. (Before / After) we see the movie, we have to buy tickets.
5. I'll call you (when / since) I get to the airport.
6. (Until / While) I was painting the kitchen, I spilled paint everywhere.
7. Luke has lost a lot of weight (since / until) he joined the gym.
8. Can you wait for me here (since / until) I finish my meeting?

UNIT 110 If it rains, she'll stay at home.

if (1) if + 현재 시제

If it rains, she'll stay at home.
비가 오면, 집에 머물 것이다.

If it doesn't rain, she'll go hiking.
비가 오지 않으면, 하이킹을 하러 갈 것이다.

If it rains, I'll stay at home.   If it doesn't rain, I'll go hiking.

1 **if**: ~하면

'~하면 …할 것이다'라는 의미로 말할 때 다음과 같이 쓴다.

If + 주어 + 현재 시제, 주어 + will/can 등 + 동사원형

- **If you do** the dishes, **I'll do** the laundry. 네가 설거지를 하면, 내가 빨래를 할게.
- **If Mr. Lewis calls, can you take** a message for me? Lewis씨가 전화하면, 메시지를 받아 주시겠어요?
- **If the restaurant is closed, we'll go** to another one.

if는 다음과 같이 문장의 중간에 쓸 수도 있다. 이때 콤마(,)를 쓰지 않는다.

- You can come to my house **if you get bored**. I'll be home all day. 심심하면 우리 집에 와도 돼.
- The sauce will taste better **if you add** more tomatoes.

2 **if** 다음에 미래의 일을 말할 때는 현재 시제를 쓴다. 이때, 미래 시제를 쓰지 않도록 주의한다.

- Will you wake me up **if you get** up early tomorrow? (내일 일찍 일어나는 것은 미래의 일이지만 if you'll get up으로 쓸 수 없음)
- **If Erin helps** us, we'll finish the work quickly. (Erin이 우리를 돕는 것은 미래의 일이지만 If Erin will help로 쓸 수 없음)

PRACTICE

A. Judy는 자신의 미래에 대해 상상하고 있습니다. if를 사용하여 예시와 같이 문장을 완성하세요.

JUDY *I will go to a design school!*

1. → study hard   *If I go to a design school, I'll study hard*   .
2. → become a famous designer   If I study hard, _____.
3. → make a lot of money   _____.
4. → help poor children   _____.
5. → feel happy   _____.

B. 괄호 안에 주어진 동사를 사용하여 문장을 완성하세요. 현재 시제로 쓰거나 will을 함께 사용하세요.

1. (take) If you like football, I *'ll take* OR *will take* you to a game.
2. (forget) I'll be upset if Holly _____ my birthday again.
3. (feel) You _____ better if you take this medicine.
4. (get) If I send this letter today, Nicole _____ it tomorrow.
5. (visit) If your sister _____ Toronto, she can stay with me.
6. (want) You should exercise more if you _____ to lose some weight.

UNIT 111
If he **had** time, he would have breakfast.

I'm late, so I won't have breakfast.

If he had time, **he would have** breakfast.
만약 시간이 있다면, 아침 식사를 할 텐데. (시간이 없어서 아침 식사를 하지 않음)

1 '만약 ~한다면 …할 텐데'라는 의미로 현재 사실과 다른 상황을 가정해서 말할 때 다음과 같이 쓴다.

If + 주어 + 과거 시제,   주어 + would(= 'd)/could 등 + 동사원형

- **If I knew** Harry's phone number, **I would call** him. 만약 Harry의 전화번호를 안다면, 전화할 텐데. (전화번호를 모름)
- **If we went** to Egypt, **we could see** the Pyramids. 만약 이집트에 간다면, 피라미드를 볼 수 있을 텐데. (이집트에 가지 않음)
- **If Donna was** here, **she would enjoy** this meal.

이때, 주어가 I/he/she/it인 경우 if 다음에 was 대신 were를 쓸 수도 있다.

- **If I were** rich, I'd travel around the world. 만약 내가 부자라면, 세계 여행을 할 텐데.
- **If Jerry were** taller, he could be a basketball player.

2 **If I were/was you, I'd ~**: 만약 내가 너라면, ~할 거야
- **If I were/was you, I'd look** for another job. 만약 내가 너라면, 다른 직장을 찾아볼 거야.
- **If I were/was you, I wouldn't see** that movie. It's boring.

PRACTICE

A. 주어진 문장과 if를 사용하여 예시와 같이 문장을 완성하세요.

| I am in Paris | ~~I have enough money~~ | I have more free time | it is sunny |

1. _If I had enough money_, I'd buy a new suit.
2. _____, I'd go to the park.
3. _____, I'd visit the Eiffel Tower.
4. _____, I could play more tennis.

B. 주어진 표현과 **If I were you, I'd ~**를 사용하여 문장을 완성하세요.

| not drink it | not drive | say sorry to her | send it to the repair shop | ~~take the subway~~ |

1. How can I get to Times Square?
2. My computer is not working again!
3. The traffic seems very bad today.
4. I had a fight with my girlfriend.
5. I bought this milk two weeks ago.

If I were you, I'd take the subway.
_____
_____
_____
_____

UNIT 112 if I do vs. if I did

if (3) if + 현재 시제와 if + 과거 시제 비교

If she **is** here, he**'ll be** very happy.
그녀가 있다면 매우 기쁠 것이다. (그녀가 있을 수도 없을 수도 있음)

If she **was** here, he**'d be** very happy.
만약 그녀가 있다면 매우 기쁠 텐데. (그녀가 없음)

1 if I do와 if I did

어떤 일이 실제로 일어날 가능성이 있는 경우에
if + 현재 시제를 쓴다.

- **If** the weather **is** warm, I**'ll go** for a walk.
  날씨가 따뜻하다면 산책할 것이다. (날씨가 따뜻할 수도 아닐 수도 있음)
- **If** we **don't have** a meeting today, we**'ll leave** work early.
  회의가 없다면 일찍 퇴근할 것이다. (회의가 있을 수도 없을 수도 있음)
- **If** Eric **asks** me to marry him, I**'ll say** yes.
- **Can** you **bring** the mail to my office **if** it **arrives**?
- You **can ask** me for advice **if** you **have** a problem.

어떤 일이 실제로 일어날 가능성이 없는 경우에는
if + 과거 시제를 쓴다.

- **If** the weather **was** warm, I**'d go** for a walk.
  만약 날씨가 따뜻하다면 산책할 텐데. (날씨가 따뜻하지 않음)
- **If** we **didn't have** a meeting today, we**'d leave** work early.
  만약 회의가 없다면 일찍 퇴근할 텐데. (회의가 있음)
- **If** Eric **asked** me to marry him, I**'d say** yes.
- Angela **would have** dinner with us **if** she **were** not ill.
- **If** today **were** a holiday, we **could go** on a picnic.

PRACTICE

A. 주어진 표현과 **if**를 사용하여 대화를 완성하세요. 현재 시제 또는 과거 시제로 쓰세요.

| Ashley is not so tired | I find it | the mall is open | ~~we leave now~~ |

1. A: What time is it?
   B: It's 6:30. *If we leave now* , we'll catch the bus.
2. A: I think I left my ring at your house yesterday.
   B: OK. _____ , I'll give it back to you.
3. A: _____ , we could go shopping.
   B: I know! But it's closed at six.
4. A: _____ tonight, she would go to the movies with us.
   B: That's OK. She can join us next time.

B. 괄호 안에 주어진 표현을 적절한 시제로 사용하여 문장을 완성하세요. 필요한 경우 **will** 또는 **would**를 사용하세요.

1. (help you) If you ask Mike, he *'ll help you* with your work.
2. (be fresh) Those vegetables look old. I would buy some if they _____.
3. (attend) If the wedding wasn't on Friday, I _____. I have an appointment that day.
4. (pick you up) If you call me at the airport, I _____.
5. (have a car) I wouldn't take the bus if I _____. The bus is always so crowded.
6. (not like coffee) If you _____, you can have tea.
7. (be healthier) I don't go to the gym regularly. If I exercised every day, I _____.
8. (not take an umbrella) If you _____ with you, you'll get wet.

UNIT 113 He knows the girl **who** won the race.

관계대명사 who, which, that (1) 주격

I know the girl **who** won the race.

He knows **the girl**. **She** won the race.
　　　　　　　　　　　주어

He knows **the girl who** won the race.
　　　　　　　　　　　관계대명사
경기에서 우승한 소녀를 안다.

1 관계대명사 **who** 또는 **which**를 써서 사람이나 사물에 대해 설명할 수 있다.

사람에 대해 설명할 때는 관계대명사 **who**를 쓴다.

	사람	who		
•	Peter is married to **a woman**	**who**	is a lawyer.	(변호사인 여자)
•	My uncle	**who**	lives in LA	is coming to visit. (LA에 사는 내 삼촌)

사물에 대해 설명할 때는 관계대명사 **which**를 쓴다.

	사물	which		
•	This is **the sweater**	**which**	was made by my mother.	(어머니에 의해 만들어진 스웨터)
•	The bus	**which**	goes to 10th Avenue	has just left. (10번가로 가는 버스)

2 관계대명사 **that**은 사람과 사물에 모두 쓸 수 있다.

	사람 · 사물	that		
•	Do you know **anyone**	**that**	knows about computers?	(컴퓨터에 대해 아는 누군가)
•	The toys	**that**	are on sale	are over there. (할인하고 있는 장난감들)

PRACTICE

A. Bill은 지금 여행 중입니다. 그림을 보고 who를 사용하여 Bill이 오늘 만난 사람들에 대한 문장을 완성하세요.

I have six children.

I play the violin.

We are very famous.

I am 99 years old.

1. Bill sat next to a woman _who has six children_.
2. He saw a man _____.
3. He met two women _____.
4. He visited a woman _____.

B. who/which/that을 사용하여 주어진 두 문장을 한 문장으로 바꾸어 쓰세요.

1. Patrick has a friend. He is from Spain. → _Patrick has a friend who (OR that) is from Spain_.
2. I bought a new sofa. It was cheap. → _____.
3. Sarah taught the students. They graduated last year. → _____.
4. The store sells fresh fruit. It's around the corner. → _____.
5. The people are very nice. They live downstairs. → _____.
6. The plane will arrive at 5:30. It left New York. → _____.

UNIT 114 They enjoyed the dinner **which** James made.

관계대명사 who, which, that (2) 목적격

We really enjoyed the dinner, James!

They enjoyed **the dinner**. James made **it**.
목적어

They enjoyed **the dinner** **which** James made.
관계대명사

그들은 James가 만든 저녁 식사를 즐겼다.

1 관계대명사 who/which/that은 목적어로 쓸 수 있다.

who/that
- Jane is **the girl** | who/that | Harry likes. (who/that을 likes의 목적어로 썼음)
- **The man** | who/that | you met in the lobby | is my boss.

which/that
- Anna often buys **clothes** | which/that | she never wears. (which/that을 wears의 목적어로 썼음)
- **The earrings** | which/that | I lost | were expensive.

2 관계대명사 who/which/that을 목적어로 쓰는 경우 생략할 수 있다.
- Most people **(who/that)** I know live in Las Vegas. (내가 아는 대부분의 사람들)
- I can't remember **the dream (which/that)** I had last night. (어젯밤에 꾼 꿈)

그러나 who/which/that을 주어로 쓰는 경우 생략할 수 없는 것에 주의한다.
- I have **a friend who** works at the hospital. (a friend works at the hospital로 쓸 수 없음)
- **The café which** is on Pine Street is always crowded. (The café is on Pine Street으로 쓸 수 없음)

PRACTICE

A. 주어진 표현을 하나씩 사용하여 예시와 같이 문장을 완성하세요.

| the book | ~~the boy~~ | the cake | + | Brian wrote | ~~I met~~ | I wore |
| the dress | the show | | | you're baking | you were watching | |

1. "Did I tell you about _the boy I met_ during the trip?" "No, tell me about him."
2. _____ to the party was too tight. It wasn't comfortable.
3. I can't wait to taste _____. It smells so good.
4. "_____ is over. Can I change the channel?" "OK."
5. _____ was good. I finished reading it last night.

B. that을 사용하여 예시와 같이 주어진 두 문장을 한 문장으로 바꾸어 쓰세요. 가능한 경우 that을 생략하세요.

1. Jamie gave me some shoes. She didn't want them. → Jamie _gave me some shoes she didn't want_.
2. I have a neighbor. He doesn't know anyone in town. → I _____.
3. We went to a restaurant. It is famous for its dessert. → We _____.
4. I took Sue to the art exhibit. It opened last night. → I _____.
5. Fred ate all of the chocolate. He bought it in Germany.
   → Fred _____.
6. My sister spent the money. She got it for her birthday.
   → My sister _____.

UNIT 115 There is a boat in the sea.

there + be동사

There is a boat in the sea.
바다에 배 한 척이 있다.

There are a lot of people on the beach.
해변에 많은 사람들이 있다.

1 '~이 있다'라는 의미로 말할 때, **there is**, **there are**를 쓸 수 있다.

there is + a package, space 등 (단수명사/셀 수 없는 명사)
- **There is a package** for you at the front desk. 안내 데스크에 당신에게 온 소포가 있어요.
- We can't buy that sofa because **there isn't enough space** in our apartment. 아파트에 충분한 공간이 없다.
- "**Is there any interesting news** in the paper?" "Not really."

there are + parties, cars 등 (복수명사)
- **There are lots of parties** during the holidays. 휴일 동안 많은 파티가 있다.
- **There aren't many cars** on the road today. 오늘 도로에 차가 많이 없다.
- "**Are there any shirts** you want to buy?" "That blue one."

2 there was/there were ~: (과거에) ~이 있었다
- **There was a bookstore** here, but it moved to Main Street. 여기에 서점이 있었는데 Main Street으로 이사했다.
- The meeting finished early because **there weren't** any questions. 질문이 없었기 때문에 회의가 일찍 끝났다.
- "**Was there** anyone in the office when you left?" "Yes, Cathy was still working."

PRACTICE

A. 그림을 보고 주어진 표현과 **there is** 또는 **there are**를 사용하여 문장을 완성하세요.

| a lake | ~~a man~~ | some fish | some people |

1. _There is a man_ at the door.
2. _____ on the bridge.
3. _____ in the water.
4. _____ in the park.

B. there is/are 또는 there was/were를 사용하여 문장을 완성하세요. 필요한 경우 부정문으로 쓰세요.

1. If you're thirsty, _there is_ lemonade in the fridge.
2. "_____ snow in the mountains when you went hiking?" "Yes, a lot."
3. I want to check my e-mail, but _____ any computers in this hotel.
4. _____ any bread to make sandwiches, so I had to go to the store.
5. "Did you have fun at the concert yesterday?" "Yes, I did. But _____ too many people."
6. "_____ any special events at the zoo this week?" "Yes, there's a dolphin show."

UNIT 116 He **gave his wife a ring**.

동사(give/make 등) + 사람 + 사물

He gave **his wife a ring**.
　　　　사람　　사물
그는 아내에게 반지를 주었다.

1 다음과 같은 동사 뒤에 **사람 + 사물**을 쓸 수 있다.

| give (~에게 …을 주다) | send (~에게 …을 보내다) | make (~에게 …을 만들어주다) |
| teach (~에게 …을 가르치다) | show (~에게 …을 보여주다) | buy (~에게 …을 사주다) |

- Sarah **sent us a wedding invitation**. She's getting married next month. Sarah가 우리에게 청첩장을 보냈다.
- Josh **made me an omelet** this morning. 오늘 아침에 Josh가 나에게 오믈렛을 만들어 주었다.
- "Can you **show me your ticket**, please?" "Sure. Here you go."

2 **to** 또는 **for**를 사용하여 다음과 같이 쓸 수도 있다. 이때, **give/teach/send/show** 뒤에는 **to**를 쓰고, **make/buy** 뒤에는 **for**를 쓴다.

동사 + 사람 + 사물　　Ralph **gave his son a ball**.
동사 + 사물 + to/for + 사람　　Ralph **gave a ball to his son**.

- Mr. Brown **teaches us science**. → Mr. Brown **teaches science to us**. Brown씨는 우리에게 과학을 가르친다.
- Can you **buy me lunch**? → Can you **buy lunch for me**?

PRACTICE

A. 그림을 보고 주어진 표현을 사용하여 예시와 같이 문장을 완성하세요. 과거 시제로 쓰세요.

| a doll | his room | ~~some flowers~~ | some tea |

These are for you.

Thank you, Mom!

This is my room.

Here you are.

1. (give) He _gave Lucy some flowers_.
2. (buy) She _____.
3. (show) He _____.
4. (make) He _____.

B. 주어진 문장의 형태를 바꾸어 쓰세요. **to** 또는 **for**를 함께 쓰세요.

1. The doctor gave Ryan some medicine.　　_The doctor gave some medicine to Ryan_.
2. Did Tim send you those gifts?　　_____?
3. My mother made me a sweater last winter.　　_____.
4. Laura teaches students yoga on weekends.　　_____.
5. Can you show me your passport?　　_____?
6. Will you buy me some milk at the store?　　_____?

UNIT 117 Come here. Let's go inside.

Come here.
이리 와라.

Let's go inside.
안으로 들어가자.

1 '~하라'라고 상대방에게 말할 때 동사원형(come, be 등)을 문장 처음에 쓴다.
- **Be** careful. The knife is really sharp. 조심해라.
- "Where is the bank?" "**Go** straight and **turn** right at the next corner."

'~하지 말아라'라고 할 때는 **don't + 동사원형**을 쓴다.
- The wall was just painted. **Don't touch** it. 그것을 만지지 말아라.
- **Don't leave** your bag there. Someone might take it.

2 '(함께) ~하자'라고 상대방에게 권유할 때 **let's + 동사원형**을 쓴다.
- **Let's take** a break for a few minutes. 몇 분 동안 쉬자.
- "I'm hungry. **Let's order** something." "OK. How about Thai food?"

'~하지 말자'라고 할 때는 **let's not + 동사원형**을 쓴다.
- We have a lot to do. **Let's not waste** time. 시간을 낭비하지 말자.
- It's going to rain this afternoon. **Let's not wash** the car today.

PRACTICE

A. 주어진 동사를 사용하여 상황에 맞게 명령문을 완성하세요. 필요한 경우 don't를 함께 쓰세요.

| be | cry | slow | tell | wake | ~~worry~~ |

1. Your roommate has a test tomorrow. He's nervous.   *Don't worry* .
2. Your friend is driving too fast.   _____ down.
3. It's already noon, but your brother is still in bed.   _____ up.
4. Your sister looks sad. She has tears in her eyes.   _____ .
5. Your friends are talking loudly in the theater.   _____ quiet.
6. You're planning a surprise party for Jane and your friend just found out.   _____ Jane.

B. 주어진 동사와 let's 또는 let's not을 사용하여 문장을 완성하세요.

| ask | ~~buy~~ | go | listen | play | watch |

1. A: This radio doesn't work.
   B: It's old. *Let's buy* a new one.
2. A: _____ to some music.
   B: Good idea. I'll play my new CD.
3. A: This movie doesn't look interesting.
   B: _____ it then.
4. A: I'm bored. _____ football.
   B: OK. I'll get the ball.
5. A: _____ jogging today. I feel tired.
   B: OK. Let's relax at home.
6. A: Do you know the answer to this question?
   B: No. _____ Philip. He might know.

UNIT 118
He **said that** I **could** use his car.

다른 사람의 말을 전달하기 (간접화법)

"**You can** use my car."

He **said that** I **could** use his car.

아빠가 차를 써도 된다고 하셨어.

1 다른 사람의 말을 전달할 때 **said (that)**을 쓸 수 있다. 이때, 주어를 바꾸고 동사의 시제는 과거로 쓴다.

어제 / 오늘

- KATIE: "**I am** so excited." → Katie **said (that)** **she was** so excited.
- JOHN: "**I want** to play outside." → John **said (that)** **he wanted** to play outside.
- The boss: "**You can** leave early." → The boss **said** **I/we could** leave early.

2 다른 사람의 말을 전달할 때 **said** 대신 **told**를 쓸 수도 있다. **told** 다음에는 사람 (+ that)을 쓴다.

- My sister **said (that)** she was ready for school. → My sister **told me (that)** she was ready for school.
  내 여동생은 학교 갈 준비가 되었다고 말했다.
- Tom **said** he needed our help. → Tom **told us** he needed our help.

단, **told** 다음에 '사람'을 생략할 수 없는 것에 주의한다.

- Lisa **told me that** she couldn't come to work today. (Lisa told that she couldn't로 쓸 수 없음)

PRACTICE

A. 다음의 사람들이 하는 말을 보고 said를 사용하여 다시 말하세요.

1. *She said (that) she was on vacation* .   3. _____ .
2. _____ .   4. _____ .

1-4번 문장을 told를 사용하여 다시 말하세요.

5. *She told me (that) she was on vacation* .   7. _____ .
6. _____ .   8. _____ .

B. said 또는 told를 써넣으세요.

1. Nicole *said* she didn't know Kim's phone number.
2. "Kevin _____ me that he could spend Christmas with us." "Really? That's great!"
3. Ms. Hill _____ that she worked at a museum.
4. "How are you getting to the airport?" "Todd _____ he would take me."
5. "I liked the book that you gave me." "I _____ you it was good."
6. Larry _____ me he could take care of our children this weekend.

UNIT 119 I like it **too**. I don't like them **either**.

too와 either

I **like** it **too**.
나도 역시 좋아해.

I **don't** like them **either**.
나도 역시 좋아하지 않아.

1 **too**: ~도 역시 …하다

too는 긍정문에 쓴다.

- Kenneth is from Canada. His wife **is too**.
  그의 아내도 역시 캐나다 출신이다.
- "I want to go to Europe this summer."
  "I **do too**." 나도 역시 가고 싶어.
- "I'm going to have coffee. What about you?"
  "I**'ll** have coffee **too**."
- "I've met Stacy."
  "I **have too**. She's very nice."

either: ~도 역시 …하지 않다

either는 부정문에 쓴다.

- "John and Jane weren't at the party."
  "Bob **wasn't either**." Bob도 역시 파티에 없었어.
- We didn't have any wine, and we **didn't** have any beer **either**. 맥주도 역시 없었다.
- "I shouldn't spend too much money today."
  "I **shouldn't either**."
- "I've never run in a marathon before."
  "I **haven't either**. This is my first time."

PRACTICE

A. too 또는 either를 써넣으세요.

1. I am _too_ .
2. I do _____ .
3. I can't _____ .
4. I did _____ .
5. I'm not _____ .
6. I have _____ .
7. I haven't _____ .
8. I don't _____ .

B. too 또는 either를 써넣으세요.

1. Cats are popular pets, and dogs are _too_ .
2. Marisa didn't pass the exam, and Liz didn't _____ .
3. "We can't go to the baseball game tomorrow." "I can't go _____ ."
4. Jake liked his old job. He likes his new one _____ .
5. I'm baking a cake. I'm baking some cookies _____ .
6. Sam hasn't finished his report, and I haven't finished mine _____ .

UNIT 120 So am I. Neither am I.

1 '∼도 역시 ⋯하다'라는 의미로 말할 때 **so**를 쓸 수도 있다. '∼도 역시 ⋯하지 않다'라는 의미로 말할 때 **neither**를 쓸 수도 있다.

| I **am** hungry. | So **am** I. |
| I **like** pizza. | So **do** I. |

| I **am not** hungry. | Neither **am** I. |
| I **don't** like pizza. | Neither **do** I. |

- "I **was** angry at Nate yesterday."
  "**So was** I." 나도 역시 어제 Nate에게 화가 났었어.
- "We **watched** the World Cup in 2006."
  "**So did** we." 우리도 역시 월드컵을 봤어요.
- "Bill **can** speak Japanese."
  "**So can** his brother. They lived in Japan."

- "I **don't** exercise often."
  "**Neither do** I." 나도 역시 자주 운동하지 않아.
- "Tina **won't** be ready until 7 o'clock."
  "**Neither will** Jack." Jack도 역시 7시까지 준비하지 못할 거야.
- "I **haven't** seen Ross for a long time."
  "**Neither have** I. He's been very busy."

2 So I am, Neither I am 등과 같은 순서로 쓰지 않도록 주의한다.
- "I'm 21 years old." "**So am I.**" (So I am으로 쓸 수 없음)
- "I'm not taking biology this year." "**Neither am I.**" (Neither I am으로 쓸 수 없음)

PRACTICE

A. 괄호 안에 주어진 단어와 so 또는 neither를 사용하여 예시와 같이 문장을 완성하세요.

1. I'm sleepy.
2. I've never gone skiing before.
3. I can ride a motorcycle.
4. Fred isn't married.
5. Sue and I are British.
6. My roommate doesn't talk a lot.
7. The soup wasn't very good.
8. Alice and Ron live in San Diego.

(I) _So am I_ .
(I) _____ .
(Brian) _____ .
(Maria) _____ .
(we) _____ .
(mine) _____ .
(the salad) _____ .
(Jim and Emily) _____ .

B. too/either/so/neither를 써넣으세요.

1. "That was such a funny movie." "I enjoyed it _too_ ."
2. Ella doesn't eat fish, and she doesn't eat meat _____ .
3. "I should get up early tomorrow." "_____ should I."
4. This soup smells great. I hope it tastes good _____ .
5. "We're going to have chicken tonight." "_____ are we."
6. We don't have a TV, and we don't have a radio _____ .
7. "I haven't talked to Ms. Williams lately." "_____ have I."
8. We visited a zoo last weekend. We went to an art museum _____ .
9. "Mark isn't good at sports." "_____ is Roy."
10. "Martin can fall asleep in noisy places." "_____ can Harry."

GRAMMAR GATEWAY BASIC

www.Hackers.co.kr

CHECK-UP TEST

지금까지 학습한 내용을 통합해서 연습할 수 있는 CHECK-UP TEST 입니다. 틀리거나 확실하지 않은 문제는 해당 UNIT으로 돌아가 복습하세요. 그럼 마무리 연습을 시작해볼까요?

TEST 1   현재와 현재진행 (UNIT 1-12)
TEST 2   과거와 과거진행 (UNIT 13-19)
TEST 3   현재완료 (UNIT 20-24)
TEST 4   미래 (UNIT 25-28)
TEST 5   조동사 (UNIT 29-36)
TEST 6   수동태 (UNIT 37-38)
TEST 7   부정문과 의문문 (UNIT 39-45)
TEST 8   -ing와 to + 동사원형 (UNIT 46-52)
TEST 9   명사와 대명사 (UNIT 53-65)
TEST 10 수량 표현 (UNIT 66-76)
TEST 11 형용사와 부사 (UNIT 77-90)
TEST 12 전치사와 구동사 (UNIT 91-104)
TEST 13 접속사와 절 (UNIT 105-114)
TEST 14 다양한 문장들 (UNIT 115-120)

TEST 1 현재와 현재진행 (UNIT 1-12)

 다양한 직업을 가진 사람들이 지금 각기 다른 행동을 하고 있습니다. 괄호 안에 주어진 동사들을 한 번씩 사용하여 문장을 완성하세요. 현재 시제 또는 현재진행 시제로 쓰세요.

1. Name: ALBERT / Job: Writer
2. Name: ANGELA / Job: Chef
3. Name: KEVIN / Job: Teacher
4. Name: SIMONE / Job: Nurse

1. (write, drink) Albert _writes_ novels. He _'s drinking_ OR _is drinking_ coffee.
2. (work, listen) Angela _____ at a restaurant. She _____ to music.
3. (read, teach) Kevin _____ a newspaper. He _____ at a high school.
4. (shop, help) Simone _____. She _____ sick people.

 괄호 안에 주어진 단어들을 적절히 배열하여 문장을 완성하세요.

5. (is / he / busy)
   Tom is working hard. _He's busy_ OR _He is busy_ today.
6. (Mom / is / pancakes / making)
   "_____?" "No, Dad is making them."
7. (do / not / we / use / it)
   Let's give Eric our camera. _____ anymore.
8. (you / know / him / do)
   "Why is that man waving at us? _____?" "Yes. He's my neighbor."
9. (are / Lisa and Anton / from England / not)
   _____. They are French.
10. (not / wear / Julia / does / glasses)
    "Are these glasses Julia's?" "No, they're Nick's. _____."

괄호 안에 주어진 단어들을 사용하여 현재 시제 또는 현재진행 시제 의문문을 완성하세요.

11. (I, late) _Am I late_ for the party?   No, you're not.
12. (you, practice) _____ the violin every day?   Yes, I do.
13. (birds, eat) _____ worms?   Yes, they do.
14. (it, rain) _____ right now?   Yes, it is.
15. (Brian, take) _____ the bus to school? No, he doesn't.
16. (you, watch) Why is the TV on? _____ it?   Yes, I am.
17. (she, work) Who is that woman? _____ here? No, she doesn't.
18. (you, ready) _____ for the meeting?   No, I'm not.

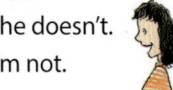

GRAMMAR GATEWAY BASIC

 보기 중 맞는 것을 고르세요.

19. "You look tired. Are you OK ?" "I _____ sick."
    a) am   b) is   c) are

20. Sally _____ a good singer. I like her songs very much.
    a) am   b) is   c) are

21. It's rainy today, but it _____ cold.
    a) am not   b) is not   c) are not

22. I _____ tall, but I'm good at basketball.
    a) am not   b) is not   c) are not

23. "I like those pants. _____ they expensive?" "No, they're not."
    a) Is   b) Are   c) Am

24. "I lost my eraser." "_____ one in my pencil case. You can use mine."
    a) I'm having   b) I'm have   c) I have

25. Andrew doesn't have a car. He _____ the subway every day.
    a) take   b) takes   c) don't take

26. In Fiji, it _____ in the winter.
    a) is not snowing   b) don't snow   c) doesn't snow

27. "_____ fish for dinner tonight?" "No, I don't like fish."
    a) Do you want   b) Are you wanting   c) You are want

28. Emma _____. Her husband makes their meals.
    a) is not cook   b) doesn't cook c) don't cook

29. I don't want to go out today. _____ too much.
    a) It's snowing b) It's not snow c) It's snow

30. "What are you and Mark doing?" "_____ a game."
    a) We're playing b) We're play   c) We play

31. Is that Bill? He _____ his glasses today.
    a) is not wearing   b) is not wear   c) doesn't wear

32. My parents _____ well. They both have a cold.
    a) are feel   b) aren't feel   c) aren't feeling

33. "_____ right now?" "No, she's reading a book."
    a) Is Margaret studying   b) Is Margaret study   c) Does Margaret study

정답 p.200

틀리거나 확실하지 않은 문제는 아래의 표를 확인하여 해당 UNIT으로 돌아가 복습하세요.

문제	1	2	3	4	5	6	7	8	9	10	11	12	13	14	15	16
UNIT	11	11	11	11	1	6	9	10	2	9	3	10	10	6	10	6
17	18	19	20	21	22	23	24	25	26	27	28	29	30	31	32	33
10	3	1	1	2	2	3	12	7	9	10	9	4	4	5	5	6

TEST 2 과거와 과거진행 (UNIT 13-19)

 프랑스를 여행 중인 Jenny가 엽서를 보내왔습니다. 주어진 동사를 사용하여 과거 시제 문장을 완성하세요.

~~arrive~~   buy   see   take   visit   walk

Dear Brian,

How are you? I'm in France!
1. I _arrived_ in Paris last Saturday.
2. On Sunday, I _____ along the river.
3. The next day, I _____ an art museum with my friend.
4. I _____ many beautiful paintings.
5. I _____ lots of photos.
6. This morning, I _____ some gifts for you.

Best wishes,
Jenny

괄호 안에 주어진 단어들을 사용하여 현재 시제 또는 과거 시제 문장을 완성하세요.

7. (I, make) _I made_ spaghetti for you.
8. (I, not see) _____ you yesterday.
9. (Susie, be) _____ your friend in college?
10. (I, have) _____ a headache.
11. (you, go) _____ to the concert last weekend?
12. (I, not know) _____ the way to city hall. Can you give me directions?
13. (he, be) Who is that handsome man? _____ a freshman?

Thanks, Grace!
I was sick.
Yes, she was.
Take this medicine.
No. I stayed at home.
Sure, follow me.

He's my brother!

 괄호 안에 주어진 단어들을 적절히 배열하여 문장을 완성하세요.

14. (was / he / not)
    Jacob didn't eat dinner. _He wasn't OR He was not_ hungry.

15. (did / Lucy / go / not)
    _____ to school yesterday. It was Sunday.

16. (Ben / clean / did)
    "_____ the bathroom yesterday?" "Yes, he did."

17. (you / were / studying)
    "I saw you at the library yesterday. _____?" "Yes. I had an exam today."

18. (waiting / were / we)
    "Why were you and Joseph at the airport last night?" "_____ for Jenna."

보기 중 맞는 것을 고르세요.

19. "What were you doing at 6 yesterday?" "I _____."
    a) am worked   b) was working   c) am working

20. Last Tuesday _____ Tracy's birthday. She's 20 years old now.
    a) was   b) were   c) is

21. Sally _____ at home this morning. She didn't answer the door.
    a) wasn't   b) weren't   c) isn't

22. "_____ jogging when you saw them last week?" "Yes, they were."
    a) Was Tom and Jane   b) Were Tom and Jane   c) Are Tom and Jane

23. "This sandwich is amazing! Did you make it?" "No, I _____ it at a store."
    a) bought   b) was buying   c) buy

24. Kyle and I _____ butterflies every day, but we're too busy these days.
    a) used to catching   b) were catching   c) used to catch

25. Jason _____ to school yesterday. He took the bus.
    a) didn't walk   b) walks   c) doesn't walk

26. "What were you doing with Mark an hour ago?" "We _____ about you!"
    a) used to talk   b) were talking   c) are not talking

27. "Sorry I called you so late last night." "That's OK. I _____ when you called."
    a) wasn't sleeping   b) was sleeping   c) am sleeping

28. "Were you playing soccer at 3 this afternoon?" "I _____ a book."
    a) used to read   b) is reading   c) was reading

29. Last night at 11, Andrew and Rachel _____ TV. They were playing video games.
    a) aren't watching   b) watched   c) weren't watching

30. "_____ you this afternoon?" "No, she didn't."
    a) Was Jennifer call b) Did Jennifer call   c) Does Jennifer call

31. "_____ when you saw him?" "Yes, he was."
    a) Was Thomas exercising b) Were Thomas exercising c) Is Thomas exercising

32. I _____ swimming lessons on Tuesdays, but I quit.
    a) take   b) used to take   c) am taking

33. "Are you hungry?" "No. I _____ dinner already."
    a) had   b) have   c) was having

정답 p.200

틀리거나 확실하지 않은 문제는 아래의 표를 확인하여 해당 UNIT으로 돌아가 복습하세요.

문제	1	2	3	4	5	6	7	8	9	10	11	12	13	14	15	16
UNIT	15	15	15	15	15	15	15	16	14	12	16	9	3	14	16	16
17	18	19	20	21	22	23	24	25	26	27	28	29	30	31	32	33
18	17	17	13	14	18	15	19	16	17	16	17	18	16	18	19	15

TEST 3   현재완료 (UNIT 20-24)

 괄호 안에 주어진 단어들을 적절히 배열하여 문장을 완성하세요.

1. (owned / a dog / you / have / ever)
   Have you ever owned a dog ?
2. (we / not / yet / eaten dinner / have)
   _____ .
3. (many concerts / has / Mark / been to)
   _____ .
4. (lived / how long / you / have)
   _____ in this city?
5. (made / some muffins / Aaron and Nick / have)
   _____ .
6. (not / Mandy / a roller coaster / ridden / has)
   _____ before.

 그림을 보고 주어진 표현을 사용하여 현재완료 시제 문장을 완성하세요. 필요한 경우 부정문으로 쓰세요.

| be sick | ~~have this camera~~ | know each other | rain |

7. I 've had this camera since 1992.

8. We _____ for 10 years.

9. It _____ since last month.

10. He _____ for two days.

 괄호 안에 주어진 동사를 사용하여 과거 시제 또는 현재완료 시제 문장을 완성하세요.

11. Do you speak French?
12. Have you talked to Cindy lately?
13. Do your parents like that TV show?
14. How long have you been in China?
15. Why are you late?
16. Your son is so tall now.
17. Where's your car?
18. When did Susan come to this company?

(study) A little. I 've studied since March.
(call) Yes. She _____ me two days ago.
(watch) Yes. They _____ it for many years.
(come) I _____ here in 2009.
(get) I _____ up late this morning.
(grow) He _____ a lot since last year.
(break) My car _____ down last week.
(work) She _____ here for three months.

138 | 예문 해석·무료 영어 학습 컨텐츠 제공 www.Hackers.co.kr

보기 중 맞는 것을 고르세요.

19. "_____ Tim and Lisa arrived at the party yet?" "Yes. They're dancing now."
    a) Have   b) Has   c) Do

20. "Have you already finished college?" "Yes. I _____ two years ago."
    a) have graduated   b) graduated   c) graduate

21. My soccer team lost again. We _____ a game since last year.
    a) haven't won   b) don't won   c) didn't win

22. I haven't seen my sister _____ five years. I miss her so much.
    a) since   b) ago   c) for

23. My daughter is at the hospital. She _____ her arm yesterday.
    a) has hurt   b) hurts   c) hurt

24. "What's wrong with the lamp?" "Jack _____ it."
    a) has broken   b) have broken   c) doesn't break

25. Jason and I _____ to the museum last Thursday.
    a) have gone   b) went   c) go

26. "Have you ever been to New Zealand?" "No. I _____ abroad."
    a) have traveled   b) haven't traveled   c) hasn't traveled

27. "_____ your homework yet?" "I'll do it tomorrow."
    a) You done have   b) Have you done   c) Have done you

28. "Let's go out for dinner." "_____ dinner already."
    a) I didn't make   b) I haven't made   c) I've made

29. "How long have you been married?" "We've been married _____ 1998."
    a) since   b) ago   c) for

30. Martin is so smart. He _____ an exam.
    a) have never failed   b) has never failed   c) hasn't never failed

31. "_____ come yet?" "Yes. It's on your desk."
    a) The mail did   b) Have the mail   c) Has the mail

32. "Am I late?" "No. The movie _____ yet."
    a) has started   b) hasn't started   c) haven't started

33. "Jessica looks upset." "_____ her watch."
    a) She has lost   b) She hasn't lost   c) Has she lost

정답 p.200

틀리거나 확실하지 않은 문제는 아래의 표를 확인하여 해당 UNIT으로 돌아가 복습하세요.

문제	1	2	3	4	5	6	7	8	9	10	11	12	13	14	15	16
UNIT	22	24	22	21	20	22	21	21	21	21	23	23	23	23	23	23
17	18	19	20	21	22	23	24	25	26	27	28	29	30	31	32	33
23	23	24	23	21	21	23	20	23	22	24	24	21	22	24	24	20

TEST 4   미래 (UNIT 25-28)

괄호 안에 주어진 단어들을 적절히 배열하여 문장을 완성하세요.

1. (like / Lisa / this ring / will)
   Will Lisa like this ring ?

2. (going / marry her / he / to / is)
   Jake loves his girlfriend so much. _____.

3. (you / are / speaking)
   _____ at the seminar? I saw your name on the list.

4. (going / are / to / watch the fireworks / you)
   "_____ tonight?" "No. I'm tired."

5. (not / will / it / I / forget)
   "The password is 0922." "OK. _____."

6. (playing soccer / are / Alex and I / not)
   _____ this weekend. We're going to the beach instead.

그림을 보고 주어진 표현과 be going to를 사용하여 문장을 완성하세요.

| drink some wine | fall | get on the train | stop at the light |

7. The tree _is going to fall_ .
8. She _____.
9. The car _____.
10. They _____.

주어진 동사와 will을 사용하여 문장을 완성하세요. 필요한 경우 부정문으로 쓰세요.

| cook | meet | open | stay | tell | touch | turn on | write |

11. These gifts are for Janice.   OK. I _won't open_ them.
12. Can I have your phone number?   Sure. I _____ it down for you.
13. You have to get up early tomorrow.   I know. I _____ up late.
14. It's so cold.   You're right. I _____ the heater.
15. I just painted that wall. It's still wet. All right. I _____ it.
16. It's a secret.   Don't worry. I _____ anyone.
17. I'm so hungry.   I _____ something for you.
18. Let's see a movie tonight.   Sure. I _____ you at the theater.

보기 중 맞는 것을 고르세요.

19. Take this medicine. You _____ better.
    a) are going to get b) were going to get c) got

20. "You can get a 10 percent discount on this coat." "Really? _____ it!"
    a) I took b) I take c) I'll take

21. "Do you have any plans for this Sunday?" "_____ my grandparents."
    a) I visited b) I visit c) I'm going to visit

22. "_____ busy tomorrow?" "I'm not sure. Why?"
    a) Do you and Nate be b) Will you and Nate be c) You and Nate will be

23. We need to hurry. The bank _____ in 10 minutes.
    a) close b) closes c) closed

24. "This steak tastes awful." "Does it? I _____ it, then."
    a) won't eat b) don't eat c) didn't eat

25. "Did you book a ticket for Tokyo?" "Yes. _____ next Wednesday."
    a) I leave b) I won't leave c) I'm leaving

26. "Hurry up!" "Don't worry. We _____ late."
    a) will be b) won't be c) are

27. _____ the meeting this afternoon. She's sick.
    a) Jenny's attending b) Jenny doesn't attend c) Jenny's not attending

28. "_____ soon?" "I don't think so."
    a) Is the rain going to stop b) Is the rain stop c) Does the rain stop

29. Tina _____ the exam next week because she studied very hard.
    a) will pass b) passes c) passed

30. "We _____ to Seattle next month." "I'm glad you're staying here."
    a) don't move b) aren't going to move c) didn't move

31. I _____ with Kim next Sunday. Do you want to go with us?
    a) am going shopping b) am not going shopping c) was going shopping

32. "_____ to my birthday party?" "Of course. When is it?"
    a) Did you come b) Do you come c) Will you come

33. "_____ the car today?" "No. You can use it."
    a) Are you going to use b) Are you use c) Did you use

정답 p.200

틀리거나 확실하지 않은 문제는 아래의 표를 확인하여 해당 UNIT으로 돌아가 복습하세요.

문제	1	2	3	4	5	6	7	8	9	10	11	12	13	14	15	16
UNIT	25	26	28	26	25	28	26	26	26	26	25	25	25	25	25	25
17	18	19	20	21	22	23	24	25	26	27	28	29	30	31	32	33
25	25	26	25	26	25	28	25	28	25	28	26	25	26	28	25	26

TEST 5   조동사 (UNIT 29-36)

괄호 안에 주어진 단어들을 적절히 배열하여 문장을 완성하세요.

1. (can / teach / you / me)
   "I want to learn Spanish. *Can you teach me* ?" "OK."

2. (not / might / he / come)
   "Is Tom coming to the beach with us?" "I'm not sure. _____."

3. (they / not / should / talk)
   Fred and Jack are at a library. _____ loudly.

4. (would / like / you / to / dance)
   "_____ with me?" "Sure."

5. (do / have to / not / I / go)
   _____ to the hospital. I'm feeling much better.

그림을 보고 주어진 표현과 조동사를 사용하여 문장을 완성하세요. 필요한 경우 부정문으로 쓰세요.

| be scared | call the police | fall down the stairs |
| fix the roof | ~~turn off the stove~~ | use the car |

6. (should) You *should turn off the stove* .

7. (can) We _____.

8. (have to) We _____.

9. (might) Watch out! You _____!

10. (have to) You _____.

11. (must) We _____.

괄호 안에 주어진 조동사를 사용하여 현재 시제 또는 과거 시제 문장을 완성하세요. 필요한 경우 부정문으로 쓰세요.

12. (must) "It's very cold today. You *must* wear a jacket!" "OK, I will."
13. (can) The view from the tower was amazing. We _____ see the entire city.
14. (have to) Hank _____ get up early yesterday. He didn't go to work.
15. (should) We _____ invite Rachel to go skiing with us. She loves to ski.
16. (must) "That's the last train! We _____ miss it." "Let's run."
17. (have to) My new sweater was too big for me. I _____ return it last weekend.
18. (can) The teacher spoke too quickly. I _____ understand him.

GRAMMAR GATEWAY BASIC

보기 중 맞는 것을 고르세요.

19. "_____ David play the guitar?" "Yes, he can."
    a) Must b) Should c) Can ✓

20. Phillip's car is very dirty. He _____ clean it often.
    a) must not b) shouldn't c) might

21. "_____ get a soda, please?" "Sure, here you go."
    a) Can I b) Would I c) Should I

22. "Where are you going on vacation?" "I haven't decided yet, but I _____ go to Miami."
    a) had to b) might c) would like

23. "Western Hotel, how can I help you?" "_____ a reservation for two nights, please."
    a) I'd like make b) Would you to make c) I'd like to make

24. Sarah _____ do the laundry last night. She was too tired.
    a) can't b) couldn't c) might not

25. The plane will land now. All passengers _____ wear seatbelts.
    a) must b) had to c) shouldn't

26. Gary failed his driving test. He _____ take it again.
    a) have to b) has to c) doesn't have to

27. "Can you finish your homework tonight?" "I don't know. I _____ finish it."
    a) shouldn't b) must not c) might not

28. "_____ order some food for us?" "Yes! I'm hungry."
    a) Would you like b) Would I c) Should I

29. I _____ wash the dishes. My sister has done it already.
    a) must not b) don't have to c) doesn't have to

30. "_____ fix my computer for me, please?" "Sure."
    a) You would b) Could you c) Should you

31. Sam broke Melinda's cup. He _____ apologize.
    a) should b) can c) could

32. Sharon missed the bus yesterday, so she _____ walk to school.
    a) has to b) might c) had to

33. "_____ more wine?" "No, thank you. I've had enough."
    a) Would you like b) Would you like to c) Should I

정답 p.201

틀리거나 확실하지 않은 문제는 아래의 표를 확인하여 해당 UNIT으로 돌아가 복습하세요.

문제	1	2	3	4	5	6	7	8	9	10	11	12	13	14	15	16
UNIT	30	31	35	36	34	35	29	33	31	34	33	33	29	34	35	34
17	18	19	20	21	22	23	24	25	26	27	28	29	30	31	32	33
33	29	29	32	30	31	36	29	33	33	31	35	34	30	35	33	36

TEST 6 수동태 (UNIT 37-38)

 그림을 보고 주어진 동사를 사용하여 수동태 문장을 완성하세요. 과거 시제로 쓰세요.

~~catch~~   make   steal   take   write

1. The thieves _were caught_ by the policeman.
2. The scarves _____ in Italy.
3. The letter _____ by Jackie.
4. The pictures _____ in New York.
5. The painting _____ by someone.

 괄호 안에 주어진 단어들을 적절히 배열하여 문장을 완성하세요.

6. (it / visited / is)
   Michael's town is famous. _It is visited_ _____ by many tourists each year.

7. (pets / allowed / not / are)
   "Can we take our dog with us?"   "No, _____ in the museum."

8. (the house / not / was / sold)
   _____ yesterday. It's still for sale.

9. (the Mona Lisa / painted / was / Leonardo da Vinci / by)
   _____.

10. (they / not / are / by / known / many people)
    This band is new. _____.

 괄호 안에 주어진 단어를 사용하여 능동태 또는 수동태 문장을 완성하세요. 과거 시제로 쓰세요.

11. (prepare) "This pasta is amazing. Who made it?"
    "All the dishes _were prepared_ by Chef Antonio."
12. (cancel) "Did you go to the meeting yesterday?"   "No, it _____."
13. (have) "Were you with Susie this morning?"   "Yes, I _____ coffee with her."
14. (break) The window _____ by the storm last night.
15. (not finish) "Did you do your homework?"   "I _____ it. I was too busy."
16. (invent) The light bulb _____ by Thomas Edison.
17. (watch) "What did Frank do on Saturday?"   "He _____ movies all day."
18. (not wash) "Has Bruce washed the car yet?"   "It _____ when I saw it this morning."

보기 중 맞는 것을 고르세요.

19. The apple pies in this bakery are fresh. They _____ every morning.
    a) baked   b) are baked   c) are bake

20. I can't read this book. It _____ in German.
    a) is written   b) was writing   c) wrote

21. I sent flowers to my friend, but they _____.
    a) were delivered   b) weren't delivered   c) don't deliver

22. "What instrument does Jane play?" "She _____ the flute."
    a) plays   b) is played   c) was played

23. Fred _____ tomatoes. He doesn't like them.
    a) isn't eaten   b) wasn't eaten   c) doesn't eat

24. "What's George's phone number?" "Sorry, I _____."
    a) don't know   b) am not known   c) wasn't known

25. "Thirty people _____ to the party, but only 10 people came." "That's too bad."
    a) invited   b) were invited   c) weren't invited

26. "Why was Jack crying this morning?" "He _____ for the soccer team."
    a) wasn't chosen   b) chose   c) isn't chosen

27. Thomas Neilson's books are very famous. They _____ every year.
    a) are read many people   b) read by many people   c) are read by many people

28. Samantha's house is very old. It _____ in 1964.
    a) was built   b) were built   c) built

29. "Where's your phone?" "I _____ it last night."
    a) am lost   b) was lost   c) lost

30. "Why does Joseph look so nervous?" "He _____ for the test."
    a) isn't studied   b) wasn't studied   c) didn't study

31. "Why were you late to work this morning?" "The road _____ by snow."
    a) blocked   b) was blocked   c) is blocked

32. "Where did you get that car?" "Tony _____ it to me."
    a) was lent   b) lent   c) is lent

33. "Who taught you math in high school?" "I _____."
    a) was taught by Mr. Adams b) was taught Mr. Adams   c) taught by Mr. Adams

정답 p.201

틀리거나 확실하지 않은 문제는 아래의 표를 확인하여 해당 UNIT으로 돌아가 복습하세요.

문제	1	2	3	4	5	6	7	8	9	10	11	12	13	14	15	16
UNIT	37	37	37	37	37	37	37	37	38	38	38	38	38	38	38	38
17	18	19	20	21	22	23	24	25	26	27	28	29	30	31	32	33
38	38	38	38	38	38	38	38	38	38	38	38	38	38	38	38	38

TEST 7 부정문과 의문문 (UNIT 39-45)

 대화를 보고 who/what/where/when을 써넣으세요.

1. _Where_ are you from? — I'm from Thailand.
2. _____ does your brother do? — He's a scientist.
3. _____ is your favorite singer? — Tracy Swift. Her songs are really good.
4. _____ did you meet your wife? — At our university. We were classmates.
5. _____ does the next bus arrive? — In 10 minutes.
6. _____ are those people in the picture? — They are my neighbors.
7. _____ can I see the doctor? — At 11 o'clock tomorrow morning.
8. _____ time does your plane leave? — At 9 p.m.

 각 사람이 궁금해 하는 내용을 보고 간접의문문을 사용하여 문장을 완성하세요.

9. Do you know _who that man is_ ?

10. Can you tell me _____ ?

11. I wonder _____ .

12. Do you know _____ ?

 괄호 안에 주어진 단어들을 적절히 배열하여 문장을 완성하세요.

13. (you / tried / have / Mexican food)
    Have you tried Mexican food before? It's really good.

14. (this necklace / much / does / cost / how)
    "_____?" "$70."

15. (does / like / Kyle / dogs / not)
    _____. He's scared of them.

16. (will / busy / whether / you / be)
    Can you tell me _____ next Saturday?

17. (go / when / Cindy / did)
    "_____ to Hong Kong?" "Last Friday."

18. (not / buy / should / it / you)
    The car is too expensive. _____.

보기 중 맞는 것을 고르세요.

19. "_____ mine?" "This one."
   a) Cup which is　　　b) Which is cup　　　c) Which cup is

20. "_____ will you arrive?" "At about 4 o'clock."
   a) When　　　b) Where　　　c) Why

21. _____ at this restaurant before. What about you?
   a) I not have eaten　　　b) I have not eaten　　　c) I have eaten not

22. "_____ do I turn on this machine?" "Press the green button."
   a) When　　　b) Who　　　c) How

23. "_____ would you like, beef or pork?" "Beef, please."
   a) Which　　　b) How　　　c) Who

24. I don't know _____ to school today.
   a) if Chris went　　　b) did Chris go　　　c) Chris went

25. "_____ are you calling?" "My boyfriend."
   a) What　　　b) Who　　　c) How

26. "Josh and Sharon just arrived." "_____ together?"
   a) They did came　　　b) Did they come　　　c) Did they came

27. _____ is my bag? I can't find it.
   a) Where　　　b) When　　　c) Why

28. "_____ from your house?" "About two miles away."
   a) How far is your school　　　b) How far your school is　　　c) How your school is far

29. "_____ did Catherine go back to the store?" "She left her purse there."
   a) When　　　b) Where　　　c) Why

30. "Can you tell me _____ for dessert?" "I want something sweet."
   a) what do you want　　　b) you want what　　　c) what you want

31. _____ to the office today. I think she's sick.
   a) Angela did not come　　　b) Angela not did come　　　c) Did Angela not came

32. "_____ lived in Sydney?" "For 20 years."
   a) How long you have　　　b) How have you long　　　c) How long have you

33. "_____ the piano?" "No, but she can play the guitar."
   a) Jamie can play　　　b) Can Jamie play　　　c) Can play Jamie

정답 p.201

틀리거나 확실하지 않은 문제는 아래의 표를 확인하여 해당 UNIT으로 돌아가 복습하세요.

문제	1	2	3	4	5	6	7	8	9	10	11	12	13	14	15	16
UNIT	43	41	41	43	43	41	43	41	45	45	45	45	40	44	39	45
17	18	19	20	21	22	23	24	25	26	27	28	29	30	31	32	33
43	39	42	43	39	44	42	45	41	40	43	44	43	45	39	44	40

TEST 8 -ing와 to+동사원형 (UNIT 46-52)

 그림을 보고 주어진 표현을 사용하여 문장을 완성하세요.

cook   go to the museum   ~~play soccer~~   read books   sing   wait in line

1. I love _playing soccer_ OR _to play soccer_ .
2. I hate _____ .
3. I practice _____ every day.
4. I enjoy _____ .
5. I plan _____ .
6. I like _____ at cafés.

괄호 안에 주어진 동사를 사용하여 대화를 완성하세요. 필요한 경우 동사를 -ing나 to+동사원형으로 쓰세요.

7. (play) "Do you go to the golf course every week?" "Yes. _Playing_ golf is my hobby."
8. (send) "Where are you going?" "I'm going to the bank _____ some money."
9. (make) "When will you return home?" "At about 6. I'll help you _____ dinner tonight."
10. (eat) "I want to lose weight." "You should avoid _____ snacks."
11. (stay) "Why didn't you come to the party?" "My dad made me _____ at home."
12. (drive) "Let's watch a movie." "I can't. Liz wants me _____ her to the hospital."
13. (learn) "I'm studying Japanese these days." "Why did you decide _____ a foreign language?"

괄호 안에 주어진 단어들을 적절히 배열하여 문장을 완성하세요.

14. (writing / finished / I / my report)
    " _I finished writing my report_ ." "Great. Can I see it?"
15. (me / use / Aaron / let / his)
    My mobile phone wasn't working, so _____ .
16. (to / buy / does / need / Kim)
    " _____ a new computer?" "Yes, hers is very old."
17. (taught / Nicole / to dance / me)
    "You're a great dancer." "Thank you. _____ ."
18. (good / swimming / is)
    _____ for your health.

보기 중 맞는 것을 고르세요.

19. "When did you decide _____ a book?" "About three years ago."
    a) to write   b) writing   c) write

20. "Jenna made Dale _____ yesterday." "What did she do?"
    a) to cry   b) crying   c) cry

21. "Mr. Smith offered _____ me chess." "That's great. You're going to enjoy it."
    a) to teach   b) teaching   c) teach

22. "Can you _____ these plants, please?" "Sure. Where should they go?"
    a) help me moving   b) help me move   c) help moving me

23. Why are you still watching TV? I told you _____ to bed an hour ago.
    a) to go   b) going   c) go

24. Sophie keeps _____ me text messages during class. I want her to stop.
    a) to send   b) sending   c) send

25. "What are you going to do next Saturday?" "I'm planning _____ Chad."
    a) visit   b) visiting   c) to visit

26. "_____ a cheesecake takes about an hour." "Really? It doesn't take very long."
    a) Bake   b) Baking   c) Baked

27. "Anna and Joe want me _____ their tennis club." "That sounds like fun."
    a) join   b) joining   c) to join

28. I don't enjoy _____ basketball outside when it's hot.
    a) to play   b) playing   c) play

29. _____ a taxi isn't easy on Fridays. Let's take a bus.
    a) Get   b) Got   c) Getting

30. "Why did you go to the supermarket in the morning?" "Emily had me _____ some milk."
    a) to buy   a) buying   c) buy

31. "I went to the library _____ a book." "What book did you borrow?"
    a) borrowing   b) borrow   c) to borrow

32. "Why did you stop _____ to the fitness center?" "I hurt my back."
    a) to go   b) going   c) go

33. "Do you have time _____ every day?" "Yes. I usually go to the gym after work."
    a) to exercise   b) exercising   c) exercise

정답 p.201

틀리거나 확실하지 않은 문제는 아래의 표를 확인하여 해당 UNIT으로 돌아가 복습하세요.

문제	1	2	3	4	5	6	7	8	9	10	11	12	13	14	15	16
UNIT	49	49	47	47	48	49	46	52	51	47	51	50	48	47	51	48
17	18	19	20	21	22	23	24	25	26	27	28	29	30	31	32	33
50	46	48	51	48	51	50	47	48	46	50	47	46	51	52	49	52

TEST 9 명사와 대명사 (UNIT 53-65)

 괄호 안에 주어진 단어들을 적절히 배열하여 문장을 완성하세요. 필요한 경우 명사를 복수로 쓰세요.

1. (dog / has / he / five)
   "Does Brian have any pets?" " _He has five dogs_____."
2. (many / attend / student / the concert)
   "Did _____ yesterday?" "No, not very many."
3. (snow / some / on / the road)
   There's _____. Please drive carefully.
4. (get / a / of / orange juice / glass)
   "Could I _____, please?" "Sure."
5. (ones / buy / new)
   "Your shoes are old!" "I know, I'm going to _____ tomorrow."

 그림을 보고 주어진 명사와 -'(s)를 사용하여 문장을 완성하세요.

| ~~book~~ | house | office | seat | suitcases |

6. It's _Jenny's book_____.
7. It's the _____.
8. It's _____.
9. It's the _____.
10. They're _____.

주어진 단어를 사용하여 문장을 완성하세요. 필요한 경우 a/an 또는 the를 함께 사용하세요.

| airport | ~~computer~~ | drums | information | money | salt | taxi | umbrella |

11. I'd like to buy _a computer_____. Could you help me choose a model?
12. "Did Clara take _____ with her? It's raining outside." "Yes, I gave her one."
13. "This soup needs some _____. Do we have any?" "Yes, we do. Here you are."
14. "We're going to be late. We should catch _____." "There's one over there."
15. "Can you play _____?" "No, I can't."
16. Mary's flight arrives in four hours. Let's wait for her at _____.
17. Can you lend me some _____? I want to get a soda.
18. "Could you give me some _____ about the test next Monday?" "Of course."

GRAMMAR GATEWAY BASIC

 보기 중 맞는 것을 고르세요.

19. "I think my eyesight is getting worse." "You should get _____."
    a) new glasses   b) a new glasses   c) a new glass

20. "Do we have an exam tomorrow?" "No, _____ is next Friday."
    a) exam   b) an exam   c) the exam

21. Michael raises many _____ on his farm for their wool.
    a) a sheep   b) sheep   c) sheeps

22. "Would you like _____?" "Yes, please."
    a) glass of milk   b) a glass of milk   c) a glass of milks

23. "Have you seen _____ in my garden?" "Yes, they're beautiful!"
    a) the flowers   b) a flower   c) flowers

24. "Is there _____ nearby?" "Yes, there's one across the street."
    a) a bank machine   b) the bank machine   c) bank machine

25. "What's the highest mountain in _____?" "Mount Everest."
    a) world   b) a world   c) the world

26. "What were you doing when I called?" "I was having _____ with Jason."
    a) dinners   b) dinner   c) the dinner

27. "Where's Lisa?" "She _____."
    a) went to a work   b) went to work   c) went to the work

28. "Why are those people smiling at you?" "I don't know. I've never seen _____ before."
    a) them   b) theirs   c) they

29. "How's the weather in Chicago these days?" "_____ has rained for five days."
    a) The weather   b) Chicago   c) It

30. This letter has your name on it. It must be _____.
    a) your   b) you   c) yours

31. "Are you wearing my earrings?" "No. _____ are mine."
    a) This   b) Those   c) These

32. Matt's company is on _____.
    a) the fifth floor of the building   b) the fifth floor's building   c) the building of the fifth floor

33. "Can I borrow one of your hats today?" "Sure. _____?"
    a) Which ones   b) Which one   c) The ones

정답 p.202

틀리거나 확신하지 않은 문제는 아래의 표를 확인하여 해당 UNIT으로 돌아가 복습하세요.

문제	1	2	3	4	5	6	7	8	9	10	11	12	13	14	15	16
UNIT	54	54	53	56	65	63	63	63	63	63	57	57	53	57	58	59
17	18	19	20	21	22	23	24	25	26	27	28	29	30	31	32	33
53	53	55	57	55	56	57	57	58	58	59	60	61	62	64	63	65

TEST 10 수량 표현 (UNIT 66-76)

  그림을 보고 some/any/no를 써넣으세요.

1. She took *some* photos.
2. There aren't _____ people in the park.
3. There are _____ apples on the table.
4. He didn't receive _____ mail today.
5. There is _____ water in the swimming pool.

  둘 중 맞는 것을 고르세요.

6. Have you had dinner?	Yes, but I didn't eat (**much** / many) food.
7. Was traffic slow this morning?	No, there were (few / little) cars on the road.
8. Did you go to bed early last night?	No, I had (much / many) things to do.
9. Do you read many books?	Yes, I usually read six books (all / every) month.
10. How's the soup?	It needs (a little / a few) salt.
11. Let's go to Europe together!	I can't. I haven't saved (much / many) money.
12. How was the beach yesterday?	Terrible. It rained (all / every) day.
13. Have you finished fixing the car?	I couldn't. I had (little / a little) time today.

괄호 안에 주어진 단어들을 적절히 배열하여 문장을 완성하세요. 필요한 경우 of를 함께 사용하세요.

14. (friends / my / day / all)
    "What are you going to do tomorrow?" "I'm meeting with *my friends all day* ."

15. (them / are / both)
    "What color are Kate's cats?" "_____ white."

16. (my / live / cousins / most)
    _____ in New York. Only one lives in Boston.

17. (has / none / he)
    "Does Brandon have any brothers?" "No, _____."

18. (mine / them / is / neither)
    "Which ball is yours, the red or blue one?" "_____. Mine is at home."

보기 중 맞는 것을 고르세요.

19. "Would you like _____ cookies?" "Yes, please. I love cookies."
    a) none   b) some ⓑ   c) no

20. "Do you have any bananas? I'd like to buy some." "I'm sorry, we have _____."
    a) no   b) none bananas   c) none

21. I haven't seen _____ movies this month. I've been too busy.
    a) any   b) some   c) no

22. _____ is knocking on the door. It might be John.
    a) Someone   b) Anything   c) Nowhere

23. "I think someone is crying. Do you hear _____?" "No, I don't."
    a) somewhere   b) anything   c) nothing

24. Jessica is popular. She has _____.
    a) many friends   b) much friends   c) all friends

25. "Do you have any rooms available?" "Yes, we have _____. Would you like to check in?"
    a) few   b) a little   c) a few

26. "How much milk do we have?" "Very _____. We should buy a carton tomorrow."
    a) a little   b) little   c) few

27. "Do you have any items on sale?" "Yes, _____ item is on sale."
    a) all of   b) all   c) every

28. Clark is very tired. He played soccer _____ day today.
    a) all   b) every   c) all of

29. I don't have to do much homework tonight. I have finished _____ it already.
    a) lot of   b) a lot   c) a lot of

30. "Did you do well on your history test?" "I think so, but _____ the questions were difficult."
    a) some   b) some of   c) most

31. I went to two different bakeries, but _____ them had bagels.
    a) neither   b) neither of   c) either of

32. "Do you want to go out for dinner or eat at home?" "_____ is fine."
    a) Both   b) Neither   c) Either

33. "Are any banks open at 6 p.m.?" "I'm not sure. _____ banks close before 5 p.m."
    a) Most   b) Most of   c) None

정답 p.202

틀리거나 확실하지 않은 문제는 아래의 표를 확인하여 해당 UNIT으로 돌아가 복습하세요.

문제	1	2	3	4	5	6	7	8	9	10	11	12	13	14	15	16
UNIT	66	66	66	66	67	69	72	69	74	71	69	73	72	73	76	75
17	18	19	20	21	22	23	24	25	26	27	28	29	30	31	32	33
67	76	66	67	66	68	68	69	71	72	74	73	70	75	76	76	75

TEST 11 형용사와 부사 (UNIT 77-90)

 그림을 보고 주어진 표현들을 하나씩 사용하여 예시와 같이 문장을 완성하세요. 형용사를 부사로 바꿔 쓰세요.

| ~~laugh~~ shout sit think | + | angry hard ~~loud~~ uncomfortable |

1. They 're laughing loudly   .
2. He _____.
3. She _____.
4. They _____.

괄호 안에 주어진 단어들을 적절히 배열하여 문장을 완성하세요.

5. (are / for / small / me / too)
   My old shirts are too small for me   . I need to buy new ones.
6. (rarely / is / crowded)
   "That café _____." "You're right. I often go there to study."
7. (to / tall / enough / not / ride)
   Thomas wanted to ride the roller coaster, but he was _____ it.
8. (tired / too / to / go)
   "I am _____ to the movies." "Let's stay at home, then."
9. (for / everyone / enough)
   "How many tickets did you buy?" "I bought _____."
10. (always / my car / can / use)
    You _____ if you need it.

괄호 안에 주어진 단어를 사용하여 문장을 완성하세요. 필요한 경우 주어진 단어를 비교급 또는 최상급으로 쓰세요.

11. (heavy) Can you help me carry these bags? They are too heavy for me.
12. (good) Something smells _____! What are we having for dinner?
13. (large) This skirt is too small for me. Do you have a _____ size?
14. (beautiful) I think roses are _____ than tulips.
15. (high) Mount Everest is the _____ mountain in the world.
16. (hot) "When is the _____ time of the day?" "Around 2 p.m."
17. (fast) "Can you run _____ than Nathan?" "No. He's the fastest in my school."
18. (strong) Susan is very strong, but she's not as _____ as her brother.

보기 중 맞는 것을 고르세요.

19. "Did you enjoy the movie?" "Yes, it was _____ the one we saw yesterday."
    a) the most interesting   b) more interesting than   c) interesting

20. "Did you make _____?" "Of course."
    a) pizza enough for the guests   b) pizza for the guests enough   c) enough pizza for the guests

21. I _____ in the ocean, but I want to try one day.
    a) never have swum   b) have never swum   c) have swum never

22. "Your shoes are so _____." "I know. I'm going to wash them tomorrow."
    a) dirty   b) dirtiest   c) dirtier

23. These pants are _____. I need shorter ones.
    a) for me too long   b) too long for me   c) for long too me

24. Ashley's house is _____ to school, so she always arrives at class first.
    a) the most close   b) more closer   c) the closest

25. My dad loves fishing. _____ me fishing on weekends.
    a) He takes often   b) Often takes he   c) He often takes

26. I'm telling you a _____ story. You have to believe me.
    a) true   b) truer   c) truly

27. Today is _____ yesterday. Let's go to the park.
    a) not as cold as   b) as not cold as   c) as cold as not

28. Troy has a stomachache. He ate dinner _____.
    a) too quickly   b) quickly too   c) too quicker

29. I finished work late yesterday. I was _____ usual.
    a) busier   b) busier than   c) the busiest

30. Did you do your homework _____ to get a good grade?
    a) enough good   b) well enough   c) enough well

31. It snowed a lot last night. You should drive _____.
    a) careful   b) carefully   c) more careful

32. "Please finish your work _____." "OK. I'll try my best."
    a) as sooner as possible   b) as soon as possible   c) as possible as soon

33. "That ring has a really big diamond." "It's _____ ring in the store."
    a) expensive   b) more expensive   c) the most expensive

정답 p.202

틀리거나 확실하지 않은 문제는 아래의 표를 확인하여 해당 UNIT으로 돌아가 복습하세요.

문제	1	2	3	4	5	6	7	8	9	10	11	12	13	14	15	16
UNIT	78	78	80	78	82	81	83	82	84	81	82	79	86	86	87	88
문제	17	18	19	20	21	22	23	24	25	26	27	28	29	30	31	32	33
UNIT	85	90	86	84	81	77	82	88	81	77	90	82	86	83	78	89	88

TEST 12 전치사와 구동사 (UNIT 91-104)

 그림을 보고 주어진 장소와 at/in/on을 사용하여 문장을 완성하세요.

| ~~a bench~~ | school | the 4th floor | the phone booth | work |

1. They are sitting *on a bench* .
2. They are _____.
3. The hair salon is _____.
4. The students are _____.
5. He is _____.

 주어진 표현들을 사용하여 문장을 완성하세요.

| behind | by | down | for | from | in | ~~next to~~ | to |

6. Is city hall near here? (that building) It's right *next to that building* .
7. When can you return my book? (this Friday) I'll return it _____.
8. How long have you known Tim? (five years) _____.
9. When does the movie start? (10 minutes) It starts _____.
10. Are you Chinese? (Korea) No, I'm _____.
11. Where are you going for vacation? (Germany) I'm going _____.
12. Where is Scott? (the curtains) He's hiding _____.
13. Is there a bathroom on this floor? (the stairs) No. It's _____.

 괄호 안에 주어진 단어들을 적절히 배열하여 문장을 완성하세요.

14. (drinking / without / water)
    Kate is very thirsty. She ran for three hours *without drinking water* .

15. (off / their / turn / cell phones)
    The play is going to start soon. Everyone should _____.

16. (about / the trip / excited)
    We're going to Disneyland next week. We're very _____.

17. (spends / on / unnecessary things / money)
    Robert likes to save money. He never _____.

18. (will / off / I / them / take)
    "Why are you wearing my shoes?" "I thought these are mine. _____."

보기 중 맞는 것을 고르세요.

19. "Where is your brother?" "He's standing _____ Colin and Ian."
    a) among   b) between   c) under

20. "Do you know where the parking lot is?" "It's _____ the white building."
    a) behind   b) from   c) to

21. "Thank you _____ me home last night." "No problem."
    a) for drive   b) for driving   c) for drive to

22. "Should we get _____ the bus at this stop?" "I'm not sure. Let me ask the driver."
    a) off   b) down   c) around

23. I finished fixing your computer. You can _____ now.
    a) switch on it b) switch it on   c) it switch on

24. "Where were you _____ 3 o'clock yesterday?" "I was at the shopping mall with Jake."
    a) in   b) on   c) at

25. The guests are coming soon. We need to finish cleaning the house _____ 20 minutes.
    a) within   b) during   c) at

26. "Are you good _____ swimming?" "No. What about you?"
    a) in   b) of   c) at

27. I went to school _____ my pencil case yesterday. I had to borrow a pen.
    a) with   b) by   c) without

28. "This question is so difficult." "How _____ Ms. Brown for help?"
    a) about ask   b) about to ask   c) about asking

29. "Don't go _____ the water. It's too cold." "OK, Dad."
    a) past   b) up   c) into

30. The theater is famous _____ its comfortable seats, but the tickets are too expensive.
    a) at   b) for   c) to

31. "I might be late for our appointment." "OK. I'll wait _____ 8 p.m."
    a) by   b) during   c) until

32. "What is Jennifer doing?" "She's talking _____ Mr. Silver."
    a) for   b) to   c) at

33. "The music is too loud. Could you _____?" "OK."
    a) turn it down b) turn down it   c) it turn down

정답 p.202

틀리거나 확실하지 않은 문제는 아래의 표를 확인하여 해당 UNIT으로 돌아가 복습하세요.

문제	1	2	3	4	5	6	7	8	9	10	11	12	13	14	15	16
UNIT	91	92	92	92	91	93	99	98	98	95	95	93	95	101	104	102
17	18	19	20	21	22	23	24	25	26	27	28	29	30	31	32	33
103	104	94	93	101	96	104	97	98	102	100	101	95	102	99	103	104

CHECK-UP TEST 12 | 157

TEST 13   접속사와 절 (UNIT 105-114)

 괄호 안에 주어진 표현과 and/but/or/so/because를 사용하여 문장을 완성하세요.

1. (they went to a café) Chris and Judy saw a movie, _and they went to a café_.
2. (should we take a bus) Do you want to drive, _____?
3. (I drank too much wine last night) I feel sick today _____.
4. (she couldn't come) Matt invited Cindy to his house, _____.
5. (she took some medicine) Christina had a headache, _____.

 괄호 안에 주어진 단어들을 적절히 배열하여 문장을 완성하세요. 현재 시제 또는 과거 시제로 쓰세요.

6. (sunny / if / it / be)
   If it is sunny OR _If it's sunny_ today, Ben will wash his car.
7. (work / finish / I / if)
   "Are you coming to the party tonight?" "I'll go _____ early."
8. (I / you / be / if)
   "My tooth hurts too much." "I'd see a dentist _____."
9. (she / since / leave / the company)
   I haven't seen Amanda _____.
10. (Martin / it / open / when)
    "What happened to our front door?" "It broke _____."
11. (while / she / on vacation / be)
    Rachel is going to stay at a resort _____ next month.

 그림을 보고 who 또는 which를 사용하여 문장을 완성하세요.

This hat cost $120 dollars.

She was on TV last night.

I met him during the trip.

Ted's dad built that house.

12. She is wearing a hat _which cost $120_.
13. He's pointing at the woman _____.
14. He's the man _____.
15. They're standing in front of a house _____.

GRAMMAR GATEWAY BASIC

> 보기 중 맞는 것을 고르세요.

16. On weekends, Evan goes to the library _____ reads some magazines.
    a) and   b) because   c) so

17. My new computer is expensive, _____ it's not very fast.
    a) so   b) but   c) while

18. "Why are you late?" "It was rush hour, _____ there were a lot of cars on the road."
    a) but   b) or   c) so

19. The girl _____ the race is my sister. I'm so proud of her.
    a) who she won   b) which won   c) who won

20. _____ I woke up, someone was knocking on the door.
    a) While   b) When   c) Since

21. Marvin is going to call Susie _____ work today.
    a) when he will finish   b) when he finish   c) when he finishes

22. He's the man _____ at Sophie's shop last week.
    a) that saw   b) which I saw   c) I saw

23. "Dad, will you buy me a new phone _____ a high score on my next exam?" "Yes, of course."
    a) if I get   b) if I'll get   c) if I got

24. _____ you if you don't finish cleaning the kitchen by noon.
    a) I help   b) I'll help   c) I would help

25. Nick _____ his friend's wedding if he weren't on a business trip.
    a) will attend   b) would attend   c) attends

26. Please turn down the music. I can't sleep _____ the noise.
    a) and   b) because   c) because of

27. Bill wanted to eat at a restaurant _____ Mexican food, but he couldn't find one.
    a) served   b) who served   c) that served

28. My uncle has taught English at this school _____ he was 25 years old.
    a) since   b) while   c) when

29. The picture _____ is great. I'll hang it on the wall in my living room.
    a) which drew   b) you drew   c) who you drew

30. You should brush your teeth _____ you go to bed.
    a) before   b) after   c) since

정답 p.203

틀리거나 확실하지 않은 문제는 아래의 표를 확인하여 해당 UNIT으로 돌아가 복습하세요.

문제	1	2	3	4	5	6	7	8	9	10	11	12	13	14	15	16
UNIT	105	105	106	105	106	110	110	111	109	107	107	113	113	114	114	105
17	18	19	20	21	22	23	24	25	26	27	28	29	30		
105	106	113	107	107	114	110	110	111	106	113	109	114	108		

CHECK-UP TEST 13 | 159

TEST 14 다양한 문장들 (UNIT 115-120)

 그림을 보고 주어진 명사와 there is a 또는 there are two/three…를 사용하여 문장을 완성하세요. 필요한 경우 명사를 복수로 쓰세요.

bird   boy   glass   table   ~~woman~~

1. _There is a woman_ _____ on the chair.
2. _____ in the tree.
3. _____ under the tree.
4. _____ on the table.
5. _____ in the water.

 괄호 안에 주어진 단어들을 적절히 배열하여 문장을 완성하세요.

6. (me / that pencil / give)
   "Could you _give me that pencil_____?" "Sure. Here you are."
7. (wanted / he / told / me)
   Mark _____ to go to the beach yesterday. Did he go?
8. (not / dinner / let's / cook)
   _____ tonight. I want to go to the Italian restaurant downtown.
9. (said / she / sleeping / that / was)
   Julia _____ when I called her.
10. (some cookies / you / I / for / made)
    "_____." "Great! Thank you."

 too/either/so/neither를 사용하여 대화를 완성하세요.

11. I love classical music. | Ian does _too_____.
12. I haven't been to Japan before. | I haven't been there _____.
13. We'll visit our parents on Christmas. | _____ will Sarah and I.
14. Kim doesn't like beer. | I don't like it _____. I prefer wine.
15. We've just had lunch. | _____ have we. Let's get some tea.
16. I wasn't good at math when I was young. | _____ was my son.
17. I didn't enjoy the movie. | _____ did I. It was boring.
18. Melvin and I watched the soccer game yesterday. | Really? I did _____.

보기 중 맞는 것을 고르세요.

19. _____ some juice in the fridge. You can drink it.
    a) There are   b) There's   c) There isn't

20. I _____ from Boston. Did you get it?
    a) sent a postcard you   b) sent you to a postcard   c) sent you a postcard

21. Ms. Kim _____ hungry, so I made her a sandwich.
    a) told me she was   b) told me she is   c) told she was

22. "_____ many people at Molly's party?" "Yes. I had a good time with them."
    a) Were there   b) Was there   c) Is there

23. Cathy will _____. Tomorrow is his birthday.
    a) buy a cake to her father   b) buy a cake her father   c) buy a cake for her father

24. Sharon likes sushi, and her husband does _____.
    a) either   b) too   c) so

25. _____! Sue looks very cute in it.
    a) This picture look   b) This picture look at   c) Look at this picture

26. Tom said you speak Chinese well. Could you _____?
    a) teach Chinese to me   b) Chinese teach me   c) teach Chinese me

27. "I can't cook very well." "_____."
    a) I can either   b) Neither can I   c) Neither I can

28. I'm worried about Mike. He _____ a cold.
    a) he has said   b) had he said   c) said he had

29. _____ the pot! It's still hot.
    a) Do touch   b) Don't touch   c) Not touch

30. Lynn _____ to her house last night, but I was too busy.
    a) said I can come   b) said I could come   c) say I could come

31. "_____ a break." "OK. Let's sit on that bench for a minute."
    a) Let's take   b) Let's taking   c) Let's not take

32. _____ any onions in the grocery store, so I couldn't make onion soup.
    a) There were   b) There weren't   c) There wasn't

33. Steve _____ the meeting was canceled, so I stayed home.
    a) said me   b) told to me   c) told me

틀리거나 확실하지 않은 문제는 아래의 표를 확인하여 해당 UNIT으로 돌아가 복습하세요.

문제	1	2	3	4	5	6	7	8	9	10	11	12	13	14	15	16
UNIT	115	115	115	115	115	116	118	117	118	116	119	119	120	119	120	120
17	18	19	20	21	22	23	24	25	26	27	28	29	30	31	32	33
120	119	115	116	118	115	116	119	117	116	120	118	117	118	117	115	118

GRAMMAR GATEWAY BASIC

www.Hackers.co.kr

부록

영어 공부에 도움이 될 기본적인 사항들과 앞 UNIT에서 다룬 내용 중 추가 설명이 필요한 부분을 부록에 담았습니다.
그럼 같이 시작해볼까요? Let's start!

1 품사와 문장 성분

2 불규칙 동사

3 주의해야 할 형태 변화

4 축약형

5 주의해야 할 명사와 the 용법

6 알아두면 유용한 형용사 + 전치사 표현

7 알아두면 유용한 동사 표현

1. 품사와 문장 성분

기초가 탄탄해야 높은 탑을 쌓을 수 있겠죠? 영어 문장의 기초를 잘 익혀두면 영어를 쉽게 이해할 수 있답니다. 그럼 영어에서 품사는 무엇인지, 문장을 구성하는 성분들은 무엇인지 알아볼까요?

A. 영어의 8가지 품사

명사 우리 주위 모든 것의 이름

girl   desk   love   music

세상의 모든 것에는 이름이 있습니다. **girl, desk**처럼 눈에 보이는 것을 부르는 이름도 있고, **love, music**처럼 눈에 보이지 않는 것을 부르는 이름도 있습니다. 이와 같이 우리 주위의 모든 것에 붙여진 이름을 **명사**라고 합니다.

대명사 명사를 대신하는 말

Jack is my brother. **He** is a doctor.
대명사

위의 문장에서 **He**는 앞에 나온 명사인 **Jack**을 반복하지 않고 대신해서 말하기 위해 썼습니다. 이와 같이 같은 명사를 반복하지 않고 대신해서 쓰는 말을 **대명사**라고 합니다.

동사 동작이나 상태를 나타내는 말

She **plays** the piano.
동사

She **likes** music.
동사

위의 문장에서 **plays**(연주하다)와 **likes**(좋아하다)는 '(누가) 무엇을 하는지' 또는 '(누가) 어떠한지'를 말하기 위해 썼습니다. 이와 같이 사람이나 사물의 동작이나 상태를 나타내는 말을 **동사**라고 합니다.

형용사 명사를 꾸며주는 말

It's a **red** car.
형용사

위의 문장에서 **red**는 명사 **car**를 꾸며서 어떤 차인지 그 특징을 말하기 위해 썼습니다. 이와 같이 명사의 상태 또는 특징을 나타내는 말을 **형용사**라고 합니다.

부사 동사, 형용사, 부사 또는 문장 전체를 꾸며주는 말

It runs **fast**.
부사

위의 문장에서 **fast**는 동사 **runs**를 꾸며서 치타가 어떻게 달리고 있는지 말하기 위해 썼습니다. 이와 같이 동사, 형용사, 부사 또는 문장 전체를 꾸며서 그 의미를 더욱 자세하게 나타내는 말을 **부사**라고 합니다.

접속사 이어주는 말

She has a dog **and** a cat.
접속사

위의 문장에서 **and**는 **a dog**과 **a cat**을 연결하기 위해 썼습니다. 이와 같이 두 가지 이상의 대상을 연결하는 말을 **접속사**라고 합니다.

전치사 명사나 대명사 앞에 쓰는 말

The telephone is **on** the table.
전치사

위의 문장에서 **on**은 '테이블 위'라는 위치를 나타내기 위해 썼습니다. 이와 같이 명사나 대명사 앞에 쓰여서 위치·장소·시간 등을 나타내는 말을 **전치사**라고 합니다.

감탄사 감정을 나타낼 때 쓰는 말

Wow!
감탄사

위의 **Wow**와 같이 기쁠 때, 놀랐을 때, 화났을 때처럼 자기도 모르게 입에서 자연스럽게 나오는 말을 **감탄사**라고 합니다.

B. 영어의 문장 성분

주어와 동사

She runs. 그녀는 달린다.
주어 동사

영어 문장에는 주어와 동사가 꼭 필요합니다. **주어**는 어떤 행동이나 상태의 주체가 되는 말로 우리말의 '누가' 또는 '무엇이'에 해당합니다. **동사**는 행동이나 상태를 나타내는 말로 우리말의 '~하다, ~이다'에 해당합니다. 위의 문장에서 **주어**는 **She**이고, **동사**는 **runs**입니다.

목적어

He plays the guitar. 그는 기타를 친다.
주어 동사   목적어

She runs와 같이 주어와 동사만으로 완전한 문장이 되는 경우도 있지만, He plays the guitar처럼 목적어를 필요로 하는 문장도 있습니다. **목적어**는 동사가 나타내는 행동의 대상이 되는 말로 우리말의 '~을/를'에 해당합니다. 위의 문장에서 그가 무엇을 연주하는지 말하기 위해 He plays 다음에 **목적어 the guitar**를 썼습니다.

보어

He is tired. 그는 피곤하다.
주어 동사 보어

He is tired와 같이 보어를 필요로 하는 문장도 있습니다. **보어**는 주어나 목적어의 성질 또는 상태 등을 보충 설명해 주는 말입니다. 위의 문장에서 그가 어떠한 상태인지를 보충 설명히기 위해 He is 다음에 **보어 tired**를 썼습니다.

수식어

She swims every weekend. 그녀는 주말마다 수영을 한다.
주어 동사   수식어

문장을 구성하는 요소에는 주어, 동사, 목적어, 보어와 같은 필수 요소 외에 수식어도 있습니다. 위의 문장은 She swims만으로도 문장이 성립되지만, **every weekend**를 써서 언제 수영을 하는지 더 자세하게 나타내고 있습니다. 이와 같이 문장을 구성할 때 없어도 되는 부가적인 요소이지만, 다른 요소를 꾸며주어 문장을 더 풍부하게 하는 말을 **수식어**라고 합니다.

2. 불규칙 동사 (UNIT 15, 20, 37)

영어에는 시제에 따라 형태가 불규칙하게 변하는 동사들도 있답니다. 자, 소리 내어 반복해 읽으면서 익혀볼까요?

현재	과거	과거분사	현재	과거	과거분사
am/is/are (be동사)	was/were	been	eat	ate	eaten
awake	awoke	awoken	fall	fell	fallen
beat	beat	beaten	feel	felt	felt
become	became	become	fight	fought	fought
begin	began	begun	find	found	found
bite	bit	bitten	fly	flew	flown
blow	blew	blown	forget	forgot	forgotten
break	broke	broken	forgive	forgave	forgiven
bring	brought	brought	get	got	got/gotten
build	built	built	give	gave	given
burn	burned/burnt	burned/burnt	go	went	gone
buy	bought	bought	grow	grew	grown
catch	caught	caught	hang	hung	hung
choose	chose	chosen	have	had	had
come	came	come	hear	heard	heard
cost	cost	cost	hide	hid	hidden
cut	cut	cut	hit	hit	hit
do	did	done	hold	held	held
draw	drew	drawn	hurt	hurt	hurt
dream	dreamed/dreamt	dreamed/dreamt	keep	kept	kept
drink	drank	drunk	know	knew	known
drive	drove	driven	lay	laid	laid

현재	과거	과거분사
lead	led	led
learn	learned/learnt	learned/learnt
leave	left	left
lend	lent	lent
let	let	let
lie 눕다	lay	lain
light	lit	lit
lose	lost	lost
make	made	made
mean	meant	meant
meet	met	met
pay	paid	paid
put	put	put
quit	quit	quit
read [riːd]	read [red]	read [red]
ride	rode	ridden
ring	rang	rung
rise	rose	risen
run	ran	run
say	said	said
see	saw	seen
sell	sold	sold
send	sent	sent
set	set	set

현재	과거	과거분사
shine	shone	shone
shoot	shot	shot
show	showed	shown/showed
shut	shut	shut
sing	sang	sung
sit	sat	sat
sleep	slept	slept
speak	spoke	spoken
spend	spent	spent
stand	stood	stood
steal	stole	stolen
swim	swam	swum
take	took	taken
teach	taught	taught
tear	tore	torn
tell	told	told
think	thought	thought
throw	threw	thrown
understand	understood	understood
upset	upset	upset
wake	woke	woken
wear	wore	worn
win	won	won
write	wrote	written

3. 주의해야 할 형태 변화 (UNIT 4, 7, 15, 20, 37, 46, 54, 78, 86, 88)

 영어의 동사, 명사, 형용사, 부사는 경우에 따라 형태가 변합니다. 복잡하게 느껴지지만, 규칙을 알면 조금도 어렵지 않답니다. 그럼 영어 단어의 형태 변화 규칙을 익혀 볼까요?

A. 동사의 형태 변화

동사에 -(e)s를 붙일 때 (현재 시제에서 주어가 he/she/it 등인 경우)

+ -s	bring → brings make → makes sleep → sleeps	eat → eats sing → sings meet → meets	walk → walks drink → drinks live → lives
-ss/-sh/-ch/-x + -es	pass → passes miss → misses kiss → kisses wash → washes wish → wishes	finish → finishes brush → brushes watch → watches catch → catches teach → teaches	reach → reaches search → searches fix → fixes mix → mixes relax → relaxes
-o + -es	go → goes	do → does	
자음 + y → y를 i로 바꾸고 + -es	study → studies carry → carries worry → worries reply → replies	copy → copies marry → marries bury → buries fly → flies	cry → cries hurry → hurries apply → applies try → tries
모음 + y → + -s	play → plays say → says	stay → stays pay → pays	buy → buys enjoy → enjoys

동사에 -ing를 붙일 때

+ -ing	go → going	be → being	know → knowing
-e → e를 빼고 + -ing	come → coming dance → dancing have → having make → making write → writing	take → taking leave → leaving live → living ride → riding shine → shining	smile → smiling prepare → preparing give → giving choose → choosing drive → driving
-ee + -ing	agree → agreeing	see → seeing	
-ie → ie를 y로 바꾸고 + -ing	die → dying	lie → lying	tie → tying
단모음 + 단자음으로 끝날 때 → 자음 한 번 더 쓰고 + -ing	run → running sit → sitting cut → cutting set → setting	put → putting hit → hitting stop → stopping swim → swimming	plan → planning shop → shopping begin → beginning refer → referring

동사에 -(e)d를 붙일 때

+ -ed	answer → answered want → wanted	help → helped watch → watched	clean → cleaned work → worked
-e/-ee/-ie + -d	create → created believe → believed	agree → agreed die → died	tie → tied lie → lied
자음 + y → y를 i로 바꾸고 + -ed	try → tried study → studied	cry → cried rely → relied	marry → married apply → applied
모음 + y → + -ed	enjoy → enjoyed	delay → delayed	play → played
단모음 + 단자음으로 끝날 때 → 자음 한 번 더 쓰고 + -ed	prefer → preferred	stop → stopped	plan → planned

B. 명사의 형태 변화

명사에 -(e)s를 붙일 때 (명사의 복수형)

+ -s	hat → hats flower → flowers	dog → dogs girl → girls	book → books tree → trees
-s/-ss/-sh/-ch/-x + -es	bus → buses glass → glasses	dish → dishes brush → brushes	sandwich → sandwiches box → boxes
-f(e) → f를 v로 바꾸고 + -es	shelf → shelves leaf → leaves	wolf → wolves wife → wives	knife → knives life → lives
자음 + y → y를 i로 바꾸고 + -es	baby → babies city → cities	lady → ladies family → families	berry → berries story → stories
자음 + o → + -es	potato → potatoes 예외) kilo → kilos	tomato → tomatoes piano → pianos	hero → heroes photo → photos
모음 + y → + -s	boy → boys	day → days	monkey → monkeys

C. 형용사/부사의 형태 변화

형용사에 -ly를 붙여 부사로 만들 때

+ -ly	careful → carefully	quick → quickly	slow → slowly
-y → y를 i로 바꾸고 + -ly	angry → angrily lazy → lazily	noisy → noisily busy → busily	sleepy → sleepily lucky → luckily
-le → -ly	probable → probably	incredible → incredibly	

형용사/부사에 -(e)r을 붙여 비교급을 만들 때

1음절* 형용사/부사 + -er	fast → faster	cheap → cheaper	high → higher
1음절* 형용사/부사가 e로 끝날 때 → + -r	nice → nicer	close → closer	wide → wider
1음절* 형용사/부사가 단모음 + 단자음으로 끝날 때 → 자음 한 번 더 쓰고 + -er	big → bigger	hot → hotter	thin → thinner
2음절* 이상 형용사/부사가 y로 끝날 때 → y를 i로 바꾸고 + -er	easy → easier early → earlier	heavy → heavier happy → happier	hungry → hungrier pretty → prettier

* 영어의 음절은 소리 나는 모음의 개수를 단위로 구분합니다. 소리 나는 모음이 1개이면 1음절, 2개이면 2음절이 됩니다. 즉, 단어의 모음 개수가 아니라 '소리 나는 모음의 개수'에 따라 음절을 구분한다는 점에 주의해야 합니다. 예를 들어, cheap은 모음이 e, a로 두 개이지만, 발음은 [tʃiːp]으로 소리 나는 모음이 iː 하나이기 때문에 1음절의 단어입니다. beautiful 역시 모음이 e, a, u, i, u로 다섯 개이지만, 발음은 [bjúːtəfəl]로 소리 나는 모음이 úː, ə, ə로 세 개이기 때문에 3음절의 단어입니다.

형용사/부사 앞에 more를 써서 비교급을 만들 때

more + 2음절 이상 형용사/부사	beautiful → more beautiful	recently → more recently

형용사/부사에 the + -(e)st를 붙여 최상급을 만들 때

1음절 형용사/부사 + -est	fast → the fastest	cheap → the cheapest	high → the highest
1음절 형용사/부사가 e로 끝날 때 → + -st	nice → the nicest	close → the closest	wide → the widest
1음절 형용사/부사가 단모음 + 단자음으로 끝날 때 → 자음 한 번 더 쓰고 + -est	big → the biggest	hot → the hottest	thin → the thinnest
2음절 이상 형용사/부사가 y로 끝날 때 → y를 i로 바꾸고 + -est	easy → the easiest early → the earliest	heavy → the heaviest happy → the happiest	hungry → the hungriest pretty → the prettiest

형용사/부사 앞에 the most를 써서 최상급을 만들 때

most + 2음절 이상 형용사/부사	beautiful → the most beautiful	recently → the most recently

4. 축약형 (UNIT 1, 2, 9, 14, 16, 20, 25)

일상 대화에서는 I am, she is 등을 I'm, she's 등과 같이 동사를 짧게 줄여서 자주 쓰는데, 이를 축약형이라고 합니다. 그럼 축약형을 함께 익혀볼까요?

A. 축약형의 형태

	be (am/is/are)	have (have/has)	will	would
I	I'm	I've	I'll	I'd
he	he's	he's	he'll	he'd
she	she's	she's	she'll	she'd
it	it's	it's	it'll	–
we	we're	we've	we'll	we'd
you	you're	you've	you'll	you'd
they	they're	they've	they'll	they'd

B. 부정어의 축약형

be	do	have	will, would 등
is not → **isn't** are not → **aren't** was not → **wasn't** were not → **weren't**	do not → **don't** does not → **doesn't** did not → **didn't**	have not → **haven't** has not → **hasn't**	will not → **won't** would not → **wouldn't** cannot → **can't** could not → **couldn't** should not → **shouldn't** must not → **mustn't**

C. 주의해야 할 축약형

is 또는 **has** → **'s**

- "Where is David?" "He**'s** in the garage. He**'s** fixing his car." (= He is in the garage. He is fixing his car.)
- My brother loves traveling. He**'s** been to almost every country in South Asia. (= He has been to ~)

yes를 써서 의문문에 짧게 답할 때는 축약형을 사용하지 않는 것에 주의합니다.

- "Are you Mr. Jones?" "Yes, **I am**." (Yes, I'm.으로 쓸 수 없음)
- "Is he a professor?" "Yes, **he is**." (Yes, he's.로 쓸 수 없음)

5. 주의해야 할 명사와 the 용법 (UNIT 53, 59)

어떤 명사들은 셀 수 있을것 같지만 셀 수 없기도 하고, the와 함께 쓰거나 함께 쓰지 않기도 합니다. 그럼, 셀 수 없는 명사들과 the를 쓰거나 쓰지 않는 명사들을 소리 내어 읽으면서 자신의 것으로 만들어 보세요.

A. 셀 수 있을 것 같지만 셀 수 없는 명사

bread	cheese	chocolate	food	fruit	meat
paper	money	wood	furniture	luggage	ice
information	advice	news	work	cash	

- "Do you want some **bread**?" "Yes, please."
- We need to order some **paper**. We don't have any for the copy machine.
- I asked Tony for **information** about the seminar.

B. the를 쓰지 않는 장소 표현

home	go home	(be) at home		
work	go to work	(be) at work	start work	finish work
school	go to school	(be) at school	start school	finish school
college	go to college	(be) in college		
bed	go to bed	(be) in bed		
church	go to church	(be) in church	(be) at church	
prison	go to prison	(be) in prison		

- Ms. Smith was very sick, so she had to **go home** early.
- Please call me after 3 p.m. I won't **be at work** until then.
- "When did your child **start school**?" "Last September."
- I **was in college** two years ago. I graduated last year.
- "I'm getting sleepy. I think I'll **go to bed**." "OK. Good night."
- The Morgans **are at church** now. They will come back in an hour.

C. the를 쓰거나 쓰지 않는 이름

the를 항상 함께 쓰는 이름

대양·바다 이름	the Pacific	the Atlantic	the Black Sea	the Mediterranean Sea
강 이름	the Amazon	the Nile	the Thames	the Mississippi River

- **The Mediterranean Sea** is north of Africa.
- **The Amazon** is the second longest river in the world.

the를 쓰지 않는 이름

산 이름	Mount Fuji　　Mount Everest　　Mount Seorak　　Mount St. Helens 예외) 산맥 이름에는 **the**를 씀 　　**the** Himalayas　**the** Alps　**the** Andes　**the** Rocky Mountains
호수 이름	Lake Michigan　　Lake Victoria　　Lake Superior　　Lake Titicaca
대륙 이름	Asia　　　　　Africa　　　　　Europe　　　　North/South America Australia　　　Antarctica
나라 이름	Italy　　　　　France　　　　Korea　　　　　Germany 예외) 연합국·공화국 이름에는 **the**를 씀 　　**the** United States of America　**the** United Kingdom　**the** Czech Republic

- **Mount Fuji** is the highest mountain in Japan.
- I want to take a trip to **the Himalayas**.
- My family visited **Lake Michigan** during our vacation.
- People in **Asia** eat a lot of rice.
- "How long does it take to fly to **Italy**?" "I can check for you."
- Washington DC is the capital of **the United States of America**.

6. 알아두면 유용한 형용사 + 전치사 표현 (UNIT 102)

 영어에서는 sorry about, good at 등과 같이 형용사와 전치사로 이루어진 표현들이 자주 쓰여요. 자, 그럼 소리 내어 반복해 읽으면서 익혀볼까요?

about	**angry about** ~에 대해 화가 난 • Mr. Meyer is **angry about** the mistakes in the report.	
	excited about ~에 대해 흥분한 • Brian is **excited about** the football game today.	
	nervous about ~에 대해 긴장되는 • "Are you **nervous about** your first day at work?" "Not really."	
	sad about ~에 대해 슬퍼하는 • Kristy is **sad about** moving. She'll miss her friends.	
	sorry about ~에 대해 미안한 • I'm **sorry about** being late. It won't happen again.	
	sure about ~에 대해 확신하는 • I asked how much the car was, but the salesman wasn't **sure about** the price.	
	upset about ~에 대해 화가 난 • We had a party, and our neighbors were **upset about** the noise.	
	worried about ~에 대해 걱정하는 • "I'm so **worried about** tomorrow's exam." "I'm sure you will do great."	
at	**angry at** ~에게 화가 난 • I'm **angry at** Betty for losing my cell phone.	
	good at ~을 잘하는 • Christine is really **good at** mathematics.	
	mad at ~에게 화가 난 • My wife is **mad at** me for forgetting our anniversary.	
	surprised at ~에 놀란 • John was **surprised at** his high score on the test.	
for	**bad for** (건강 등)에 나쁜 • Coffee isn't **bad for** your health if you don't drink too much.	
	crazy for ~을 매우 좋아하는 • Monica is **crazy for** romance novels.	
	famous for ~으로 유명한 • This restaurant is **famous for** its pasta.	
from	**different from** ~과 다른 • "How is this apartment **different from** the other one?" "This one has an extra bathroom."	
in	**dressed in** ~을 입은 • Edward is usually **dressed in** a suit at his office.	
	interested in ~에 관심 있는 • I'm **interested in** art, so I often go to galleries.	

of	**afraid of** ~을 무서워하는	
	• You don't have to be **afraid of** my dog. He won't bite.	
	certain of ~을 확신하는	
	• Erica loves me. I'm **certain of** it.	
	full of ~으로 가득 찬	
	• "Why is the store **full of** people?" "There's a sale today."	
	jealous of ~을 질투하는	
	• A lot of people are **jealous of** Kenny because he's so popular.	
	proud of ~을 자랑스럽게 여기는	
	• My sister won a prize. I am very **proud of** her.	
	sick of ~에 싫증이 난	
	• I'm **sick of** eating the same thing every day. Let's try a new restaurant.	
	tired of ~에 질린	
	• Brent was **tired of** waiting for his friend, so he went home.	
to	**clear to** ~에게 분명한	
	• The instructions for my new camera aren't **clear to** me.	
	identical to ~과 똑같은	
	• "What do you think of my new laptop?" "It looks **identical to** Jeremy's."	
	married to ~와 결혼한	
	• Jeff has been **married to** his wife for six years.	
	nice to ~에게 잘해주는	
	• Matt, you should be **nice to** your younger sister.	
	similar to ~과 비슷한	
	• Your shoes look **similar to** mine.	
with	**angry with** ~에게 화가 난	
	• I'm sorry I broke your glasses. Please don't be **angry with** me.	
	busy with ~으로 바쁜	
	• Brenda had to quit the softball team. She was too **busy with** work.	
	careful with ~을 조심하는	
	• Be **careful with** that plate. It's hot.	
	familiar with ~에 익숙한	
	• I'm **familiar with** this neighborhood. I've lived here for a long time.	
	happy with ~에 대해 행복해하는	
	• Thomas is very **happy with** his new bicycle.	
	pleased with ~에 대해 기뻐하는	
	• "Are you **pleased with** your birthday gifts?" "Yes! I love them."	
	wrong with ~에 문제가 있는	
	• What's **wrong with** the TV? It doesn't work.	

7. 알아두면 유용한 동사 표현 (UNIT 103, 104)

 영어에서는 talk about, look at 등과 같이 두 단어로 이루어진 동사 표현들이 자주 쓰여요. 자, 그럼 소리 내어 반복해 읽으면서 익혀볼까요?

about	**care about** ~에 관심이 있다	
	• I don't **care about** music much.	
	hear about ~에 대해 듣다	
	• "Have you watched the movie *Titan*?" "No, but I **heard about** it from my friend."	
	talk about ~에 대해 이야기하다	
	• Everyone was **talking about** Clara's new car.	
	think about ~에 대해 생각하다	
	• Donna **thought about** changing jobs, but she decided to stay.	
	worry about ~에 대해 걱정하다	
	• "I'm sorry I'm late." "Don't **worry about** it. I didn't wait long."	
at	**arrive at** ~에 도착하다	
	• We **arrived at** the station on time.	
	laugh at ~을 듣고 웃다, ~을 비웃다	
	• I **laughed at** my friend's funny story.	
	look at ~을 보다	
	• The visitors are **looking at** paintings in the gallery.	
	smile at ~에게 미소 짓다	
	• Look! The baby is **smiling at** us.	
around	**go around** ~을 돌아가다	
	• **Go around** the corner and you'll see the bank.	
	look around (~을) 둘러보다, (~을) 구경하다	
	• "How can I help you?" "I'm just **looking around**."	
	pass around (물건 등)을 돌리다	
	• Andy, could you **pass around** the snacks to the guests?	
	show around ~을 둘러보도록 안내하다	
	• Could you **show** me **around** the city?	
	take around ~을 데리고 다니다, ~을 산책시키다	
	• Follow me, and I will **take** you **around** the museum.	
	turn around 회전하다, 뒤돌아보다	
	• We're driving the wrong way! We have to **turn around**.	
away	**go away** 떠나다, 사라지다	
	• I want to **go away** for my vacation.	
	keep away ~을 피하다, ~을 가까이하지 않다	
	• Please **keep away** from that wall. The paint is still wet.	
	pass away 돌아가시다, 사망하다	
	• My grandmother **passed away** last year.	

	put away ~을 치우다	
	• Could you **put away** your books?	
	run away 도망가다	
	• The dog jumped over the fence and **ran away**.	
	throw away ~을 버리다	
	• I **threw away** my old furniture before I moved here.	
back	**come back** 돌아오다	
	• "When will you **come back**?" "In two hours."	
	get back 돌아가다, 물러나다	
	• We **got back** from our trip to Rome this morning.	
	go back 되돌아가다	
	• Can we **go back** home to get my bag?	
	look back 뒤돌아보다, (~을) 회상하다	
	• I **looked back**, but nobody was there.	
	pay back ~에게 돈을 갚다	
	• Can I borrow $50? I can **pay** you **back** tomorrow.	
	take back ~을 반품하다, ~을 되찾다	
	• This laptop isn't working. I'm going to **take** it **back** to the store.	
	turn back 돌아오다, ~을 되돌리다	
	• The traffic was bad, so we had to **turn back**.	
down	**break down** (자동차·기계 등이) 고장 나다, 분해하다	
	• The photocopier **broke down**, so I couldn't copy the report.	
	calm down 진정하다, 가라앉히다	
	• Ms. Ling told her children to **calm down** and be quiet.	
	fall down 넘어지다	
	• Thomas **fell down** and hurt his leg.	
	lie down 눕다	
	• I'm not feeling well. I'm going to **lie down** for an hour.	
	look down 내려다보다	
	• **Look down** there! There are ducks under the bridge.	
	pass down ~을 물려주다	
	• My older sister's clothes were **passed down** to me.	
	put down ~을 내려놓다, ~을 적어놓다	
	• **Put down** that vase! You will break it.	
	shut down ~을 끄다, ~을 닫다	
	• Make sure to **shut down** the computer before you leave.	
	slow down 속도를 줄이다	
	• You need to **slow down**. You're driving too fast.	
	sit down 앉다	
	• Please **sit down** and wait for a few minutes.	

	take down (주소·전화번호 등을) 적어 놓다	
	• "Did you **take down** the salesman's phone number?" "Yes."	
	turn down (TV·음악 등)의 소리를 줄이다	
	• "Dan, the music is too loud." "Sorry, I'll **turn** it **down**."	
	write down ~을 적다	
	• I'll **write down** some directions for you.	
for	**apply for** ~에 지원하다	
	• Ms. Miller **applied for** the bank job, but she didn't get it.	
	care for ~을 돌보다, ~을 좋아하다	
	• My mom **cares for** me when I'm sick.	
	look for ~을 찾다	
	• "What are you **looking for**?" "My wallet."	
	search for ~을 찾다	
	• I **searched for** my keys all morning, but I couldn't find them.	
	wait for ~을 기다리다	
	• Don't **wait for** me. I'm going to be late.	
	work for ~에 근무하다	
	• Mr. Donald **works for** the restaurant.	
in	**bring in** ~을 들여오다, ~을 가져오다	
	• "It's raining now." "Really? We have to **bring in** the laundry!"	
	check in (숙박·탑승) 수속하다, 체크인하다	
	• Please **check in** at least an hour before your flight.	
	fill in (빈칸 등)을 채우다	
	• You need to **fill in** the blanks with your name and address.	
	get in (택시·승용차 등)에 타다, ~에 들어가다	
	• Hurry up and **get in** the car. It's getting late.	
	hand in (서류 등)을 제출하다	
	• Students must **hand in** their homework after class.	
	stay in (나가지 않고) 안에 머무르다	
	• It was snowing too hard, so we **stayed in**.	
off	**call off** (계획 등)을 취소하다	
	• Derek **called off** the party because he was sick.	
	drop off (사람·짐 등)을 도중에 내려놓다	
	• Can you **drop** me **off** at the mall? I need to buy some clothes.	
	fall off 떨어지다	
	• Cindy **fell off** the bicycle and hurt her knees.	
	get off (버스·기차 등)에서 내리다	
	• Daniel **got off** the train at Central Station.	
	put off ~을 미루다	
	• Mr. Jenkins **put off** the meeting. He changed it to next Monday.	

	switch off (스위치 등을 눌러서) ~을 끄다 • Please **switch off** your phones during the flight.	
	take off (의복)을 벗다, 이륙하다 • Please **take off** your shoes at the front door.	
	turn off (전기 · TV 등)을 끄다, (수도 · 밸브 등)을 잠그다 • Did you **turn off** the heater when you left home?	
on	**carry on** ~을 계속하다 • The teacher told Jenny to be quiet, but she **carried on** talking.	
	get on (버스 · 기차 등)에 타다 • That's our bus. Let's **get on**.	
	go on 계속하다 • "Is my story too long?" "No. It's very interesting. Please **go on**."	
	hold on 기다리다 • "May I speak to Mr. Grey, please?" "**Hold on** and I'll connect you."	
	keep on ~을 계속하다, ~을 유지하다 • "Where's the bank?" "**Keep on** walking straight ahead."	
	put on ~을 입다 • Don't forget to **put on** your coat. It's very cold outside.	
	switch on ~을 켜다 • Don't **switch on** the light. I'm trying to sleep.	
	try on ~을 입어보다 • "Can I **try on** this shirt?" "Sure."	
	turn on ~을 켜다 • Dad **turned on** the TV to watch the news.	
out	**bring out** (상품 등)을 내놓다 • The company will **bring out** a new product next month.	
	eat out 외식하다 • "Shall we **eat out** tonight?" "That sounds good. What about Italian?"	
	find out ~을 알아내다 • Did you **find out** what happened to Sammy?	
	give out ~을 나눠주다 • My parents **give out** gifts every Christmas.	
	go out 나가다, 외출하다 • "What are you doing tonight?" "I'm **going out** with some friends."	
	hand out ~을 나눠주다 • We'll **hand out** the party gifts after the dinner.	
	look out 조심하다, 주의하다 • **Look out**! There's a car coming!	
	put out (불 등)을 끄다 • The men **put out** the fire at the office building.	

	run out 다 써버리다, 다 떨어지다 • We need to go to the gas station. We might **run out** of gas.	
	take out ~을 가져가다, ~을 꺼내다 • Would you **take out** the dishes from the dishwasher?	
	watch out 주의하다, 조심하다 • **Watch out**! There's a bee by your head.	
	work out 운동하다 • Todd **works out** at the gym every evening.	
over	**get over** ~을 극복하다, ~을 넘다 • Andrew **got over** his cold after only two days.	
	go over ~을 복습하다 • Kimberly **went over** her notes before the test.	
	read over ~을 자세히 읽다, ~을 다시 읽다 • We **read over** your report. It's very good.	
	turn over (~을) 뒤집다, (~의) 방향을 바꾸다 • The pancake was cooked on one side, so Judy **turned** it **over**.	
through	**get through** ~을 통과하다, (전화 등으로) 연결되다, ~을 끝내다 • Traffic was bad, and it took 10 minutes to **get through** the tunnel.	
	go through ~을 통과하다, ~을 겪다 • This train **goes through** Boston.	
to	**belong to** ~의 것이다, ~에 속하다 • "Whose car is that?" "It **belongs to** Tim."	
	reply to ~에게 답하다 • I asked Brenda a question, but she didn't **reply to** me.	
	talk to ~에게 말하다, ~와 대화하다 • I **talked to** the neighbors about the noise.	
up	**break up** 헤어지다, 이별하다 • Did you hear? Chad and Lisa **broke up**!	
	bring up (문제 등)을 제기하다, ~을 기르다 • You **brought up** a good point at the meeting.	
	clean up ~을 청소하다 • Marina **cleaned up** the kitchen this morning.	
	get up 일어나다 • When do you usually **get up** in the morning?	
	give up ~을 포기하다 • I want to **give up** smoking soon.	
	grow up 성장하다 • When Timmy **grows up**, he wants to be a singer.	
	hang up (전화를) 끊다 • Randy **hung up** the phone without saying goodbye.	

hurry up 서두르다
- Bob, you need to **hurry up**. The train leaves in 10 minutes.

look up ~을 찾아보다
- "What does this word mean?" "**Look** it **up** in the dictionary."

pick up ~을 집다, ~을 들어올리다
- Joey, please **pick up** your toys. Your room is a mess.

speak up 큰 소리로 말하다
- You need to **speak up**. I can't hear you well.

stand up 일어서다
- At the wedding, everyone **stood up** when the bride entered the room.

stay up 깨어 있다
- I never **stay up** late on weekdays.

turn up (TV · 음악 등)의 소리를 높이다
- I like this song! Could you **turn up** the volume, please?

wake up 잠이 깨다, ~을 깨우다
- Tony, **wake up**! It's time for breakfast.

GRAMMAR GATEWAY BASIC

www.Hackers.co.kr

정답

PRACTICE Answers

CHECK-UP TEST Answers

PRACTICE Answers

UNIT 1

A
2. is a photographer
3. are in their car
4. are on the stage
5. is a repairman

B
2. I'm OR I am
3. the weather is
4. we're OR we are
5. You're OR You are
6. It's OR It is

UNIT 2

A
2. This water isn't OR This water is not
3. you're not OR you aren't OR you are not
4. Mark isn't OR Mark is not
5. We're not OR We aren't OR We are not
6. The exam isn't OR The exam is not
7. she's not OR she isn't OR she is not
8. My books aren't OR My books are not

B
2. 'm not
3. 're
4. aren't
5. 's
6. 'm not
7. 's not OR isn't
8. 're

UNIT 3

A
2. Is it
3. Am I
4. Are you
5. Is today
6. Are Joel and Mary
7. Is she
8. Are we

B
2. No, I'm not
3. No, he's not OR No, he isn't
4. Yes, they are
5. No, it's not OR No, it isn't

UNIT 4

A
2. is playing the violin
3. is entering the bank
4. are flying in the sky
5. is standing at the bus stop

B
2. He's having OR He is having
3. Mitchell is practicing
4. The children are helping
5. They're running OR They are running
6. I'm tying OR I am tying

UNIT 5

A
2. isn't moving OR is not moving
3. 'm not enjoying OR am not enjoying
4. 're not wearing OR aren't wearing OR are not wearing
5. isn't speaking OR is not speaking
6. 're not swimming OR aren't swimming OR are not swimming

B
2. 're not playing soccer OR aren't playing soccer OR are not playing soccer; 's raining OR is raining
3. 's driving OR is driving; 's not talking on the phone OR isn't talking on the phone OR is not talking on the phone

UNIT 6

A
2. Is Glen looking
3. Are you calling
4. Am I talking
5. Are you and Vicky making

6. Is the wind blowing
7. Is Emily wearing
8. Are your brothers riding

B
2. No, she's not OR No, she isn't
3. No, I'm not
4. Yes, they are
5. No, he's not OR No, he isn't
6. Yes, it is

UNIT 7

A
2. calls
3. listens
4. close
5. gets
6. ride
7. costs
8. work

B
2. does
3. has
4. speak
5. play
6. finishes
7. cries
8. buy

UNIT 8

A
2. leaves home
3. starts work
4. goes to lunch
5. finishes work

B
2. need
3. likes
4. sleep
5. plays
6. bakes

UNIT 9

A
2. doesn't understand Chinese OR does not understand Chinese
3. don't look well OR do not look well

4. don't have a lot of homework OR do not have a lot of homework
5. doesn't watch OR does not watch
6. don't make much noise OR do not make much noise
7. doesn't clean OR does not clean
8. doesn't run after midnight OR does not run after midnight

B
2. have
3. remembers
4. don't want OR do not want
5. doesn't like OR does not like

UNIT 10
A
2. Does Ann have a boyfriend
3. Do you read the newspaper
4. Does Jack play any sports
5. Do your parents call you
6. Do you own a bicycle
7. Does the bus usually arrive
8. Do your kids like dogs

B
2. No, you don't
3. No, he doesn't
4. Yes, I do
5. No, she doesn't
6. Yes, they do

UNIT 11
A
2. is riding; works
3. is playing; designs
4. paints; 's sleeping OR is sleeping

B
2. Angela goes
3. I'm looking OR I am looking
4. The post office doesn't deliver OR The post office does not deliver
5. We buy
6. Jason and Frank aren't studying OR Jason and Frank are not studying
7. he's not answering OR he isn't answering OR he is not answering

UNIT 12
A
2. 're swimming OR are swimming
3. spends
4. Do; remember
5. 's attending OR is attending
6. play

B
2. O
3. shop → 're shopping OR are shopping
4. O
5. isn't having → doesn't have OR does not have
6. don't sleep → 'm not sleeping OR am not sleeping

UNIT 13
A
2. The stars were
3. Andy was
4. My friends and I were
5. These gloves were
6. he was
7. It was
8. We were

B
2. was; 'm OR am
3. were
4. was
5. was; Is
6. were
7. are; were
8. was; 's OR is; 's OR is

UNIT 14
A
2. was asleep
3. wasn't on time OR was not on time
4. was angry
5. wasn't happy OR was not happy

B
2. Were you
3. Was Howard
4. They were
5. Was the party
6. My parents were
7. The sky was
8. Were you

UNIT 15
A
2. played
3. invited
4. cried
5. went
6. worked

B
2. It closes
3. Laura and Nick got
4. The Earth travels
5. Everyone laughed
6. I forgot
7. He flies
8. I need

UNIT 16
A
2. She didn't read the newspaper OR She did not read the newspaper
3. She went to the gym
4. She didn't wash the car OR She did not wash the car
5. She attended the cooking class
6. She had dinner with Jackie

B
2. Did Sarah pass
3. Did you read
4. Did someone knock
5. Did you get
6. Did we miss
7. Did Dave grow
8. Did the Smiths buy

UNIT 17
A
2. was eating
3. were waiting

4. were attending
5. were playing
6. was crossing

B

2. Jim and Monica were drinking
3. Alice was lying
4. I was visiting
5. Becky and I were doing
6. The phone was ringing
7. We were standing
8. It was snowing

UNIT 18

A

2. weren't sitting OR were not sitting
3. was carrying
4. were having
5. wasn't wearing OR was not wearing

B

2. Was Victor practicing
3. Eric and I weren't working OR Eric and I were not working
4. We were making
5. Were you walking
6. Nick wasn't riding OR Nick was not riding

UNIT 19

A

2. used to be
3. used to like
4. used to live

B

2. exercises
3. remember
4. used to listen
5. used to go
6. used to ride

UNIT 20

A

2. went; gone
3. stopped; stopped
4. talked; talked

5. ate; eaten
6. played; played
7. wrote; written
8. made; made
9. drove; driven
10. knew; known
11. watched; watched
12. met; met

B

2. haven't eaten OR have not eaten
3. has grown
4. hasn't spoken OR has not spoken
5. 've ridden OR have ridden
6. haven't seen OR have not seen
7. haven't found OR have not found
8. 's attended OR has attended

UNIT 21

A

2. have been married for
3. hasn't rained since OR has not rained since
4. has driven his car for
5. has lost 10 pounds since
6. hasn't eaten anything since OR has not eaten anything since

B

2. How long has he collected
3. How long have they gone
4. How long has she taken
5. How long has he been
6. How long have you had

UNIT 22

A

2. I've (never) played chess before
3. I've (never) lived in the country
4. I've (never) ridden a roller coaster
5. I've (never) seen a kangaroo

B

2. Have you ever watched an opera
3. Have you ever gone skiing
4. Have you ever swum in the ocean
5. Have you ever been to Paris
6. Have you ever run a marathon

UNIT 23

A

2. 's worked OR has worked
3. invented
4. 've studied OR have studied
5. saw
6. has grown

B

2. O
3. has visited → visited
4. knew → 've known OR have known
5. O
6. didn't use → haven't used OR have not used
7. O
8. did you play → have you played

UNIT 24

A

2. 's just dived OR has just dived
3. has just opened
4. 've just met OR have just met

B

2. I haven't found a job yet OR I didn't find a job yet
3. I've already had some OR I already had some
4. Has Lily called you back yet OR Did Lily call you back yet
5. Dave has already finished his painting OR Dave already finished his painting
6. Have you visited him yet OR Did you visit him yet

UNIT 25

A
2. It won't take OR
   It will not take
3. Will you drive
4. I won't wear OR
   I will not wear
5. Will you meet
6. You'll find OR You will find

B
2. 'll explain OR will explain
3. listens
4. 'll love OR will love
5. went
6. snows

UNIT 26

A
2. They're going to get OR
   They are going to get
3. I'm not going to go OR
   I am not going to go
4. Are you going to buy
5. Brian isn't going to join OR
   Brian is not going to join
6. Is Tina going to meet

B
2. 's going to play golf OR
   is going to play golf
3. 're going to have a sale OR
   are going to have a sale
4. 's going to take an exam OR
   is going to take an exam

UNIT 27

A
2. I'll pay
3. We're going to go
4. I'll make
5. We're going to visit
6. She's going to bake

B
2. 're going to walk there OR
   are going to walk there
3. 'll get my coat OR
   will get my coat
4. 're going to buy some snacks
   OR are going to buy some
   snacks

5. 'll buy some wine OR
   will buy some wine

UNIT 28

A
2. 's seeing a movie OR
   is seeing a movie
3. 's taking a swimming lesson
   OR is taking a swimming
   lesson
4. 's visiting her grandparents
   OR is visiting her grandparents
5. 's attending Karen's wedding
   OR is attending Karen's
   wedding
6. 's leaving for Brazil OR
   is leaving for Brazil

B
2. leaves at 2:15
3. arrives at 2:00
4. begins at 9:00

UNIT 29

A
2. Can; talk
3. can eat
4. Can; attend
5. can't lift OR cannot lift
6. can fix

B
2. couldn't see
3. can walk
4. could buy
5. can't remember
6. couldn't cook

UNIT 30

A
2. Can I take this seat
3. Can I have some water
4. Can I close the window

B
2. Could you come to my office
3. Could you sign this form
4. Could you move your car
5. Could you read me another
   story

UNIT 31

A
2. might travel by train
3. might go to Martin's
   wedding
4. might move next month

B
2. might help
3. might not come
4. might try
5. might not fit
6. might not like
7. might invite
8. might not buy

UNIT 32

A
2. must practice
3. must miss
4. must like
5. must hurt
6. must be

B
2. must feel
3. must not sell
4. must not cook
5. must not have
6. must need
7. must read
8. must not understand
9. must know
10. must not allow

UNIT 33

A
2. have to ask
3. has to wear
4. have to use
5. had to stop
6. has to attend

B
2. must
3. had to
4. must
5. had to
6. must
7. had to
8. had to

UNIT 34

A
2. must stop
3. must not smoke
4. must not take
5. must turn off

B
2. must not look
3. don't have to run
4. don't have to bring
5. must not swim
6. must not throw

UNIT 35

A
2. should buy
3. should speak
4. should wash

B
2. Should I change
3. Frank shouldn't smoke
4. We should take
5. Should I stay
6. Children shouldn't watch
7. You should be
8. We shouldn't make

UNIT 36

A
2. Would you like to go shopping
3. Would you like some cookies
4. Would you like a map
5. Would you like to see the menu
6. Would you like to play golf

B
2. I'd like to study biology
3. I'd like a ticket
4. I'd like to invite you
5. I'd like that blue sweater
6. I'd like to visit Europe

UNIT 37

A
2. are packed
3. aren't required OR are not required
4. 's written OR is written
5. aren't used OR are not used
6. isn't collected OR is not collected

B
2. His paintings are displayed
3. it was canceled
4. The road is blocked
5. It was moved
6. These photos were taken

UNIT 38

A
2. were sent
3. hit
4. was grown
5. found

B
2. Many accidents are caused by icy roads
3. Sandra was taught by Professor Kim
4. This place is visited by many tourists
5. Those houses were designed by Michael Smith
6. The television was invented by John Baird

UNIT 39

A
2. haven't been to Venice OR have not been to Venice
3. can't speak French OR cannot speak French
4. weren't studying at 10 o'clock OR were not studying at 10 o'clock
5. hasn't snowed a lot in Vancouver OR has not snowed a lot in Vancouver
6. won't make pizza OR will not make pizza
7. doesn't open on Sundays OR does not open on Sundays
8. didn't have any money OR did not have any money

B
2. wasn't OR was not
3. didn't OR did not
4. isn't OR is not
5. hasn't OR has not
6. doesn't OR does not
7. 'm not OR am not
8. haven't OR have not

UNIT 40

A
2. The cookies are
3. Has Ted done
4. Mitchell lives
5. Did you pass
6. Was Julie sleeping
7. We should take
8. Have you found

B
2. Have
3. Does
4. Did
5. Is
6. Has
7. Were

UNIT 41

A
2. What did John send
3. Who did they visit
4. What did he eat

B
2. What was your major
3. Who did Barry call
4. Who did you see
5. What flavor is that cake
6. Who should I contact

UNIT 42

A
2. Which book
3. Which car
4. Which shirt

B
2. What
3. Which
4. What
5. What
6. Who
7. Which

8. Who

UNIT 43

A
2. Where
3. When
4. Why
5. Where
6. When
7. Why
8. Why

B
2. When will your parents be
3. Where do you live
4. When did he buy
5. Why are you wearing
6. Where is Susan
7. Why is the mall closed
8. When does Ralph leave

UNIT 44

A
2. How are you feeling
3. How do you make
4. How can I turn off
5. How was the concert
6. How is your son doing

B
2. How old
3. How often
4. How much
5. How long
6. How far

UNIT 45

A
2. Do you know where they lived before
3. Do you know why they've come here
4. Do you know what Tony does
5. Do you know how many children they have
6. Do you know what their hobbies are

B
2. if/whether Joey can play the violin
3. if/whether Annie is going to visit us tomorrow
4. if/whether you've seen my brother
5. if/whether many people came to the party
6. if/whether Hannah has gone home

UNIT 46

A
2. Swimming
3. Losing
4. Wearing
5. Driving
6. Eating

B
2. Riding a roller coaster is exciting OR Riding a roller coaster is scary
3. Taking a taxi is cheap OR Taking a taxi is expensive
4. Walking alone at night is safe OR Walking alone at night is dangerous
5. Playing chess is fun OR Playing chess is boring

UNIT 47

A
2. driving
3. reading
4. taking
5. opening
6. solving
7. hitting
8. wearing

B
2. finish packing
3. keep losing
4. mind sharing
5. avoid drinking
6. practice speaking
7. give up teaching
8. suggest getting

UNIT 48

A
2. hope to find
3. choose to become
4. want to watch
5. learn to ride
6. promise to wash

B
2. opening the door
3. cleaning the bathroom
4. to buy this house
5. to play the flute
6. looking at me

UNIT 49

A
2. going
3. feeling OR to feel
4. to join
5. painting
6. fixing
7. to use
8. driving OR to drive

B
2. stop laughing
3. stop to ask
4. Stop worrying
5. stop to buy
6. stop to take

UNIT 50

A
2. want us to have
3. want me to move
4. want you to clean

B
2. allowed Jamie to use the camera
3. told Brian to answer the phone
4. expected David to call back soon
5. wanted Nick to speak louder
6. advised Nancy to go to bed

UNIT 51

A
2. him buy

3. me drive
4. us stay
5. them pay
6. her bake

B

2. help you find OR
   help you to find
3. help you carry OR
   help you to carry
4. help you answer OR
   help you to answer
5. help you wash OR
   help you to wash

UNIT 52

A

2. post office to send a package
3. hospital to visit his friend
4. library to return a book
5. zoo to see the pandas

B

2. place to sit
3. time to visit
4. questions to ask
5. book to read

UNIT 53

A

2. rice
3. music
4. a postcard
5. a computer
6. a pen
7. salt
8. a man
9. milk
10. snow

B

2. butter
3. movie
4. money
5. apples
6. time
7. years
8. song
9. house
10. air

UNIT 54

A

2. feet
3. days
4. photos
5. children
6. shelves
7. brushes
8. tickets
9. potatoes
10. bedrooms
11. parties
12. wives

B

2. a book
3. babies
4. tomatoes
5. an umbrella

UNIT 55

A

2. cookies
3. fish
4. a key
5. sheep
6. babies

B

2. money
3. pajamas
4. scissors
5. glasses
6. sandwiches

C

2. five caps
3. three pairs of jeans
4. four skirts
5. a pair of pajamas

UNIT 56

A

2. two cartons of milk
3. a piece of cake
4. three cans of soda
5. a loaf of bread

B

2. O
3. two box of cereals →
   two boxes of cereal

4. O
5. three deers → three deer
6. a jean → jeans OR
   a pair of jeans
7. 10 scissors → 10 pairs of scissors
8. O
9. table → a table
10. sugars → sugar

UNIT 57

A

2. an
3. a
4. an
5. the
6. The
7. the
8. A

B

2. a question
3. The water
4. a problem
5. the keys
6. a good restaurant
7. an umbrella
8. the mountains

UNIT 58

A

2. the radio
3. golf
4. the moon
5. math

B

2. the ocean
3. history
4. the Internet
5. The government
6. baseball
7. breakfast
8. the world

UNIT 59

A

2. work
3. the station
4. home
5. the bank

6. the theater

B
2. go home
3. go to work
4. go to the movies
5. go to the airport
6. go to the bank

UNIT 60

A
1. me
2. her; She
3. He; him
4. They; them

B
2. It
3. him
4. us
5. you
6. We

UNIT 61

A
2. It's 12:30
3. It's warm
4. it's close
5. It's December 1st

B
2. It
3. they
4. you
5. It
6. We
7. It

UNIT 62

A
2. my bag
3. your key
4. our dog
5. his ball

B
2. Whose glasses; his
3. Whose sandwich; mine
4. Whose pen; yours
5. Whose scarf; hers
6. Whose kids; theirs

UNIT 63

A
2. Laura's husband
3. Our neighbor's garden
4. your brother's boat
5. Richard's voice
6. artists' paintings

B
2. Scott's
3. the Andersons'
4. Lucy's
5. Kevin's

UNIT 64

A
2. that
3. Those
4. this
5. These

B
2. How much are those socks
3. How much is that cake
4. How much are these spoons
5. How much is this perfume
6. How much are those sunglasses

UNIT 65

A
2. ones
3. one
4. one
5. ones

B
2. some black ones
3. a bigger one
4. an important one
5. some chocolate ones
6. some cheap ones

UNIT 66

A
2. any snow
3. some paper
4. any sports
5. any trains
6. some friends

B
2. any
3. some
4. any
5. any
6. some

UNIT 67

A
2. no plans
3. no bread
4. No students
5. no money
6. no tickets

B
2. No
3. none
4. any
5. no
6. any

UNIT 68

A
2. something
3. Someone OR Somebody
4. somewhere

B
2. nowhere
3. someone OR somebody
4. anything
5. anywhere
6. No one OR Nobody
7. nothing

UNIT 69

A
2. There isn't much space
3. There isn't much money
4. There are many students
5. There isn't much bread

B
2. much interest
3. much furniture
4. many cups
5. many dogs
6. much information

UNIT 70

A
2. a lot of money
3. a lot of fun
4. a lot of difficulty
5. a lot of people

B
2. much OR a lot of
3. a lot of
4. a lot of
5. much OR a lot of
6. much OR a lot of
7. a lot of
8. much OR a lot of

UNIT 71

A
2. a little water
3. a few roses
4. a few tickets

B
2. A little
3. a few
4. a few
5. a little
6. a little

UNIT 72

A
2. little information
3. Few cars
4. little sugar
5. little space
6. few letters

B
2. little
3. a little
4. a few
5. few
6. little

UNIT 73

A
2. all seafood
3. all floors
4. all month
5. All luggage
6. all day

B
2. All languages have
3. All rain comes
4. All flights are
5. All babies need
6. All advice is

UNIT 74

A
2. Every student
3. Every flower
4. Every seat
5. Every man

B
2. everywhere
3. Everyone OR Everybody
4. everything
5. everyone OR everybody
6. everywhere

UNIT 75

A
2. Most of them
3. None of them
4. Most of them
5. Some of them
6. All of them

B
2. Some animals
3. None of my children
4. Most trees
5. all of them

UNIT 76

A
2. Both
3. either
4. Both
5. Neither
6. both
7. either
8. neither

B
2. Both of our cars
3. Neither of my dogs
4. either of the restaurants
5. neither of us
6. both of my legs

UNIT 77

A
2. important meeting
3. cold weather
4. pink roses
5. empty seats

B
2. 's tall
3. are heavy
4. is long
5. are small

UNIT 78

A
2. quickly
3. nervously
4. comfortably
5. brightly

B
2. easily
3. terribly
4. perfectly
5. noisily
6. well

UNIT 79

A
2. smart
3. excitedly
4. interesting
5. completely
6. badly
7. strange
8. regularly

B
2. smells delicious
3. feel scared
4. sounds good
5. tastes great
6. look happy OR feel happy

UNIT 80

A
2. fast
3. beautifully
4. hard
5. early
6. happily

7. long
8. exciting
9. nervous
10. carefully

B
2. O
3. regular → regularly
4. comfortably → comfortable
5. noisy → noisily
6. O
7. amazingly → amazing
8. hardly → hard
9. easily → easy
10. O

UNIT 81

A
〈샘플 정답〉
2. I often exercise OR
   I rarely exercise
3. I usually watch movies OR
   I never watch movies
4. I often travel OR
   I rarely travel
5. I sometimes go shopping
   OR I rarely go shopping
6. I often listen to music OR
   I rarely listen to music

B
2. She's always smiling
3. Nick often plays
4. I'm usually free
5. You should never leave
6. Danny sometimes meets his cousins
7. You can always call
8. We rarely finish

UNIT 82

A
2. too fast
3. too dark
4. too long
5. too high

B
2. too sick to go
3. too difficult to answer
4. too spicy for us
5. too warm for me
6. too busy to take

UNIT 83

A
2. large enough
3. tall enough
4. long enough

B
2. clear enough to see
3. big enough for two people
4. sweet enough for me
5. old enough to drink
6. lucky enough to meet

UNIT 84

A
2. enough jobs
3. close enough
4. long enough
5. enough light
6. hard enough
7. enough paper
8. enough energy

B
2. enough biology books for the students
3. enough time to get
4. enough exercise to lose
5. enough bedrooms for your family

UNIT 85

A
2. smaller
3. louder
4. darker
5. older

B
2. shorter than David
3. warmer than New York
4. longer than the Amazon

UNIT 86

A
2. thinner
3. worse
4. nicer
5. more dangerous
6. lower
7. busier
8. bigger
9. easier
10. farther
11. more interesting
12. closer
13. better
14. cheaper
15. more comfortable

B
2. more expensive than the brown cap
3. farther than Seattle
4. faster than the man
5. heavier than the white box

UNIT 87

A
2. the kindest man
3. the strongest animals
4. the highest score
5. the freshest vegetables
6. the quietest girl

B
2. David is the oldest
3. Jason is the fastest
4. Bob is the youngest
5. David is the shortest

UNIT 88

A
2. more beautiful; most beautiful
3. better; best
4. higher; highest
5. nicer; nicest
6. hotter; hottest
7. happier; happiest
8. more important; most important
9. worse; worst
10. colder; coldest

B
2. more expensive than; the most expensive
3. the youngest; younger than
4. better than; the best

UNIT 89
A
2. as tall as
3. as heavy as
4. as expensive as
5. as fast as
6. as old as

B
2. as carefully as possible
3. as often as possible
4. as loud as possible
5. as short as possible

UNIT 90
A
2. isn't as cold as
3. isn't as new as
4. is as strong as

B
2. isn't as old as Katie
3. isn't as far as the mall
4. doesn't go to work as early as Judy
5. doesn't last as long as the bus tour

C
2. is older than Eric
3. is farther than the park
4. goes to work earlier than Sally
5. lasts longer than the train tour

UNIT 91
A
2. on
3. at
4. in
5. at
6. in
7. on

B
2. in
3. At
4. on
5. on
6. at
7. on
8. in

UNIT 92
A
2. at a birthday party
3. in the sky
4. on the bus

B
2. at
3. on
4. at
5. on
6. in

UNIT 93
A
2. by OR next to
3. behind
4. in front of
5. behind

B
2. next to
3. at
4. by
5. behind
6. next to
7. on
8. in front of
9. in front of
10. in
11. by
12. behind

UNIT 94
A
2. over
3. among
4. under
5. between

B
2. next to
3. between
4. behind
5. among
6. by
7. under
8. over
9. in front of

10. among
11. under
12. over

UNIT 95
A
2. 're getting out of
3. 's diving into
4. is going over
5. 's walking down

B
2. up
3. out of
4. under
5. over
6. to
7. down
8. into

UNIT 96
A
2. is going past
3. 's falling off
4. 's walking across
5. is driving around

B
2. around
3. into
4. under
5. out of
6. on
7. off
8. through

UNIT 97
A
2. at 7:18 p.m.
3. in 1879
4. at night
5. on April 10

B
2. in February
3. at breakfast
4. at 10 a.m.
5. on Sunday
6. in 2005
7. in the morning
8. on weekdays

UNIT 98
A
2. During the weekend
3. For eight years
4. During lunchtime
5. During winter
6. For five minutes
7. For about four months
8. During the holidays

B
2. in
3. during
4. for
5. during
6. within
7. for
8. in

UNIT 99
A
2. from June to July
3. from 10 a.m. to 7 p.m.
4. from Monday to Friday
5. from April 20 to May 5

B
2. by
3. until
4. by
5. by
6. until

UNIT 100
A
2. without his glasses
3. with his dog
4. with a swimming pool
5. without a helmet

B
2. by subway
3. with brown hair
4. without a ticket
5. by plane
6. on foot
7. without my wallet

UNIT 101
A
2. without stopping
3. before leaving
4. after watching the movie
5. about getting a promotion
6. for visiting me at the hospital

B
2. falling
3. waking
4. looking
5. breaking
6. reading

UNIT 102
A
2. at
3. about
4. of
5. to
6. with
7. in
8. for
9. of
10. with

B
2. different from
3. proud of
4. full of
5. sure about

UNIT 103
A
2. 're looking at
3. 's asking for
4. 's writing to

B
2. apply for
3. answer
4. depend on
5. belong to
6. reach
7. shout at
8. discuss

UNIT 104
A
2. work on
3. go out
4. turn up
5. get off

6. come back

B
2. hand in this report OR hand this report in
3. clean it up
4. take them away
5. turn off the heater OR turn the heater off
6. write down the address OR write the address down

UNIT 105
A
2. but
3. or
4. and
5. or
6. but
7. and
8. but

B
2. or do you need more time
3. and it hurt a lot
4. but he couldn't attend
5. but it tasted terrible
6. or do you want to drive yours

UNIT 106
A
3. so he got very tired
4. He got very tired because he ran for an hour
5. because she had a headache
6. She had a headache, so she took some medicine

B
2. because of
3. because
4. because
5. because of
6. because of

UNIT 107
A
2. While he was sitting on the chair
3. while the movie was playing

4. when he woke up

B
2. 'll get
3. 'll see
4. make
5. 'll buy
6. cleans

UNIT 108

A
2. after I took a shower
3. Before Andy goes home
4. before I ordered a cup of coffee
5. After the visitors checked out of the hotel

B
2. after reading
3. before the exam
4. before driving
5. after the show
6. after our wedding

UNIT 109

A
3. until he moved to Seoul
4. since he moved to Seoul
5. until she bought a car
6. since she bought a car

B
2. After
3. Since
4. Before
5. when
6. While
7. since
8. until

UNIT 110

A
2. I'll become a famous designer
3. If I become a famous designer, I'll make a lot of money
4. If I make a lot of money, I'll help poor children
5. If I help poor children, I'll feel happy

B
2. forgets
3. 'll feel
4. will get
5. visits
6. want

UNIT 111

A
2. If it were sunny OR If it was sunny
3. If I were in Paris OR If I was in Paris
4. If I had more free time

B
2. If I were you, I'd send it to the repair shop
3. If I were you, I wouldn't drive
4. If I were you, I'd say sorry to her
5. If I were you, I wouldn't drink it

UNIT 112

A
2. If I find it
3. If the mall were open OR If the mall was open
4. If Ashley weren't so tired OR If Ashley wasn't so tired

B
2. were fresh
3. 'd attend
4. 'll pick you up
5. had a car
6. don't like coffee
7. 'd be healthier
8. don't take an umbrella

UNIT 113

A
2. who plays the violin
3. who are very famous
4. who is 99 years old

B
2. I bought a new sofa which (OR that) was cheap
3. Sarah taught the students who (OR that) graduated last year
4. The store which (OR that) is around the corner sells fresh fruit
5. The people who (OR that) live downstairs are very nice
6. The plane which (OR that) left New York will arrive at 5:30

UNIT 114

A
2. The dress I wore
3. the cake you're baking
4. The show you were watching
5. The book Brian wrote

B
2. have a neighbor that doesn't know anyone in town
3. went to a restaurant that is famous for its dessert
4. took Sue to the art exhibit that opened last night
5. ate all of the chocolate he bought in Germany
6. spent the money she got for her birthday

UNIT 115

A
2. There are some people
3. There are some fish
4. There is a lake

B
2. Was there
3. there aren't
4. There wasn't
5. there were
6. Are there

UNIT 116

A
2. bought Jen a doll
3. showed Kim his room
4. made Jake some tea

B

2. Did Tim send those gifts to you
3. My mother made a sweater for me last winter
4. Laura teaches yoga to students on weekends
5. Can you show your passport to me
6. Will you buy some milk for me at the store

UNIT 117

A

2. Slow
3. Wake
4. Don't cry
5. Be
6. Don't tell

B

2. Let's listen
3. Let's not watch
4. Let's play
5. Let's not go
6. Let's ask

UNIT 118

A

2. They said (that) they were getting married
3. He said (that) he had a headache
4. He said (that) he'd call later
6. They told me (that) they were getting married
7. He told me (that) he had a headache
8. He told Betty (that) he'd call later

B

2. told
3. said
4. said
5. told
6. told

UNIT 119

A

2. too
3. either
4. too
5. either
6. too
7. either
8. either

B

2. either
3. either
4. too
5. too
6. either

UNIT 120

A

2. Neither have I
3. So can Brian
4. Neither is Maria
5. So are we
6. Neither does mine
7. Neither was the salad
8. So do Jim and Emily

B

2. either
3. So
4. too
5. So
6. either
7. Neither
8. too
9. Neither
10. So

CHECK-UP TEST Answers

TEST 1

2. works; 's listening OR is listening
3. is reading; teaches
4. is shopping; helps
6. Is Mom making pancakes
7. We don't use it OR We do not use it
8. Do you know him
9. Lisa and Anton aren't from England OR
   Lisa and Anton are not from England
10. Julia doesn't wear glasses OR
    Julia does not wear glasses
12. Do you practice
13. Do birds eat
14. Is it raining
15. Does Brian take
16. Are you watching
17. Does she work
18. Are you ready
20. b)   21. b)
22. a)   23. b)
24. c)   25. b)
26. c)   27. a)
28. b)   29. a)
30. a)   31. a)
32. c)   33. a)

TEST 2

2. walked
3. visited
4. saw
5. took
6. bought
8. I didn't see OR I did not see
9. Was Susie
10. I have
11. Did you go
12. I don't know OR I do not know
13. Is he
15. Lucy didn't go OR Lucy did not go
16. Did Ben clean
17. Were you studying
18. We were waiting
20. a)   21. a)
22. b)   23. a)
24. c)   25. a)
26. b)   27. a)
28. c)   29. c)
30. b)   31. a)
32. b)   33. a)

TEST 3

2. We haven't eaten dinner yet OR
   We have not eaten dinner yet
3. Mark has been to many concerts
4. How long have you lived
5. Aaron and Nick have made some muffins
6. Mandy hasn't ridden a roller coaster OR
   Mandy has not ridden a roller coaster
8. 've known each other OR
   have known each other
9. hasn't rained OR has not rained
10. 's been sick OR has been sick
12. called
13. 've watched OR have watched
14. came
15. got
16. 's grown OR has grown
17. broke
18. 's worked OR has worked
20. b)   21. a)
22. c)   23. c)
24. a)   25. b)
26. b)   27. b)
28. c)   29. a)
30. b)   31. c)
32. b)   33. a)

TEST 4

2. He's going to marry her OR
   He is going to marry her
3. Are you speaking
4. Are you going to watch the fireworks
5. I won't forget it OR I will not forget it
6. Alex and I aren't playing soccer OR
   Alex and I are not playing soccer
8. 's going to drink some wine OR
   is going to drink some wine
9. is going to stop at the light
10. 're going to get on the train OR
    are going to get on the train
12. 'll write OR will write
13. won't stay OR will not stay
14. 'll turn on OR will turn on
15. won't touch OR will not touch
16. won't tell OR will not tell
17. 'll cook OR will cook
18. 'll meet OR will meet
20. c)   21. c)
22. b)   23. b)
24. a)   25. c)

26. b)   27. c)
28. a)   29. a)
30. b)   31. a)
32. c)   33. a)

TEST 5

2. He might not come
3. They shouldn't talk OR
   They should not talk
4. Would you like to dance
5. I don't have to go
7. can't use the car OR
   cannot use the car
8. have to call the police
9. might fall down the stairs
10. don't have to be scared OR
    do not have to be scared
11. must fix the roof
13. could
14. didn't have to OR did not have to
15. should
16. must not
17. had to
18. couldn't OR could not
20. a)   21. a)
22. b)   23. c)
24. b)   25. a)
26. b)   27. c)
28. c)   29. b)
30. b)   31. a)
32. c)   33. a)

TEST 6

2. were made
3. was written
4. were taken
5. was stolen
7. pets aren't allowed OR
   pets are not allowed
8. The house wasn't sold OR
   The house was not sold
9. The Mona Lisa was painted by Leonardo da Vinci
10. They aren't known by many people OR
    They are not known by many people
12. was canceled
13. had
14. was broken
15. didn't finish OR did not finish
16. was invented

17. watched
18. wasn't washed OR was not washed
20. a)   21. b)
22. a)   23. c)
24. a)   25. b)
26. a)   27. c)
28. a)   29. c)
30. c)   31. b)
32. b)   33. a)

TEST 7

2. What
3. Who
4. Where
5. When
6. Who
7. When
8. What
10. where I can put this
11. why you bought this hat
12. when Erica will get here
14. How much does this necklace cost
15. Kyle doesn't like dogs OR
    Kyle does not like dogs
16. whether you'll be busy OR
    whether you will be busy
17. When did Cindy go
18. You shouldn't buy it OR
    You should not buy it
20. a)   21. b)
22. c)   23. a)
24. a)   25. b)
26. b)   27. a)
28. a)   29. c)
30. c)   31. a)
32. c)   33. b)

TEST 8

2. waiting in line OR to wait in line
3. singing
4. cooking
5. to go to the museum
6. reading books OR to read books
8. to send
9. make OR to make
10. eating
11. stay
12. to drive
13. to learn
15. Aaron let me use his

16. Does Kim need to buy
17. Nicole taught me to dance
18. Swimming is good
20. c)   21. a)
22. b)   23. a)
24. b)   25. c)
26. b)   27. c)
28. b)   29. c)
30. c)   31. c)
32. b)   33. a)

TEST 9

2. many students attend the concert
3. some snow on the road
4. get a glass of orange juice
5. buy new ones
7. principal's office
8. David's seat
9. Andersons' house
10. Sam's suitcases
12. an umbrella
13. salt
14. a taxi
15. the drums
16. the airport
17. money
18. information
20. c)   21. b)
22. b)   23. a)
24. a)   25. c)
26. b)   27. b)
28. a)   29. c)
30. c)   31. c)
32. a)   33. b)

TEST 10

2. any
3. some
4. any
5. no
7. few
8. many
9. every
10. a little
11. much
12. all
13. little
15. Both of them are
16. Most of my cousins live
17. he has none

18. Neither of them is mine
20. c)   21. a)
22. a)   23. b)
24. a)   25. c)
26. b)   27. c)
28. a)   29. c)
30. b)   31. b)
32. c)   33. a)

TEST 11

2. 's sitting uncomfortably
3. 's thinking hard
4. 're shouting angrily
6. is rarely crowded
7. not tall enough to ride
8. too tired to go
9. enough for everyone
10. can always use my car
12. good
13. larger
14. more beautiful
15. highest
16. hottest
17. faster
18. strong
20. c)   21. b)
22. a)   23. b)
24. c)   25. c)
26. a)   27. a)
28. a)   29. b)
30. b)   31. b)
32. b)   33. c)

TEST 12

2. at work
3. on the 4th floor
4. at school
5. in the phone booth
7. by this Friday
8. For five years
9. in 10 minutes
10. from Korea
11. to Germany
12. behind the curtains
13. down the stairs
15. turn off their cell phones OR
    turn their cell phones off
16. excited about the trip
17. spends money on unnecessary things
18. I'll take them off

20. a)   21. b)   30. b)   31. a)
22. a)   23. b)   32. b)   33. c)
24. c)   25. a)
26. c)   27. c)
28. c)   29. c)
30. b)   31. c)
32. b)   33. a)

TEST 13

2. or should we take a bus
3. because I drank too much wine last night
4. but she couldn't come
5. so she took some medicine
7. if I finish work
8. if I were you OR if I was you
9. since she left the company
10. when Martin opened it
11. while she's on vacation
13. who was on TV last night
14. (who) she met during the trip
15. (which) Ted's dad built
17. b)   18. c)
19. c)   20. b)
21. c)   22. c)
23. a)   24. b)
25. b)   26. c)
27. c)   28. a)
29. b)   30. a)

TEST 14

2. There is a bird
3. There is a table
4. There are three glasses
5. There are four boys
7. told me he wanted
8. Let's not cook dinner
9. said that she was sleeping
10. I made some cookies for you
12. either
13. So
14. either
15. So
16. Neither
17. Neither
18. too
20. c)   21. a)
22. a)   23. c)
24. b)   25. c)
26. a)   27. b)
28. c)   29. b)

GRAMMAR GATEWAY BASIC

www.Hackers.co.kr

Index

영문 **Index**

한글 **Index**

영문 Index

Index에 있는 숫자는 UNIT 번호입니다. 괄호 안에 있는 숫자는 UNIT 내 섹션 번호입니다.

a/an	54(1), 57
a/an과 the	57
across	96(1)
a few	71-72
a few와 few	72(2)
after	108
a little	71-72
a little과 little	72(2)
all	73, 75
all of ~	75
along	96(1)
a lot (of)/lots of	70
already	24
always/usually/often 등	81
am/is/are	1-6, 28, 37
am/is/are + -ing	4-6, 부록 3
미래를 나타내는 am/is/are + -ing	28(1)
am/is/are + 과거분사	37(1), 38, 부록 2-3
among	94(1)
and	105
any	66-68
any와 some	66
not ~ any	67(2)
anyone/anybody/anything/anywhere	68(1-2)
around	96(1)
as ~ as	89-90
not as ~ as	90
at	91-92, 97
at + 장소	91(1), 92(1)
at + 시간	97(1)
be going to	26-27
be going to와 will	27
because (of)	106(2)
before	108
behind	93(1)
between	94(1)
both (of)	76(1), 76(4)
but	105
by	38, 93, 99-100
수동태와 by	38(2)
by + 위치	93(2)
by + 시간	99(2)
by + 교통수단	100(3)
can/could	29-30
Can/Could I ~ ?, Can/Could you ~ ?	30
down	95(1)
during	98(1)
either	76, 119
either of ~	76(4)
enough	83-84
형용사/부사 + enough	83
enough + 명사	84
ever	22(2)
every	74
everyone/everybody/everything/everywhere	74(2)
few	72
few와 little	72(1)
few와 a few	72(2)
for	21, 98
현재완료와 for	21(1)
for + 시간	98(1)
from	95, 99
from + 방향	95(1)
from ~ to	99(1)
give	116
give + 사람 + 사물	116(1)
give + 사물 + to + 사람	116(2)
have	12, 20-24, 33-34, 51
have와 be having	12(2)
have/has + 과거분사	20-24, 부록 2-3
have/has been (to ~)	22(2)
have to	33(2), 34(2)
had to	33(3)
have + 사람 + 동사원형	51(1)
help	51
help + 사람 (+ to) + 동사원형	51(2)
how	21, 44
how long have you ~ ?	21(2)
I/we/you 등	60
if	45, 110-112
간접의문문과 if	45(2)
in	91-92, 97-98
in + 장소	91(2), 92(2)
in + 시간	97(3), 98(2)

in front of	93(1)
into	95(2)
it	60-61
대명사 it	60
비인칭 주어 it	61
-ing	4-6, 11, 17-18, 28, 46-47, 49, 101, 108, 부록 3
동명사 -ing	46-47, 49, 부록 3
am/is/are + -ing	4-6, 11
was/were + -ing	17-18
미래를 나타내는 am/is/are + -ing	28(1)
전치사 + -ing	101, 108(2)
just	24
let	51, 117
let + 사람 + 동사원형	51(1)
let's (not)	117(2)
little	72
little과 few	72(1)
little과 a little	72(2)
make	51, 116
make + 사람 + 동사원형	51(1)
make + 사람 + 사물	116(1)
make + 사물 + for + 사람	116(2)
many	69
me/us/you 등	60
might	31
mine/ours/yours 등	62(2)
more	86(2)
most	75, 88(2)
most of ~	75
much	69
must	32-34
must (강한 확신)	32
must와 have to (의무)	33
must not과 don't have to	34
my/our/your 등	62(1)
neither	76(3), 120
neither of ~	76(4)
never	22, 81
현재완료와 never	22(2)
next to	93(2)
no	67-68
no one/nobody/nothing/nowhere	68(3)
none	67(3), 75

none of ~	75
of	63(2)
off	96(2)
on	91-92, 96-97
on + 장소	91(3), 92(3)
on + 방향	96(2)
on + 시간	97(2)
one/ones	65
or	105
out of	95(2)
over	94-95
over + 위치	94(2)
over + 방향	95(2)
past	96(2)
's	63
said (that)	118
should	35
since	21, 109(1), 109(3)
현재완료와 since	21(1)
so	106(1), 120
some	66, 68, 75
some과 any	66
someone/somebody/something/somewhere	68(1-2)
some of ~	75
tell	50, 118
tell + 사람 + to + 동사원형	50(2)
told + 사람 (+ that)	118(2)
than	85(2), 90(2)
that	64, 113-114
that/those	64
관계대명사 that	113(2), 114
the	57-59, 87
the와 a/an	57
the를 쓰는 경우와 쓰지 않는 경우	58-59, 부록 5
최상급과 the	87(1)
there is/are, there was/were	115
this/these	64
through	96(1)
to	46, 48-52, 95
to + 동사원형	46(3), 48-52
to + 방향	95(1)

Index | 207

too ·· 82, 119

toward ···································· 96(2)

under ······································ 94-95
  under + 위치 ························ 94(2)
  under + 방향 ························ 95(2)

until ·················· 99, 109(2-3)
  until + 시간 ·························· 99(3)

up ·· 95(1)

used to ·································· 19

want ····························· 12, 48, 50
  현재진행 시제로 쓰지 않고 현재 시제로 쓰는 want ··· 12(1)
  want + to + 동사원형 ············· 48
  want + 사람 + to + 동사원형 ··· 50(1)

was/were ················· 13-14, 17-18, 37-38
  was/were + -ing ················· 17-18
  was/were + 과거분사 ·········· 37(2), 38, 부록 2-3

what ·· 41-42
  what ~ ? ···························· 41(2-3)
  what과 which 비교 ············· 42(3)

when ······························· 43, 107
  when ~ ? ······················ 43(2), 43(4)
  접속사 when ························ 107

where ························ 43(1), 43(4)

whether ·································· 45(2)

which ···························· 42, 113-114
  which ~ ? ····························· 42
  which와 what 비교 ············· 42(3)
  관계대명사 which ··············· 113(1), 114

while ·· 107

who ···························· 41, 113-114
  who ~ ? ························ 41(1), 41(3)
  관계대명사 who ················· 113(1), 114

whose ···································· 62(3)

why ·· 43(3-4)

will ······························· 25, 27, 110
  will과 be going to ················ 27
  if와 will ······························· 110(1)

with ·· 100(1)

within ···································· 98(2)

without ·································· 100(2)

would ····························· 36, 111
  Would you like (to) ~ ? ········ 36(1)
  I'd like (to) ·························· 36(2)

  if와 would ··························· 111(1)

yet ··· 24

한글 Index

Index에 있는 숫자는 UNIT 번호입니다. 괄호 안에 있는 숫자는 UNIT 내 섹션 번호입니다.

간접화법 ··· 118

과거 ··· 13-19, 23, 111-112, 부록 2-3
   be동사 was/were ··· 13-14
   과거 시제 ··· 15-16, 부록 2-3
   과거진행 시제 ··· 17-18
   used to ··· 19
   과거 시제와 현재완료 시제 비교 ··· 23
   if + 과거 시제 ··· 111
   if + 과거 시제와 if + 현재 시제 비교 ··· 112

관계대명사 ··· 113-114
   주격 관계대명사 who, which, that ··· 113
   목적격 관계대명사 who, which, that ··· 114

관사 ··· 57-59, 부록 5
   a/an과 the ··· 57
   the를 쓰는 경우와 쓰지 않는 경우 ··· 58-59, 부록 5

구동사 ··· 104, 부록 7

대명사 ··· 60, 62, 64-65
   사람과 사물을 가리키는 대명사 (I, me 등) ··· 60
   소유대명사 (mine, ours 등) ··· 62(2)
   this/these와 that/those ··· 64(1)
   one과 ones ··· 65

동명사 (-ing) ··· 46-47, 49, 101, 108
   동명사를 주어로 쓸 때 ··· 46
   동명사를 목적어로 쓰는 동사 ··· 47
   동명사와 to부정사 모두 뒤에 올 수 있는 동사 ··· 49(1)
   stop + 동명사 ··· 49(2)
   전치사 + 동명사 ··· 101, 108(2)

수동태 ··· 37-38, 부록 2-3
   수동태와 능동태 비교 ··· 38(1)
   수동태와 by ··· 38(2)

명령문 ··· 117(1)

명사 ··· 53-56
   셀 수 있는 명사와 셀 수 없는 명사 ··· 53, 부록 5
   단수와 복수 ··· 53(2), 54
   단수, 복수에 주의해야 할 명사 ··· 55
   단위를 나타내는 표현 (a glass of ~ 등) ··· 56(1)

미래 ··· 25-28
   will ··· 25
   be going to ··· 26
   will과 be going to 비교 ··· 27
   미래를 나타내는 현재진행과 현재 시제 ··· 28

부사 ··· 78-83, 89-90, 119-120, 부록 3
   부사와 형용사 비교 ··· 79
   주의해야 할 형용사와 부사 ··· 80
   빈도부사 (always, often 등) ··· 81
   too ··· 82
   enough ··· 83
   (not) as ~ as ··· 89-90
   too와 either ··· 119
   so와 neither ··· 120

부정문 ··· 2, 5, 9, 14, 16, 18, 39
   be동사 am/is/are 부정문 ··· 2
   현재진행 시제 부정문 ··· 5
   현재 시제 부정문 ··· 9
   be동사 was/were 부정문 ··· 14(1)
   과거 시제 부정문 ··· 16(1)
   과거진행 시제 부정문 ··· 18(1)

비교급 ··· 85-86, 90(2), 부록 3
   비교급과 than ··· 85(2)

비인칭 주어 it ··· 61

소유를 나타내는 표현 ··· 62-63
   소유격 (my, our 등) ··· 62(1)
   whose ··· 62(3)
   명사의 소유격 ··· 63

수량표현 ··· 66-67, 69-76
   some과 any ··· 66
   no와 none ··· 67
   many와 much ··· 69
   a lot of, lots of ··· 70
   (a) few와 (a) little ··· 71-72
   all ··· 73
   every ··· 74
   all/most/some/none of ~ ··· 75
   both/either/neither (of) ··· 76

의문문 ··· 3, 6, 10, 14, 16, 18, 40-45
   be동사 am/is/are 의문문 ··· 3
   현재진행 시제 의문문 ··· 6
   현재 시제 의문문 ··· 10
   be동사 was/were 의문문 ··· 14(2)
   과거 시제 의문문 ··· 16(2)
   과거진행 시제 의문문 ··· 18(2)
   who, what, which ··· 41-42
   where, when, why ··· 43
   how ··· 44
   간접의문문 ··· 45

조동사 ··· 29-36
   can과 could ··· 29, 30
   might ··· 31
   must (강한 확신) ··· 32
   must (의무) ··· 33(1), 34(1)
   have to ··· 33(2), 34(2)
   had to ··· 33(3)
   should ··· 35
   Would you like (to) ~ ? ··· 36(1)
   I'd like (to) ··· 36(2)

전치사 ·· 91-103, 108, 부록 6, 부록 7
  장소 전치사 at, in, on ······················· 91-92
  위치 전치사 (in front of, between 등) ········· 93-94
  방향 전치사 (from, through 등) ··············· 95-96
  시간 전치사 (at, during, from ~ to 등) ········ 97-99
  기타 전치사 (with, by 등) ······················ 100
  전치사 + 동명사 ···························· 101, 108(2)
  형용사 + 전치사 ······························ 102, 부록 6
  동사 + 전치사 ································ 103, 부록 7

접속사 ··· 105-112
  and, but, or ··· 105
  so와 because (of) ··································· 106
  when과 while ······································· 107
  before와 after ······································· 108
  since와 until ··· 109
  if ··· 110-112

최상급 ··· 87-88, 부록 3

현재 ······················· 1-12, 28, 107, 109-110, 112
  be동사 am/is/are ······································ 1-3
  현재진행 시제 ································· 4-6, 부록 3
  현재 시제 ······································ 7-10, 부록 3
  현재진행 시제와 현재 시제 비교 ······················· 11
  현재 진행 시제로 쓰지 않고 현재 시제로 쓰는 동사 ······ 12
  미래를 나타내는 현재진행과 현재 시제 ················ 28
  when과 while 다음에 미래의 일을 말할 때 ········ 107(2)
  until 다음에 미래의 일을 말할 때 ················· 109(2)
  if + 현재 시제 ···································· 110(1)
  if 다음에 미래의 일을 말할 때 ···················· 110(2)
  if + 현재 시제와 if + 과거 시제 비교 ················ 112

현재완료 ····································· 20-24, 부록 2-3
  현재완료 시제와 for, since ························ 21(1)
  How long have you ~ ? ··························· 21(2)
  현재완료 시제와 ever, never ······················ 22(2)
  have/has been (to ~) ····························· 22(2)
  현재완료 시제와 과거 시제 비교 ······················ 23
  현재완료 시제와 just, already, yet ·················· 24

형용사 ································· 77, 79-80, 89-90, 102
  형용사와 부사 비교 ··································· 79
  주의해야 할 형용사와 부사 ···························· 80
  (not) as ~ as ······································ 89-90
  형용사 + 전치사 ····································· 102

to부정사 (to + 동사원형) ······················ 48-52, 82-83
  to부정사를 목적어로 쓰는 동사 ······················· 48
  to부정사와 동명사 모두 뒤에 올 수 있는 동사 ······· 49(1)
  stop + to부정사 ·································· 49(2)
  want, advise 등 + 사람 + to부정사 ·················· 50
  help + 사람 + to부정사 ··························· 51(2)
  목적을 나타내는 to부정사 ···························· 52
  too + 형용사 + to부정사 ·························· 82(2)

  형용사 + enough + to부정사 ······················ 83(2)
  enough + 명사 + to부정사 ························ 84(1)

초보를 위한 기초 영문법

개정 3판 17쇄 발행 2025년 10월 13일
개정 3판 1쇄 발행 2013년 5월 1일

지은이	David Cho ǀ 언어학 박사, 前 UCLA 교수
펴낸곳	㈜해커스 어학연구소
펴낸이	해커스 어학연구소 출판팀
주소	서울특별시 서초구 강남대로61길 23 ㈜해커스 어학연구소
고객센터	02-537-5000
교재 관련 문의	publishing@hackers.com
동영상강의	HackersIngang.com
ISBN	978-89-6542-028-6 (13740)
Serial Number	03-17-01

저작권자 ⓒ 2017, David Cho
이 책 및 음성파일의 모든 내용, 이미지, 디자인, 편집 형태에 대한 저작권은 저자에게 있습니다.
서면에 의한 저자와 출판사의 허락 없이 내용의 일부 혹은 전부를 인용, 발췌하거나 복제, 배포할 수 없습니다.

외국어인강 1위,
해커스인강(HackersIngang.com)

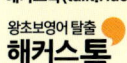해커스인강

· 예문 해석 및 교재 정답 자료
· 교재에 수록된 예문을 듣고 따라하는 **예문 음성 MP3**
· 해커스 스타강사의 **본 교재 인강**

영어 전문 포털,
해커스영어(Hackers.co.kr)

해커스영어

· 영어의 기본원리가 이해되는 **본 교재 핵심포인트 무료 인강**
· 누구나 쉽게 학습할 수 있는 **말하기/듣기/읽기/쓰기 무료 학습자료**

'영어회화 인강' 1위,
해커스톡(talk.Hackers.com)

왕초보영어 탈출
해커스톡

· 쉽고 재미있게 학습하는 **기초 영어회화 동영상강의**
· **데일리 무료 복습 콘텐츠, 무료 레벨테스트** 등 다양한 무료 학습 콘텐츠

[외국어인강 1위] 헤럴드 선정 2018 대학생 선호브랜드 대상 '대학생이 선정한 외국어인강' 부문 1위
[영어회화 인강 1위] 헤럴드 선정 2018 대학생 선호 브랜드 대상 '대학생이 선정한 영어회화 인강' 부문 1위